MANAGING PEOPLE

EFFECTIVE MANAGEMENT SKILLS

SKILLS

MANAGING PEOPLE

JOHN SCOTT & ARTHUR ROCHESTER

Sphere/British Institute of Management

First published by
Sphere Books Ltd/BIM 1984

Printed and bound in Great Britain by
Cox & Wyman Ltd, Reading

Cartoons by Bill Belcher
End of Chapter patterns by John Plumb

Contents

Preliminaries

The manager is someone who has enormous influence in our society. Almost every part of our lives is touched in one way or another by the organisations he runs — whether they are businesses or the agencies of national or local government. We're affected as customers or users of their services, as employees, as managers ourselves (in which case we're still being managed by the people over us). So the way managers manage people isn't just a private matter of each organisation's internal workings. It's something that concerns us all. Managers have a big responsibility to the society that sustains their organisations, a duty to manage people well. *How* they can do that is the point this book explores.

We aren't trying to argue that this is all there is to management, of course. This and the other books in this series aim to put together a broad view of what management is about — a view that is coherent, that makes practical sense for anyone in a management job from the supervisor upwards, and that is reasonably easy reading. It's a view on the manager's role from different angles: his management of work, of people and of money. The first book, *What is a Manager?* explained why we're taking these as the three priorities of management, primarily because they're what any managed organisation is itself about — and managers are creatures of organisations. No organisations, no managers.

This particular book has a special significance. The way our organisations are managed generally leaves a lot to be desired. But if there's one aspect that's more ineptly managed than any other, it's this one — the management of *people*. That's bad for several reasons.

> One reason: organisations are only as good as the performance of the people in them. Entrepreneurial flair, financial wizardry, technical brilliance, administrative efficiency aren't enough to enable them to flourish. Their managers also have to be able to harness their people's talents and energies.

> Another reason: bad management affects millions of people's lives. Stresses, indignities, boredom and feelings of futility are created on a grand scale by bosses whose people-management is a crude affair of carrot-and-stick or a feeble let-things-drift.

> Yet another reason: there's really very little excuse. Managing people well begins with plain old-fashioned common-sense about how to treat others. It's not so very difficult to be at one and the same time courteous and clear about what you want to get done. And that's the root of it.

One point we'll simply repeat from the opening of the first book. It's a practical problem to do with sex and English pronouns. A lot of managers are women, but to keep the style of writing simple you've got to choose your pronoun. Do you call a manager 'him' or 'her'? We offer our apologies to all the she-managers we might have insulted, but we've opted for 'him' pretty well throughout. Please take this as a problem of language, not an attempt to cut half the human species out of management.

To start off, here's a quiz similar to that in the first book, if you've read it (if not, we strongly recommend it). Its purpose is just to get you thinking about some of the key issues we're going to deal with. Choose which of the three answers to each question you agree with most. You may agree partly with them all or wholly with none. But which comes closest to your view? Later you'll be able to look back and see if your ideas have changed at all.

People-management quiz

1 Which is the most important thing a manager can do to increase his people's motivation?
   a) Offer them rewards for doing what he wants done.
   b) Create opportunities for them to achieve things they feel are worthwhile.
   c) Keep his relationships with them pleasant and friendly.

2 To what extent should a manager concern himself with his people's personalities?
   a) Enough to recognise any differences in the ways he should manage each of them.
   b) Not at all. Personalities shouldn't be allowed to interfere with the way people do their work.
   c) Enough to get them to change awkward aspects of their personalities where necessary.

3 What attitude should a manager take to the amount of pressure his people work under?
   a) The more pressure the better. It brings out the best in people.
   b) People need a certain amount of pressure. But it must be regulated to suit the individual.
   c) All pressure is bad. It makes it more difficult for people to do a good job.

4 Which of these qualities is most likely to make a manager a good leader?
   a) A strong personality and a commanding manner.
   b) A capacity for hard work that wins his people's respect.
   c) A natural interest in people and a keen sense of purpose.

5 Which is most likely to help the manager turn his people into a team?
   a) He finds ways for them to collaborate in working out aims and priorities.
   b) He gets rid of people who don't fit in so that everyone gets on well together.

c) He talks to them regularly about ways they can pull together.

6 What gives the best indication that a manager is a good communicator?
a) People usually agree with him because his arguments are so persuasive.
b) People talk to him freely because he's interested in their views on his plans and ideas.
c) People always understand him because he speaks and writes clearly and logically.

7 Which of these is the best way for a manager to control the meetings he chairs?
a) He requires everyone to address their remarks through the chair so that open conflicts of view are avoided.
b) He uses summaries to make progress clear to all and to move the discussion on stage by stage.
c) He insists that each member keeps his contribution short so that no time is wasted.

8 Which quality is most likely to help a manager make good decisions in selecting applicants for a job?
a) The toughness that lets him frame questions that search out any weaknesses in applicants.
b) The intuition that enables him to pick a winning applicant early on in an interview.
c) The interest in the applicants that encourages them to talk candidly about their past experiences.

9 Which is the most important thing to concentrate on in an annual appraisal interview with a subordinate?
a) Identifying ways he can be helped to improve his present performance.
b) Assessing his potential for further promotion in the organisation.
c) Pointing out his past weaknesses so that he realises the scope for improvement.

10 What is the best way a manager can develop a subordinate's abilities?
a) By keeping up the pressure on him to do a better job.
b) By nominating him for any training course he wants to attend.
c) By helping him learn from the experiences he gets in his job.

1. People and performance

How do you see your job? In our first book in this series we devoted a lot of space to discussing what management is — and what it isn't. We exposed a number of popular wrong notions about management; for example, those which confuse it with status in an organisation, with administration, with manipulation for private interest, and so on. And we tried to crystallize a simple yet revealing concept of real management, summed up in the phrase: 'getting things done economically through the efforts of your people'.

As a definition of management, something very close to that has been around for a long time. Perhaps the dimension that hasn't always been included is the economic one. We added it because it's hard to think of any management job which shouldn't be concerned with the value — and therefore the cost — to the organisation of the things that 'get done' (whether the managers *doing* the job realise it or not). All managers need to be able, at least to some extent, to manage money. But that's the subject of another book altogether.

Putting that important consideration aside for the moment, we're left with the definition of management which, in various forms, has been quoted and taught in countless books and courses for decades. It really has two halves: first, 'getting things done' and, second, 'through the efforts of your people'. Managing *work*, and managing *people*. Actually it's far harder to separate these two elements than it is to isolate the money angle. Anything you say about one almost automatically has some relevance to the other. Perhaps it's wrong — and unnecessary — even to try to separate them. The question is really one of emphasis. The trouble is that so many managers get the emphasis wrong.

The task is all

Some see their jobs *only* in terms of 'getting things done'. Their management is full of action plans, control systems, sanctions and penalties, tangible incentives, close supervision and constant exhortation. A lot of the time they get results and because they drive themselves as hard as their people, a good deal of perhaps grudging respect.

This 'style' of management is most often based on ideas which are left-overs from the dawn of management thinking, in the aftermath of the industrial revolution. They centre around the concept of people as 'resources', in effect as another kind of machine — more unpredictable, temperamental and unreliable than man-made machinery, but nevertheless to be scheduled, controlled and manipulated in much the same way. (Perhaps it's no accident that one of the pieces of business-school jargon to gain popularity in very recent years is the term 'human resources'.)

'Scientific management'

The approach which developed from such thinking in the 1930s is extremely well-documented. It is clearly based on a particular set of assumptions about the nature of 'working people' and their behaviour. These are: that they are influenced primarily by personal gain (chiefly financial); although emotions sometimes overcome this self-interest, they are fundamentally lazy and lacking in self-discipline.

These assumption naturally led to a system of management based on financial incentives to achieve results, and restrictions and controls to eliminate or minimise the effect of individual's emotions. You will still find this style of management flourishing in a good many present-day organisations. You can recognise it by the extreme emphasis on:
— efficient planning of work
— financial rewards related to productivity
— close control and supervision
— stringent rules and disciplinary measures
— authoritarian attitudes on the part of individual managers.
No one is likely to deny that such measures *can* and do get results. But if you work or have worked in such an organisation you will have experienced for yourself some of the drawbacks of this approach.

Yesterday's management today

One is the effect which it tends to have on attitudes in the workforce. Having become used to the idea that the only rewards they can expect are monetary, they look for higher and higher returns and become militant in their demands. This behaviour, of course, reinforces their managers' assumptions. Much of the militancy seen in certain industries today is the legacy of decades of management of this kind.

Another drawback is that most industries today are experiencing technological advances which make jobs more and more complex. This in turn increases the need for such qualities as judgement, initiative, innovation and creativity — precisely the qualities which this type of management positively discourages. People suddenly asked to make this kind of contribution find the adjustment difficult, if not impossible.

Managers who (consciously or unconsciously) perpetuate

7

the 'scientific management' philosophy have also failed to realise the nature of the modern worker — what someone called the 'new subordinate'. Changes in living-standards, educational opportunities and social customs have created very different expectations. People of all kinds now demand recognition of their individuality. They no longer accept authority for its own sake (and, despite the unemployment situation in the 1980s, are no longer driven by the fear of punishment or dismissal). They seek outlets for their creative intelligence which, if not available within the work, they will find in outside activities, to which their best efforts will then be diverted.

The 'human relations' school

This would seem to point to the need for a different management style, one which grew in popularity throughout the nineteen-sixties. It really consists of the opposite emphasis being given to that definition. Unfortunately many managers get this wrong too.

Those who believe that the all-important words are 'through the efforts of your people' seem also often to conclude that this means just keeping people happy. Their management is concerned solely with harmonious working relationships, the removal or relief of job pressures, exercising great sensitivity to people's feelings and taking great care over their welfare.

The problem is, of course, that when these become a sole pre-occupation they often preclude any real drive towards the achievement of results! Such managers become, in effect, what one authority described as the 'happy failures' — 'it's true we're not achieving our objectives, but look how happy my people are'. Ultimately, by neglecting organisational priorities, and objectives, they do not even serve the real interests of their people.

The balancing act

What's needed, obviously, is the ability to balance the two halves of this management concept, the achievement of results with the involvement and satisfaction of the people. You have to meet both these aims — for that is what they really are — so that each supports and reinforces, not outweighs or inhibits, the other.

A much wordier definition of management was produced around the 1940s by the American Management Association. Their aim was to have a definition universally applicable to any form of enterprise — management not only in industry but, for example, in government, in the medical profession, in the Church, in labour unions, etc. In pursuit of this they ended up, perhaps inevitably, with a form of words rather too unwieldy for practical use, but not without value in expanding our understanding of the subject.

It talks about 'Guiding human and physical resources (people and things) into dynamic organisation units' (here the word dynamic is used, we think, accurately to mean having force or motive power) 'which achieve their objectives' (ah!) 'to the satisfaction of those served' (customers? shareholders? ratepayers? hospital patients? union members?) 'and with a high degree of morale and sense of attainment on the part of those rendering the service' (the organisation's people). Despite its obvious verbosity, this does have the virtue of emphasising (whether intentionally or not) that management's aim has to satisfy *two* groups of people involved: those receiving the service which is the organisation's reason for existing, *and* those providing it.

Definitions of management — and there have been many others we've not mentioned — are inevitably limited in their acceptability and application. What we're trying to establish at the outset of this book is not a definition but an understanding of management. No-one can deny that its underlying purpose is to achieve results (what *kind* of result is another question). But if there is one feature which distinguishes management from other human activities it is the need to fulfil that aim by influencing, guiding and co-ordinating the efforts of other *people*. You can achieve relatively little (and nothing at all *as* a manager) without this ability.

Management is concerned with performance. Economic performance in terms of value for money; operational performance in terms of efficiency; above all, personal performance in terms of effectiveness. Managing people means being able to get *high* performance from people. Not just when special circumstances require it, but consistently over a sustained period. Not only as individuals, but also as a team — including, of course, you as the manager or team-leader.

Let's take a closer look at that word 'performance'. You know in your department, section, unit or whatever, what *you* would accept and expect. But what decides people's level of performance? Why do some always do a better job than others? Why do the high performers sometimes do a rotten job? Why do your lost causes occasionally astonish you by bringing home the bacon? What actually determines how well any one of your people does his job?

No doubt you could make a very long list, ranging from the

way someone's feeling on any particular morning, to the state of the weather, or the fortunes of the local football or cricket team. Indeed, the list is likely to be so long and so diverse that it gives you very little help in finding out which particular influences are at work at any one time. We need to sharpen our thinking a bit. Examine carefully the performance of any one of your subordinates. Male or female, it doesn't matter, but as we have to choose a pronoun we'll follow our usual practice and make it 'him'. Probably you'll find that the multiplicity of things which affect his performance could be sorted out under relatively few headings.

The external influences

Many of them are aspects of the person himself — what he has to offer as an individual and the things within him that cause him to offer or to withhold it, to different degrees and at different times. Other things which influence his performance are external — mostly in the job itself and the environment in which it's done. For want of a better general term we'll call it his 'situation'. However able or willing an individual may be, a poor situation can at best restrict and at worst destroy his output.

It consists of three principal influences:

1. *His job*
Thousands of people suffer in relative silence jobs which in themselves cause any capable person to perform poorly. Look closely at your subordinate's job:
- The *kind of work* may be wrong for him. Although right for others, it may not suit *his* temperament or aptitudes. It may be too undemanding. It may be downright boring. It may even be work for which little of his experience has prepared him.
- The *purpose* of the job may give him nothing to achieve that he can feel is worthwhile. The job may even seem purposeless or parasitic to him: he may not be able to identify with its goals.
- The *amount of responsibility* may be too much for him to handle — or too small for his personal ability. In the first case, he'll settle for working at his own natural level and the whole job won't get done. In the second he may grow careless and apathetic, or work out his frustration with negative and disruptive behaviour.

— The *growth potential* in the job may not offer him the development he is capable or, or may be beyond his personal capacity.

2. *The working atmosphere*

Jobs are done, for the most part, not in isolation but in company with others. What features of the working atmosphere might limit your subordinate's capacity for effective performance?

— The *behaviour code* that pervades the organisation may be anti-performance. It may not be the 'done thing' to take a pride in one's work, to give loyalty to one's organisation or one's boss, to do anything that is not written into the job-description.

— The *relationships between people* may be negative or sour. There may be little sense of team-work, but a great deal of playing politics and point-scoring.

— *Management leadership* may be weak. You may be guilty of complacently accepting low performance as the norm, letting merit go unrecognised, allowing individuals to be bullied by their colleagues or shop-floor militants, and generally ignoring a poor state of morale throughout your organisation.

— The *organisation of work* may be ineffective. It may weaken commitment by causing conflict between overlapping responsibilities or by setting people at cross-purposes. (Some managers actually try deliberately to create these conditions from a mistaken belief in 'competition'.)

3. *The pressure system*

Every job has one — a framework of demands, expectations and sanctions that condition anyone's behaviour in it. Rarely put into words, often not explicitly recognised, but real for all that. It governs what gets attention in the job, what the person doing it feels he must do. It has been called 'The Law of the Situation'.

What features of the pressure system might misdirect your subordinate's efforts?

— *Pressures within the job*: its moment-by-moment demands may cause him to ignore important longer-term needs. The work-load may be too heavy for him to act effectively, or to light to maintain his interest in the job. Persistent routines may reduce his capacity to apply judgement and initiative when required.

— *Pressures from management*: your management style may make him over anxious to avoid mistakes rather than confident in exercising skill and judgement. Your orders may be given with little understanding of their practical implications. Controls may stress measurable aspects of performance and ignore important but less quantifiable aspects.

— *Pressures from organised labour*: as, say, a supervisor or foreman, general abdication of authority by management may leave him with little effective control over key responsibilities of his job. 'Custom and practice' may limit his freedom to improve working methods. The unpredictability of the work-force's reactions may lead him to play safe in his decision making. As a union member he may be constrained to avoid the risk of his union representatives' or workmates' displeasure or ridicule.

Any or all of these things may have a specific effect at any given time. By and large, though, these are things which don't change very greatly from day to day (although they may certainly change, for better or worse, over a longer period of time). They form a background, a pattern against which a general level of performance develops and becomes established. For that very reason their effect is not always recognised. Managers spend their time exhorting people to perform better without recognising the fundamental limitations which the situation is imposing.

Many of these factors are directly within your control as your people's boss. The way you organise their work, the kind of leadership you provide, how you interpret and apply the pressure system — all these can improve or worsen your people's situation. Others are things which you may be able to influence only indirectly or over a long period, such as people's relationships with each other and pressures from other sources. Some of them you can do little more than recognise and try to mitigate their effects as far as possible. However, the fact remains that as your people's immediate boss you probably have more direct influence over their situation, good, bad or indifferent, than anyone else in the organisation.

The inner forces

His situation alone does not, of course, determine entirely the way your subordinate performs his job. Probably the more important factors are those which exist, not in the environment, but within the person himself. Again you'll be able to recognise the distinction between three sets of key factors:

1. *His calibre*

This is a question of the powers he brings to his job — his capacity to cope with responsibility in general, and with the demands of the job in particular. Several personal qualities are relevant:

- His *intelligence*: his capacity for thinking things out for himself; his learning powers; his speed of uptake.
- His *temperament*: his powers of concentration; his capacity to maintain emotional stability when under pressure.
- His *force of personality*: his characteristic behaviour and its effect on others.
- His *maturity and common-sense*: the extent of his self-understanding; his capacity to cope with disappointments; the judgement with which he applies his intelligence to practical situations.
- His *tolerance of uncertainty*: his ability to keep an open mind, to avoid jumping to over-hasty conclusions; his capacity to maintain his decisions through the period before their validity is proved by results.

Many of these qualities grow gradually with age. None of them are things you can 'manage' by deliberate acts of will, apart from offering the scope and stimulation for them to develop and patiently awaiting results. Matching a person's calibre to the level of responsibility in a job is done primarily in *job placement*. He may be perfectly competent in one job, but perform poorly when promoted into a job that's too big for him or which demands aptitudes he doesn't possess. The really poor performer is the manager who put him there.

2. *His commitment*

This is a question of his attitude to the job — the amount of interest and effort he is willing to put into its performance. The popular term is 'motivation', often used to mean what is done to someone rather that what he himself brings to the job:

- *His personal goals*: the extent to which things like security, ease and comfort, companionship, self-respect, status, power or personal development are important to him; what he regards as 'being successful'.
- *His values*: acquired from upbringing and from people who have been big influences in his life: conscience, sense of responsibility, courage, etc.
- *His emotional drive*: the level of determination and persistence he has to offer.

— *His attitudes to others*: his capacity to trust other people, his reactions to authority, the extent to which he seeks to conform or to stand apart.

Most of these attributes are deeply entrenched in anyone's character. None can be deliberately manufactured or bought off by incentives. What you can do is to try to manage the situation (or your people's understanding of it) so that it draws out whatever commitment they are capable of.

Selection is the key point at which you can control your people's capacity for commitment. Managers who are casual about probing job-applicants' attitudes in their previous employment buy a great deal of trouble for themselves and their organisations.

3. *His know-how*

This is the range of knowledge, skills and habits the person has that is relevant to the particular job. Much of it he brings with him when he enters the job — his basic skills of thinking and communication, his general knowledge, his previous experience, appropriate technical qualifications etc. But most of the finer points he picks up once he is in the job.

— *His knowledge*: of the job and the organisation ('knowing the ropes'); of what to do and what not to do in different situations; of how to apply broad principles to the particular problems he meets.

— *His skills*: the physical skills required to manipulate the equipment he uses; the social skills appropriate to the people he has to deal with; the mental skills needed for the communication, problem-solving and decision-making he has to do.

— *His acquired habits*: the way his role conditions him to think and behave; the norms of work tempo and quality he subconsciously comes to accept; the disciplines and social codes that become second nature to him; his feelings of comfort about doing accustomed things in accustomed ways — his 'comfort zones'.

All of these things are *learned.* Which is not to say they are the result of formal training. In practice, most of this know-how is gained in actually doing the job — 'learning by experience'.

A person's know-how is his one attribute that can be *directly* controlled in the course of his work. You can guide what your people learn in their day-to-day experience of their jobs. Through your management of them, you can help ensure they develop the know-how that enables them to perform well — or you can choose to ignore what they are learning or not learning. Take no interest in what your people are learning from their jobs and you pay a heavy penalty in their poor performance.

Know-how is important not only for its direct effect on performance. It also decides how much of a person's *calibre* is usable in his job: unless he *knows* enough to do the job his calibre may be if little value. It also influences his *commitment* to the job: if his knowledge and skills are well-developed, they become for him an investment that he can take pride in possessing and exercising to good effect. So increasing people's know-how is a crucial management responsibility and a key way of getting high performance.

Your people's performance in their jobs is the product of these influences — those within the individuals and those in their situation. For consistently high performance it's vital that the two are well-matched: the right individual in the right situation, *and* the situation tailored, as far as possible, to fit the individual. Achieving this match is one of your most difficult and yet most fundamental tasks in managing people.

The way to approach it is the way we shall follow in this book. To examine critically each of the six principal influences on people: their jobs, the working atmosphere and the pressure system: their calibre, commitment and know-how. And then to see how you can *manage* each of these factors constructively for the benefit both of the people themselves and of your organisation.

People and performance

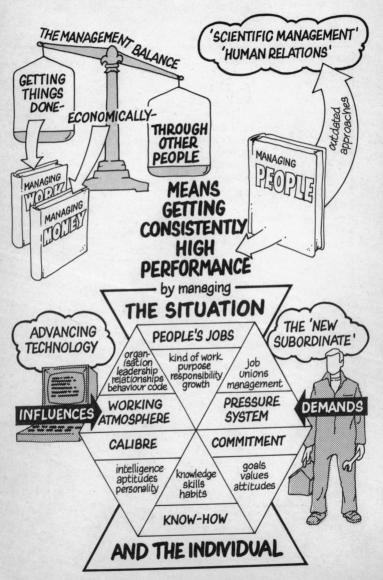

THE MANAGEMENT BALANCE

'SCIENTIFIC MANAGEMENT'
'HUMAN RELATIONS'

GETTING THINGS DONE—

ECONOMICALLY—

THROUGH OTHER PEOPLE

MANAGING WORK

MANAGING MONEY

MANAGING PEOPLE

outdated approaches

MEANS GETTING CONSISTENTLY HIGH PERFORMANCE

by managing
THE SITUATION

ADVANCING TECHNOLOGY

THE 'NEW SUBORDINATE'

PEOPLE'S JOBS

organisation
leadership
relationships
behaviour code

kind of work
purpose
responsibility
growth

job
unions
management

INFLUENCES

WORKING ATMOSPHERE

PRESSURE SYSTEM

DEMANDS

CALIBRE

COMMITMENT

intelligence
aptitudes
personality

knowledge
skills
habits

goals
values
attitudes

KNOW-HOW

AND THE INDIVIDUAL

2. Managing the situation

A lot of the job of managing people isn't in fact coping with the problems of human psychology and cussedness. It's setting the situation up so that you don't get the cussedness in the first place. In other words, it's to do with the way you arrange the anatomy of your people's jobs; it's how you keep the atmosphere in which they work sweet and wholesome; it's the way you regulate the pressures on them so they're not too much to cope with, but not so weak that your people feel no sense of challenge.

The anatomy of a job

The degree of personal satisfaction people find in their jobs naturally varies from one to another. It's the *calibre* of the individual — which we'll look at more closely later — which decides what kind of job suits that particular person best. Such things as his ability to accept and cope with responsibility, his grasp of broad issues or his attention to detail, his need for a variety of tasks or for concentration on a narrow range — all these and more will guide you in trying to pick 'horses for courses'. As a manager there may not be too much you can do to change the *type* of work your people have to do. What you can control far more easily is the *size* and *shape* of their jobs.

Here again, as so often in management, you're faced with a sort of balancing act. On the one hand you need to ensure that the job is big enough for the individual. Not just in terms of activity to fill every minute, but rather in terms of its ability to provide at least a reasonable amount of interest, involvement and even challenge. Very few of us are lucky enough to have a job which is totally satisfying all the time. But if a job can't provide *some* opportunity for personal satisfaction, you're not likely to find many people who will perform it to a consistently high standard. On the other hand, when the demands on people's time and energies are such that they are at full stretch all the time and still find it impossible to meet all the job's requirements, sheer exhaustion if nothing else will eventually ensure that performance falls off.

Actually the problem, all too often, is not really that people find their jobs too big or too small. It is that they don't really know how big or small they ought to be. There's no clear definition of jobs, and the efforts people make to sort out for themselves who should be doing what result in disagreements, rivalries, confusion and, sometimes, demoralisation.

Why define people's jobs?

Some managers deliberately avoid defining their people's jobs. They believe that if people have precise job descriptions they will then refuse to do anything which is not actually spelled out. Apart from the fact that such attitudes are usually a symptom of something fundamentally wrong in the way people are being managed, this is one of many misconceptions about the purpose and the form of job descriptions.

A job is defined in people's heads, not on paper. It is the way someone's work is understood by different people — by the person himself, by you his boss, by his colleagues and co-workers across the organisation, by his subordinates if he has any, by anyone else his work brings him into contact with. The written job description is an attempt, sometimes a poor attempt, to put these understandings into words on paper.

So why write it down? One reason is that the different people involved may have conflicting views on what the job is supposed to be. If the written description is clear and specific it can help resolve these conflicts. Another reason is that the person doing the job may never have been encouraged really to think it through. If he is involved in the writing it can help him to clarify his ideas about the job. But the key reason should be to improve the performance of work by *increasing* the scope for initiative and intelligence, not to regulate or control.

A lot of the confusion about job descriptions centres around what kind of document should be produced. All kinds of terminology is heard in different organisations — job descriptions, job specifications, job statements, management guides and so on. They may range from a sketchy half-page generalisation to a comprehensive attempt to specify every last detail of the work. Unfortunately the one thing many have in common is that they are of very little use to the person actually trying to *do* the job (we know of one company where job descriptions are kept in a locked filing cabinet in the personnel department and no-one else is allowed to see them!). There's no one 'right' way to define a job on paper. The need is first to be clear about what you're trying to achieve and then to select or design the method which will best accomplish that purpose. As a manager you should understand the differences between some common approaches to job definition.

What form of description?

Many job descriptions are written only when the need arises to recruit someone to do that particular job. We call these *ability specifications*, although they're also called man specifications, personnel specifications or, confusingly, job specifications. They may contain, depending on the thoroughness with which they're prepared, details of the qualifications, experience, knowledge, skills, temperament and personal qualities needed by the potential job-holder. What they usually do not — and need not — contain is any real guidance as to how the job should actually be tackled. Yet, in many organisations, especially in the public sector, these are the only written descriptions of jobs in existence.

Another area of confusion is with *job evaluations*. Their purpose is to set relative rates of pay for different jobs. A common approach is to assess a points rating for each of several standard factors in a job: the value of assets controlled, the number of subordinates, the possible cost of faulty decisions, etc. This is usually done on selected 'bench-mark' jobs. The difference between their points scores are used to establish pay differentials. For other jobs, pay levels are set on the basis of bench-mark jobs. A job evaluation may be a very important and useful document. However, by its very nature it is limited to those specific factors affecting the job's 'value' and may be of little practical use in deciding *how* the job should be done.

Increasingly organisations are also making use of *job analyses*. These attempt to show how the content of jobs and the methods of doing them can be improved. The assessment of management ability, for example, invariably begins with a detailed job analysis. Using some quite sophisticated research techniques we interview people doing the job, their bosses and their subordinates, to develop a list of the key abilities affecting a person's success in that job. This may help with selection or promotion decisions but is primarily aimed at determining individual training and development needs. As such it serves an enormously valuable but again strictly limited purpose.

None of these documents really help you directly to define people's jobs from the point of view of the organization of their work. The kind of job description we're after is a management tool, not a personnel record. Its purpose is to develop people's thinking about their jobs and to increase their effectiveness by giving them a clearer understanding of their particular role and contribution.

The 'job profile'

For this purpose a simple but specific form of job description is needed. At the risk of introducing a further piece of terminology we distinguish it from others by calling it a *job profile*. To get the full benefits of job profiling you have to be sure it satisfies four conditions:

1. *The person in the job should write the first draft*
Not an outsider — someone in Personnel, say, or a management consultant. He probably really understands neither the job itself not the different concepts of it that the people involved might have. Not you either, otherwise you may not discover where you and your subordinate have differences to resolve. The *person* begins the process by writing up his own view of his job. Then you discuss with him any differences of view that are revealed and work out solutions that you both agree. Then his *colleagues* can see whether there are any gaps, overlaps or inconsistencies between their jobs and his. Finally his *subordinates*, if he has any, can gain from it an understanding of how *their* jobs contribute.

2. *It should be written in clear language and with a logical structure*
After it has been written, circulated and discussed, everyone concerned should feel they understand the job more clearly than before. This isn't possible if the description is a list of conventional management clichés, or a muddle of activities, tasks, responsibilities, objectives, relationships, authority limits, performance requirements, prohibitions and exhortations.

3. *It should be designed for a specific management purpose*
It should be a *profile* of the job viewed from *one* angle, not an attempt to cover every conceivable aspect. What angle is chosen depends on the specific need the exercise is intended to meet. For example, the purpose of the exercise may be to strengthen the pattern of delegation. In this case the job profile might define the areas of responsibility and authority and the methods of accountability of each job. Or the purpose may be to identify aims and priorities. In this case the job profile should spotlight the problems and opportunities relevant to the job, the order of priority of its various objectives, and the tasks that should get most attention. But the purpose must be clear to all concerned before the process is begun.

4. *It should be regularly updated*
A three-year old job description is a historical document not a

management tool. With time, jobs change and the organisation changes around them. At least once a year, job descriptions should be reviewed and amended — totally rewritten if necessary. The annual round of appraisal interviews is as good a time as any for doing this. Although the document itself, when finally agreed, is a useful management tool, it is really the process of reaching the agreement which is of the greatest value. The discussions you have with your people in profiling their jobs will be very revealing and have all kinds of worthwhile side effects.

The language of job definition

One problem you will undoubtedly encounter when you embark on job profiling is sorting out the terminology. So many job descriptions are filled with vague abstractions or management jargon. Terms like aims, objectives, tasks, responsibilities, authority and accountability are sprinkled around in a way that belies any clear understanding of exactly what they are intended to convey. Often they are used in ways which are at best confusing, and at worst, contradictory. Even organisation 'experts' differ about the precise meaning of some of these terms. To help people understand their jobs you have to know — and be able to explain — the differences. It's not so much a matter of finding dictionary definitions as of having an acceptable, agreed understanding between all the people involved.

One of the very first things anyone needs to know about his job is what he should be trying to achieve. What are the *aims?* An aim describes a *state of affairs you want to achieve*. If the state of affairs is specified and a date is set for its achievement, it is often called an *objective*. For example:

— an *aim* for an area sales manager might be 'to match the frequency of visits to each customer to his business potential for us'.

— one of his *objectives* may be: 'within three months to achieve a 10% improvement in the call-rate on category A customers'.

If your people have a good sense of their *aims* it may be unnecessary to specify very exactly the *tasks* to be undertaken in meeting those aims. If you do decide you have to list tasks, for heaven's sake limit the profile to the *key* tasks — those that it's really important to recognise and fulfil.

A task is *a specific series of actions with a definable end-point*. The end point can be defined in terms of time and result, and often isn't specified. The task may be regularly repeated, or it may be done once only — when it is often called a *project*. The general term *activities* has more to do with how you spend your time. Some activities may be components of tasks, others may be minor and perhaps scrappy bits of the job. For example:

— a *task* of a production manager may be: 'to produce a monthly analysis of machine down-time'.

— a *project* he undertakes might be: 'to install the new milling equipment and train the work-force in its use'.

— one of his *activities* may be: 'to attend meetings with the suppliers of the milling equipment'.

Rather than filling your job profile with tasks, it will usually be more constructive to concentrate on the *responsibilities* of the job.

A responsibility is *an area of action for which you feel a continuing personal obligation*. You may well have aims in dealing with it, and perform tasks and activities in fulfilling it. But in defining the responsibility you are more concerned with marking out *the area in which you act of your own accord* — and similarly your subordinates with their responsibilities. The manager who takes the trouble to carve out areas of responsibility for each of his subordinates needs to give far fewer orders. His people become largely self-directing.

Responsibilities can be defined in general or particular terms. The trouble with general terms is that they may be too vague, and so fail to distinguish between different people's areas of action. If responsibilities are over-particularised, the list becomes too long. Judgement is needed to choose the right level.

For example, these might be some of the *responsibilities* for:

an area sales manager:	'planning the geographical coverage of the sales area'
	'gaining the commitment of the area sales team to achieving their sales targets'
a production manager:	'avoid damage being caused to plant by poor operator practices or failure to report faults'
	'economising in materials usage'
a training officer:	'organising courses to satisfy the training needs of operating departments'
	'post-course follow-through with course participants' superiors'.

Having a responsibility doesn't mean physically doing it all yourself. You may delegate much or most of the action by setting up smaller, more specific responsibilities for your subordinates. But you still carry the can for what is done.

Incidentally, here lies the answer to those managers who fear an implacable refusal by their subordinates to undertake anything not spelled-out in the job description. Where this happens, the job descriptions are usually at fault in listing tasks rather than responsibilities. If you try to write down every task your subordinates might be required to perform, it's not really surprising if they react adversely to the ones you forgot or failed to include. Nor is it the answer, in our experience, to try to cover these by the 'dustbin' category at the end — 'any other duties as required by his superior'. This may meet the letter of the law but won't help you much with people's attitudes. If, instead of specifying people's tasks, you tell them what they're *responsible for achieving*, and leave them to use a little intelligence and initiative in deciding (under your guidance) how to fulfil these responsibilities, you'll be far less likely to experience this problem.

If your subordinates are themselves managers in any sense, a very important aspect of their job which they need to know is the extent of their *authority*. Authority is the *freedom to decide the use of specified resources*. The decisions may be on the use of money, materials, equipment and other people's time (particularly subordinates' time), on the making of agreements, on the conduct of operations, on the organisation of work and on the passing-on of authority to subordinates within the area of responsibility.

For example, there might be ways of indicating the specific *authority* of:

an area sales manager:	'allocating geographic sales territories to representatives within his area' 'authorising promotional expenditure within his area up to a limit of £500 per month'
a production manager:	'scheduling machine shut-down periods for routine maintenance to meet laid-down requirements' 'authorising essential overtime up to a total of 72 hours weekly'
a training officer:	'mounting additional courses to meet excess demand up to the

limit of the training department's capacity'

'authorising purchase of visual aid materials up to a limit of £50 each month'.

An overriding principle of managing people is that authority must match responsibility. Authority without responsibility is privilege; responsibility without authority is hell! It's no good asking someone to accept the responsibility for achieving some aim if you then deny him the authority to make the decisions he must make in order to reach it.

To make this principle work, authority must not only be passed down to a manager from his boss. It must also be granted upward from his subordinates: they have to accept his right to make decisions on their work, to control their performance. If you can't maintain your authority you can't fulfil your responsibilities, and it may be your fault. You may have got authority mixed up with the exercise of personal power over your people, and that's what they resent and resist. Some managers fail to protect their authority in an effort to avoid this pitfall. Again they're missing the distinction between authority, which is necessary to the organisation, and constant hounding of people, which stems from the manager's misinterpretation of his role (and probably from his own insecurity).

Perhaps the key factor in making organisation work is this business of passing authority from one management level to another — the principle of *delegation*. We'll have more to say about this later, because it's an important element of the pressure system. However, there's one important point worth making here and now. Whatever authority you delegate, you can no longer use it yourself! This is the difference between authority and responsibility: when you delegate, you can no longer use the delegated authority — and you must restrain yourself from interfering with your subordinates' use of it. But *you* still have the responsibility for its use.

A very common failure in managing people is to abdicate rather than delegate authority. This is what happens when your people are not clear about their *accountability*. Accountability is *your control over the authority you have delegated* to your immediate subordinates. You define with them how they are to account to you for its use, just as you have to account to your boss for the authority he's delegated to you. This is an essential principle of delegation. Without it, you're not delegating at all — you're dumping.

For example, *accountability* might be expressed in these ways for:

an area sales manager: 'report quarterly to sales manager on all customers upgraded to key account status'
'report monthly to sales manager on results of promotional activity in his area'

a production manager: 'discuss with production director weekly production summaries'
'report to productivity director all equipment failures due to ineffective maintenance'

a training officer: 'discuss monthly with personnel and training manager the % utilisation of training facilities'
'report to personnel training manager all cases of dissatisfaction with courses expressed by line management'.

By giving your people a clear advance understanding of exactly how much you wish to know about their decisions and actions, you keep yourself informed and demonstrate a genuine interest in their activities. You also relieve them of the necessity to decide when and where not to report to you and avoid the equal and opposite dangers of over-involvement or loss of control. Also, you are now able to be properly accountable to *your* boss for what's happening in your part of the organisation.

Aims, tasks, responsibilities, authority and accountability are the key things that your people need to understand about their jobs. But the most important thing is that their understanding should be the same as yours. If there's confusion about the aims of a job, the responsibilities it entails, the tasks to be performed, the degree of authority it carries or the way in which the person is to be held accountable for it, then you're treading an organizational minefield. Any step may touch off argument, resentment, inefficiency and, at worst, chaos. Hence the need for every job to be defined clearly. This is the first step in getting high performance from your people.

Before we leave this crucial aspect of your people-management let's get a little practical experience with the idea of the job profile. The one job you know *really* well is your own. Or is it? When did you last pause to think objectively about it, in the sort of terms we've described?

When did you last talk about it with your boss — the whole job, not just one specific operational aspect of it? Let's find out how clear your ideas are by completing a profile of your own job.

As we've said, the first thing to decide is the *purpose* which job profiling can most usefully serve in your case. We've already suggested two — to improve the pattern of delegation or to identify aims and priorities. Possibly neither of these is the most relevant to your present situation. If not, think carefully about what you *do* want to achieve — and write it down. Then decide on the elements which the job profile should contain and draw it up.

As a guide, on the following pages are two job profile blanks designed to meet the purposes we suggested. Take the time to complete one — or both, or one of your own devising — as carefully and thoroughly as you can. Don't try to do it at one sitting. After your initial effort, allow your brain time to work subconsciously on the problem and you'll find you can add to and improve it more easily the second time around. Refer back to the earlier part of this chapter to clarify your thinking.

When your profile is as complete as you can make it, take it to your boss. Pick a moment when there's time to explain exactly what you're up to (perhaps he may like to read this chapter so that you're both on the same wavelength) and ask him to comment. Keep your mind open and listen carefully to *his* understanding of your job. From there it's a matter of reaching agreement, hopefully by a little give and take on both sides, as to the final form the profile should take. We predict that you'll find life a lot easier from then on and may well experience a better working relationship — providing you're prepared to do your bit by moving in his direction where it seems necessary.

We hope the experience will encourage you then to extend the exercise to your own subordinates, with similarly worthwhile results.

Delegation-centred job profile

This profile looks at the way responsibility is allocated and authority delegated down through your organisation. It is intended to show how clearly people's responsibilities are defined, and whether they are given adequate authority to fulfil each responsibility. Putting together the job profiles of people in the organisation can also reveal where there are gaps or overlaps in the structure.

This is how each part should be completed:

Job profile – Delegation-centred

Job title:		Date prepared:
Role:		Review dates:
Responsibilities	Authority	Accountability

Role: write a brief but specific statement of the main contribution your job makes. What would be missing from the organisation if the job didn't exist?

Responsibilities: list the areas of action you are responsible for. Show how they are different from the responsibilities of superiors and colleagues. Keep the list reasonably short — not more than a dozen items say. Concentrate on the real responsibilities, not on unimportant details.

Authority: list the kinds of decision you can take that best define the extent of your freedom of action, your power to get things done in your areas of responsibility. How far can you go in taking these decisions, and what are the points at which you must defer to someone else's authority? Although authority will be related to responsibilities, the relationship need not be one-to-one.

Accountability: against each kind of decision, show how your boss eventually finds out whether your authority has been properly used, not exceeded. Is it by his positive checks, by your reporting back, or by the absence of problems or complaints? Here a one-to-one relationship is needed, a method of accountability for each area of authority.

Priority-centred job profile

This profile identifies where a person should concentrate his efforts to improve the way his function performs — or to

Job profile – Priority-centred

Job title:		Date prepared:			
Function:		Review dates:			
Problems	Aims	Key tasks			

maintain its performance in the face of difficulties. It aims to establish an order of priority for the different things he should be working towards.

Function: a 'function' is something performed by you as a manger plus all the people below you in the organisation structure — although sometimes it may be represented by an individual in a specialist non-management role in the organisation. This is a brief statement of the main contribution the function makes. What would be missing from the organisation if the whole function didn't exist?

Problems: a 'problem' is the difference between the way something *is* and the way it *could* and *should* be. So this is a list of any difficulties or inefficiencies that reduce the function's effectiveness (or that may do in the future), and of its opportunities and possibilities — areas where its performance could be improved in some way. Some problems may lie within the function, others may be due to external factors. But all should be things you can actually *do* something about.

Aims: a list of your goals in tackling the problems. To enable concentration of effort, the list should be fairly short — not more than say six or seven aims. Each one should be realistic (i.e. capable of achievement) and specific enough to know when it has been achieved. List the aims *in order of priority* — most important first, next most important second, etc.

Key Tasks: A list of the main things you have to do to achieve the aims — a simple statement in each case. Don't include non-essentials. This should be a list of *key* tasks.

A healthy atmosphere

Legislation forces employers' attention to the physical environment in which their people work. Many go beyond the dictates of the law in ensuring acceptable standards of temperature, light and air. Yet many more fail to perceive that their people labour under the handicap of a psychological 'atmosphere' which stifles their initiative and morale as surely as an airless office or factory would affect their physical well-being.

Your people's working atmosphere is affected by four principal influences: the complex and subtle network of unwritten laws which constitute the organisation's *behaviour code*; the feelings of mutual liking, respect and dependence which characterises personal *relationships*; the quality of *leadership* which you and your management colleagues provide; and the strength of the formal and informal communication links created by the *organisation* of work. Any one of these — or, more likely, a combination of them — may be creating a working atmosphere which continually undermines your people's co-operation and team-work and reduces their joint performance. Conversely, you may be fortunate (or skilful) enough to enjoy a working atmosphere in which these influences positively reinforce your efforts to maximise your team's performance.

Some of these influences are wholly or partly within the control of the individual manager. Others are the product of practices and prejudices built up over many years and beyond managers' ability to affect directly. *None* of them are susceptible to sudden change or simple solutions.

Deciphering the behaviour code

For some managers the most difficult problem is to become aware of the true causes of a restrictive behaviour code. Symptoms such as poor co-operation, diminishing pride in work well done and generally obstructive behaviour are easier to attribute to the 'bloody-mindedness' of staff or workers. It's harder to look for the underlying grievances and dissatisfactions, long-suffered and fatalistically accepted, which are at the root of such attitudes.

Usually the existence of an anti-performance behaviour code is the result of people's failure to perceive past rewards for their performance as matching their efforts. In this sense, rewards don't mean solely money — although the feeling of being inadequately or unfairly paid, when it exists, is obviously a severe handicap. More often, it is the simple feeling that effort has not been recognised or appreciated by the organisation in general or by particular bosses, which nurtures the 'why bother?' philosophy. And, naturally, there will frequently be those few individuals who, for a variety of reasons, seize upon every opportunity to sap the loyalty and conscientiousness of the majority.

When managers are asked why they don't show appreciation, they often reveal one of two fears: that praise of any kind may produce complacency and slackness, or that it may be interpreted as 'flannel' and damage respect. Certainly there is little evidence that praise *in itself* actually increases performance. To do that other means have to be applied, which we will discuss later. But neither does praise have to result in a general resting on laurels. The trick is to make the praise *specific* — to give credit where it is due — and to avoid over-doing it. In this way recognition will be seen as having been *earned* — and reinforce, not diminish, the standard of performance.

Showing appreciation is not limited to praising people's work or thanking them for a job well done. It has to be demonstrated in many little ways which are impossible to enumerate. And, of course, it has to be balanced by an appropriate response when performance falls short of what could be achieved. It is when praise is used in a manipulative way and is at odds with the manager's general attitude that people perceive and react to insincerity — one of the most disliked qualities in a boss.

If the behaviour code is working against you in your organisation you have a lengthy and difficult task ahead to change it. But it's a task that can't be shirked if you want to improve performance. There are few hard and fast rules about how to tackle it, except perhaps one. A head-on clash is unlikely to produce results. You may be able to compel people to meet minimum performance standards, but what you really want is that extra effort which has to be offered freely. You'll find more help in this area when we discuss commitment later on.

The effect of relationships

The prevailing behaviour code in a team is closely linked to the relaionships which exist within it. Few groups of people at work are without occasional disagreements or differences. A limp and spineless harmony may in fact be less productive than healthy rivalry. But the performance of the team will suffer if mutual suspicion, political point-scoring or just plain dislike one for another is the norm rather than the exception.

Getting people working together *as* a team is one of your key tasks as a manager. Again, it's something we'll deal with specifically as a part of gaining people's commitment. The *basis* for teamwork, however, is people's feelings towards each other. A useful list of the factors affecting group atmosphere has been produced by an American researcher named Fred Fiedler. He uses a questionnaire which asks people to describe their working group in the following ways:

- how friendly the members of the group are to each other
- how well accepted each member feels by the others
- how much satisfaction they get from the group's activities

- how enthusiastic team members are
- how productive they are within the group
- how co-operative they are with each other
- how supportive they are of each other
- how interesting each member is to the others
- how successful each member is in achieving goals set by the group.

Fiedler uses the answers to these questions, in the form of a numerical score, to determine the style of leadership to which a group is likely to respond. (He combines it, incidentally, with two other factors: the structure of the group's tasks and the 'position-power', or perceived authority, of the leader. Significantly, he concludes that group atmosphere is the most important influence.)

Your first reaction to that list may be that few of the qualities mentioned are ones that you can hope to change. Many of them depend on the personalities of the people involved and their reactions to each other. Don't lose sight of the fact, though, that in talking about a relationship we are considering *all* the members of the team — including you, a very influential member, as its leader. If you can't influence it, who can?

The forces of leadership

Leadership is an aspect of management about which more has been written in recent years than almost any other. We'll review some of the more relevant and practical theories later. In terms of a group's working atmosphere, however, it's sensible to examine what we call the forces of leadership.

Because of your *position*? They are submissive to your status in the hierarchy rather than to you as a person. They are in awe of authority. The force is one of convention or inertia: "we always do as our superior officers tell us".

Because you *domineer* them? They are nervous of the consequences of displeasing you. Your manner may be overbearing or distant. You may be unconcerned, even contemptuous of their feelings and interests. They lack the power or will to retaliate.

Because you are *popular*? You act in a warm and likeable way towards them, and your leadership avoids any conflict with their wishes or expectations. They are happy to go along with someone they regard as "really just one of us".

Why people follow your lead

Because they *respect* you? They may not like you, but they admire your integrity and character. They may also have a high regard for other qualities: Your competence in the work? Your courage? Your energy? Your determination? Above all, they "know where they stand" with you.

Because they *trust* you? You may not always give them exactly what they want, but they believe you understand them, are concerned to see they get fair treatment, have the ability to protect and support them. Through you they gain in self-respect and self-confidence to stand on their own feet.

Because you have *charisma*? You have a natural 'presence', a dominant personality and a reputation as a 'winner'. They feel safe when you are around, and may be flattered to feel they share in your personal power and prestige. You may even give them a 'cause' they can believe in and become committed to.

What makes you a leader? Essentially, the fact that people are prepared to follow you. The real question is why they respond to your lead.

These forces are not mutually exclusive. Several may be affecting your relationship with your people. Domineering leaders sometimes have the respect of their people. You can have both charisma and your people's trust. And so on. But in your leader-led relationship one force is likely to predominate. And this will undoubtedly be having a profound effect on the working atmosphere. Ask yourself:

which force is uppermost in my leadership? What evidence do I have for this? What are the pros and cons of that force? On balance, does it get the best from my people in the situation we're working in? Could a different force draw more from them? How can I go about developing the most effective relationship with my people — how can I build their trust and win their respect?

The organisation of work

Your group's working atmosphere may be damaged by the behaviour code, poor internal relationships or ineffective leadership. Quite often, however, even when these factors are positive in their effect, a fourth influence still limits achievement. Commitment is weakened and co-operation restricted by deficiencies in the way the work is organised.

Part of good organisation is the proper definition of people's jobs, which we've already examined quite thoroughly. Clear, written job descriptions (and the discussions inherent in the process) will help to eliminate overlapping responsibilities or gaps in coverage of the workload. However, the effective performance of each individual will depend also to some extent on the structure by which individual jobs are linked.

Structuring an organisation is, of course, usually the prerogative of fairly senior management. Perhaps some 'experts' or specialists, either within or from outside the enterprise, may be involved. But the view from the lofty pinnacle of the corporate mountain is not always sharply-focused enough to produce sound, detailed decisions about what should actually be happening in the foothills. True, the best top managers do descend from time to time, to a point from which observation of the nursery slopes can be reasonably accurate.

Even so, they're usually wise enough to rely for detailed organisational decisions on the people closest to the action — the 'subordinate' managers who really know the up-to-date demands of the work at and around their own levels.

So organised structure — if you like, deciding who does what, with whom, and where, when and how — is a concern for *every* manager or supervisor. And one which directly affects his success in managing his people. At the lower levels of management it's true that the scope for organisation (or re-organisation) may be limited to relatively minor adjustments to people's job responsibilities and workloads, or to small practical improvements in the working systems and procedures. However, don't underestimate the effect of (and necessity for) this kind of fine-tuning. The front-line manager who believes that such decisions are the sole prerogative of his superiors may be neglecting an important component of the overall control of his operation.

Of course, all managers need also to be able to judge when *not* to re-organise. You may well have read this much-quoted complaint:

> 'We trained hard, but it seemed that every time we were beginning to form up into teams, we would be re-organised. I was to learn later in life that we tend to meet any new situation by re-organising, and a wonderful method it can be for creating the illusion of progress while producing confusion, inefficiency and demoralisation'.

If that has you nodding in agreement and guessing which industrial enterprise it refers to, you may be intrigued to learn that its author was Gaius Petronius Arbiter, a Roman Governor under Nero! Unfortunately, it still rings true of many modern undertakings, where hardly anybody has time to become familiar with the current organisation structure before the next change. Conversely, others continue to labour under the handicap of an unwieldly and outdated structure which has long since outlived its usefulness. And either of these equally unfavourable situations can apply to a supervisor and his six-man team as easily as to a mammoth commercial or industrial enterprise.

Getting the structure right

The point of organisation is that a group of people working towards a common objective should be able to produce more than they could if each worked in isolation. So one of the key contributions of management is to enable that to happen by co-ordinating. This means putting people's different talents and abilities to the best use and providing them with the links they need, in all directions, to create a truly co-operative effort. Good

37

organisation represents, if you like, the mechanical linkage; co-ordination is the lubrication which keeps it working smoothly.

As with job definition, the important thing about an organisation structure is not the piece of paper on which it is formally described. The more significant factor is, once again, people's *understanding* of how the organisation works — from whom they take their lead, who they communicate with for specific purposes, who is able to provide help and advice and how all these common-sense links are maintained and used. This understanding represents the *informal* organisation structure — the way things actually happen. Informal structure always exists and it is foolish either to ignore or to fight it. On the contrary, the manager who understands organisation positively nurtures and develops the informal links which get the work done.

However, if the informal picture is too far removed from the formal structure, obvious problems may result: the usurping of authority, the by-passing of necessary reporting relationships, the break-down of accountability and ultimately the loss of control. Informal relationships, direct information exchanges and common-sense working collaborations must exist within the formal pattern of known responsibility, authority and accountability. They must complement and enhance, not challenge or undermine, the formal structure.

For this reason it is necessary for the organisation structure to be logically thought-through and then depicted in a way which is available and understandable to all. Usually this means an *organisation chart*. This shows the positions in the organisation, their levels of responsibility and the lines of *formal* communication — those concerned with authority and accountability. Some organisation charts also attempt to suggest such refinements as relative status or informal lines of communication. But the purpose of an organisation chart is to help everyone get a picture of the organisation and to make it possible to spot and analyse structural problems, work out solutions to them and plan future changes.

This highlights an important need in organisation structure: that it should be dynamic, as opposed to static. One of the problems in representing organisation graphically is that it almost automatically creates a reluctance to change the picture. Yet the detail of the structure itself may (indeed, should) change quite frequently in response to the changing demands on the organisation — demands of varying workloads and changing activities, of untimely difficulties and unforeseen turns of events. One authority in the field says that we should think of the organisation chart not as a picture, but as one frame in a film. We know that each succeeding frame is going to be slightly different, and we know that there's going to be an enormous difference between the first frame and the last. Perhaps that's overstating the case for dynamism, but it serves to underline the need for flexibility in organisation structures.

Principles of organising

If you happen to be a first-line manager with a small team you won't, perhaps, have too many worries about organisation structure. As soon as you begin to move up the promotion ladder, however, acquiring new areas of responsibility and more subordinates with more diverse talents, it becomes essential for you to understand and apply some basic principles of organisation.

The first is that the structure should grow from the *demands of the work*, not from the characteristics of the people in it. It needs a logical base that won't be disrupted by changes in its membership. Obvious, perhaps, but many a structure has been shaped more to accommodate personalities past or present than to suit the work. Certainly a structure has to be adjusted for the people in it, but *first* it should be properly engineered for the work to be done.

Secondly, the structure should be based on a *division of responsibility*. This is not the same thing as allocation of activities. It is poor organisation to give people a succession of things to do rather than a sense of their responsibilities. As we said earlier, a 'responsibility' is a person's feeling of obligation for a specified aspect of the work or its management, his understanding of what he has to act on *without being told to*.

The third principle is that *'spans of control'* should not be too wide. Each manager is responsible for co-ordination between the jobs of his subordinates. He has to see that the communication system between them works, and to arbitrate when co-operation fails. But if he has too many subordinates he cannot do this effectively. So how many people should be directly accountable to each manager? The answer depends partly on the work, partly on the people:

— for the work, the question is how complex are the inter-relationships between the jobs. At higher levels, complex inter-relationships often make spans of more than six or seven subordinates ineffective. Lower down, the simpler relationships may allow wider spans.
— for the people, the question is one of team-sense.

Eleven or twelve people are probably the most that can feel themselves to be a unified team.

Spans of control can also be too narrow. A number of one-to-one boss-subordinate relationships is often the sign of poor organisation and of jobs which have too little to interest or occupy the people in them.

Fourthly, there should be no more *levels* than necessary in the structure. As a general rule the fewer the better, to keep lines of communication and control short. But this has to be balanced against the need to avoid over-wide spans of control. Only real levels count. Not deputies or assistants who aren't carrying a full managerial responsibility, nor managers who merely pass their bosses' instructions down the line. At each *real* level, the managers have full authority for decisions about their subordinates' work.

And lastly, *boundaries between jobs* should be made clear. This is a question of how the organisation structure operates. At one extreme is the rigid *'mechanistic'* structure: strict boundaries between the activities of different jobs, people very conscious of what each must and mustn't concern himself with, much awareness of jobs' status. At the other extreme is the flexible *'organic'* structure: boundaries defined more by the aims and priorities of different jobs, people more concerned for co-operation and teamwork than for overstepped boundaries, open expression of views etc. uninhibited by differences in status.

Any organisation (or any department in it) will be somewhere between these extremes. As the world becomes tougher for our organisations and the pace of change increases, the organic pattern is proving to be the better for organisational survival.

These are the things which principally determine the *working atmosphere* in which your people operate — the behaviour code, relationships between people, the strength of management leadership and the organisation of work. Even small improvements in any of these areas will be handsomely repaid. But well-understood and clearly-defined jobs, and a favourable working atmosphere must be complemented by one further set of considerations — those relating to what we called the pressure system.

Regulating the pressure system

When you jump into your car to run down to the shops or

wherever, the series of actions you go through are pretty automatic — certainly if you're an experienced driver. Having started the engine, selected first gear and checked it's safe to move off, you set the car in motion by the opposite action of your two feet (assuming you don't drive an automatic!). The right presses down on the accelerator as the left is lifted from the clutch pedal. The two movements are skilfully co-ordinated to produce a smooth take-off. At the same time your hands move the steering wheel one way or the other to control the direction of travel.

Without really thinking about it, you are using three different *pressures* (or, in one case, the release of pressure), automatically from long practice and experience. Without any one of those pressures, all the power of the engine may be useless, or dangerously misdirected. At the first hazard or obstacle you meet, pressure is applied again, this time to the brake (and simultaneously to the clutch, in order to keep the engine power available to increase speed again).

Although the analogy is not perfect, the pressures on people at work are not too dissimilar from this accelerator/clutch/steering wheel/brake arrangement. Some exist within the work itself and others come from other people — from their bosses, colleagues, subordinates, customers, even wives and families! They may be of many kinds and act in various ways.

Together they make up the 'pressure system' of your organisation. Properly adjusted, it can help to ensure that the motive power within your people is harnessed to the best effect. Wrongly applied it can result in that power being dissipated or dangerously misused in unwanted directions.

Some of the pressures within your people's jobs we've already looked at. Perhaps the most obvious is the workload that each one carries. If it is too heavy, too many conflicting demands to be fitted into too little time, it may be impossible to cope effectively. On the other hand, if you've ever had a job in which there was *no* pressure of work, too little to do, you'll know how demoralising that can be. Some jobs, or course, have fluctuating workloads which move from one extreme to the other. The uncertainty this creates is in itself another kind of pressure, more easily tolerated by some than others.

The effects of widely fluctuating or badly distributed workloads can be quite severe. Check your own operation for any tell-tale signs. Sometimes work has to be done twice because mistakes slip through without being checked. Important deadlines are missed and results delayed because of the time taken for routine processing. Information can't always be found when its needed. These problems are sometimess quite serious and cause considerable temporary upheaval in your department. Most of the time they're not much more than pinpricks — it's easy to shrug them off as inevitable or to miss the signs altogether. But what you're experiencing is often evidence of too little attention having been given to an important aspect of your people's and your own situation.

Checking the systems

The work of your department, section, unit or whatever may be quite routine and repetitive; it might be very creative and innovative; more probably, it's somewhere between these two extremes. Wherever it fits on the scale, in order to get it done at all you have to rely, at least to some extent, on the implementation (perhaps almost unconsciously) of laid-down *systems*: clerical systems, measurement systems, recording systems, communication systems — even tea and coffee-making systems.

Sometimes these systems are the very stuff of the job itself and just following the system seems to be the main aim of the work. In other cases the systems are almost incidental and unnoticed, but nevertheless provide a foundation without which much of the innovative effort could be largely wasted. Either way, these systems are critical in their effect on people's efficiency and morale. One of your responsibilities as a manager is continually to be looking for opportunities to improve them, or at very least be sure that they continue to meet your organisation's changing needs.

Systems design is today an increasingly complex and sophisticated business. Large undertakings will have specialist departments offering services to management such as Organisation and Methods Study, Work Study, Operational Research and so on. As a manager you will benefit from taking the trouble to acquire a working knowledge of those that are relevant to your area of responsibility, if only to be able to interpret intelligently the ideas they put forward and use them to the best practical advantage.

However, nothing more than application of a little common sense is needed to ensure that the systems you and your people regularly use are helping and not hindering your progress. To spot where systems are needed in places that haven't had them before and to see where doing away altogether with an unnecessary system will save time and effort.

Asking the right questions

The need is for a questioning attitude, even towards areas of the operation which seems to be running smoothly. How long will they go on that way? Is there an even better approach? And of course apply the same thinking to the more obvious problem areas — information bottle-necks, work overloads, time-wasting, inexplicable delays, missed targets and low standards. Look for the causes and analyse the problems.

This questioning attitude in itself requires a sort of system — or at least a systematic application. Whether attempting to solve a pressing problem or to re-appraise an apparently satisfactory process, the following checklist will help you to identify the key facts about any system:

WHY   does the system exist? Is it still necessary? Could it achieve its purpose better? Should its purpose be changed?

WHAT   does it achieve? Could it achieve more? Does it attempt to achieve too much?

HOW   does it work? Could it be simpler? More flexible? Is there any duplication of effort? Unnecessary refinements? Does it overlap with any other system?

WHO   benefits from the system? Do they still need it? Are they getting what they need from it? Could anyone else benefit from it?

WHEN   does it apply? Should the frequency be reduced — or increased?

WHERE   else could it be usefully applied? Where are there other problems or needs that could be tackled by introducing a similar or a different system?

The answers to these questions may suggest immediate changes. At least they'll pinpoint the areas in which you need to seek help and advice. When you decide to change systems, however, remember that they all involve people. Ask yourself a few additional questions. Who started this system? Does anyone still have a feeling of ownership? How will different people react to the change? Who will have to be consulted, who convinced, who placated?

Remember too that few people welcome change. For some it represents a positive threat. Changes in systems usually mean that people have to change, if only slightly, their working practices, even their habits. Some changes take time. Don't expect instant results — allow time for the personal adjustments that are needed. This is the strongest argument for planning changes well ahead of the point where they become emergencies.

Don't change too much too often. And don't change unless you're reasonably sure there's a visible, tangible benefit to be gained. Consistency and familiarity with systems are benefits to be nurtured and the manager who's constantly tinkering with systems to no good effect not only becomes unpopular with his people but seldom achieves anything worthwhile.

Don't get the question of systems out of proportion either. The manager who devotes all — or most — of his attention to devising and maintaining systems is trying to make them do things which can really only be done by leadership. But the leader ignores systems at his peril. Really the two are indivisible: a large part of good management is to make it as easy as possible for people to achieve worthwhile results, but the systems by which you try to do that will only be followed intelligently when people respond to your leadership. Managing people is largely a question of the things we've yet to discuss in detail — increasing their motivation, improving communication and developing their abilities. None of these is really possible if you're struggling eternally to overcome poor job understandings, ineffective structure or unworkable systems. Without leadership, the best organisations have been known to fail. But without good organisation, the best leadership is eventually hamstrung.

The pressures created by the organisation's systems are, of course, by no means the only kind experienced by your people. So far we've tended to use the word pressure as though it were an evil to be avoided, or at least relieved as far as humanly possible. Managers who try to remove *all* the pressure from their people, leaving aside the impossibility of such an aim, are missing an important point. Relieved of all pressure the human being has no motivation (or will be motivated towards other activities than his work). The aim should be to apply the right *kind* of pressure in the right way.

Most people want their managers to manage. Not just tell them what to do, but to create conditions in which they have worthwhile responsibilities, the necessary authority to carry them out *and* know how they are to be held accountable for the results. This is pressure of the right kind, applied through the use of one of the key skills in managing people — the skill of delegation.

Are you delegating enough?

As we've already said, the principle here is that authority must match responsibility. Unfortunately this principle is widely misunderstood and badly applied by a great many managers. Delegation isn't intended to allow you a life of idleness or the time to improve your golf handicap. Its purpose is to strip you of unnecessary work so that you can devote your attention to your bigger responsibilities. Managers should be busy. But they should be busy doing important things: defining aims, planning and organising their operations, listening and analysing, foreseeing problems, maintaining their people's morale and commitment, developing their subordinates for the future. To maintain the impression of great importance by rushing about performing tasks that your subordinates could (and should) handle better is merely foolish.

There are few hard and fast rules that will help you decide what to delegate. But these are some good guidelines:

— delegate what you are *used to doing* or are skilled at doing. You can train and control subordinates far more effectively in a task that you know well than in a task you have only recently learned to cope with. Don't penalise your own effectiveness by hanging on to tasks that are comfortable, but not suitable

— delegate those tasks for which your subordinates have *better knowledge* and information than you have. Decisions are better taken by those who have the knowledge than by those who have only the formal authority.

— delegate whatever *authority* your subordinates need to fulfill the responsibilities you give them. Don't ask them to do something where it is not in your power to give them the power to match — like expecting them to get information from other departments that even you haven't the power to demand. Remember that 'responsibility without authority' is a definition of hell.

— delegate *some big decisions*. They are what help your subordinates grow. Choose those that mean a lot to them and that have an important impact on their effectiveness — their methods of sharing work or of co-ordination, say, or improvements in systems or procedures. Draw up whatever limits you think are necessary. But don't merely delegate ape-work.

— delegate to the *maximum of each subordinate's ability* to carry responsibility. Even if you do occasionally find you have delegated a two-ulcer task to a one-ulcer man, that is a smaller fault in a manager than failing to delegate at all.

Managers are often criticised for not delegating enough. Perhaps we should be equally critical of the manager who delegates too much too quickly — the manager who doesn't know the difference between delegating authority and dumping it. Delegation isn't handing a job over and then forgetting about it. You must first be sure that your subordinate has acquired the knowhow, judgement and confidence needed. Secondly you must have built in the controls that give you a regular check on your subordinate's performance — otherwise you know neither who are the poor performers not who are the good performers.

Are you really delegating?

If you feel that you're already delegating effectively, perhaps it would be a good idea to carry out a check. Ask yourself whether you can truthfully give a 'yes' response to each of these statements:

1. *I am willing to let go*
Do not go on making decisions for the job you have left behind. The clerk who becomes Office Manager should not meddle with the clerical work that is now his subordinates' concern.

(There is a kind of managerial law here: a manager makes himself effective when he concentrates his own efforts on managerial tasks and delegates operational tasks — *even though he is better at the operational tasks than his subordinates are*. This law is difficult to observe. But it is vital for good leadership.)

2. *I am willing to give my subordinates' ideas a chance*
The less NIH factor you have, the better. (NIH = 'Not Invented Here' and therefore 'No Good'). Good ideas often look strange at first sight.

3. *I am willing to set up standards and controls*
You can delegate only as far as you can accept responsibility for results. This means setting up controls that limit your own freedom of action: whatever tasks you *retain* you have to run by plan, not by ear.

4. *I am willing to let others make mistakes*
In the process of learning how to do things, people must be free to make mistakes. A baby that was beaten every time it fell over would never acquire much of a taste for walking.

You can reduce the risks by standard setting, by matching responsibility to ability, by guidance and coaching. But mistakes will happen. Use them to build on for the future, not to find whipping-boys: ask 'What can we learn from the mistake?' 'Who is to blame?' (it may well be you anyway).

5. *I am willing to keep my people in the picture*
This takes time and effort. But if you keep them in the dark — either accidentally or deliberately — you sabotage delegation. It is your responsibility to give them whatever information you have, not their responsibility to ask for it.

Five 'yes' answers and you're a real delegator. Any 'no' indicates an area you should think carefully about — and then act.

Improve your delegation

If you're not entirely satisfied with your delegation but find it hard to know where or how to improve it, here's an exercise that will help you to give yourself more time for your real management priorities, allow yourself more scope to organize your own work effectively, develop your subordinates' abilities and commitment and ensure there is proper cover for your absence.

Start by thinking through the things you perhaps *ought* to be doing as a manager. For instance, are you giving enough time and attention to:
— thinking ahead and planning?
— keeping in touch with what is going on in your areas of responsibility?

— talking with your people and listening to them?

— identifying actual or potential problems and trying to reduce or prevent them in the future?

— improving the way your operation runs?

— increasing your people's abilities and commitment?

— developing your subordinates to cope with bigger responsibilities in the future?

If the answer to any of these questions is no, or if you're continually short of time to do these things, here's how to go about improving the situation by a three-stage analysis.

Stage I

Identify the *tasks and responsibilities* you *ought* to delegate. Are you, for example, getting too involved in:

— work that is really part of your subordinates' jobs?

— 'DIY' tasks you find personally interesting?

— time-consuming routine or straightforward activities?

— detailed administrative or clerical operations?

— 'polishing up' things already done by your staff?

— fighting fires your people should be able to cope with?

— tasks that cause problems in your absence?

— responsibilities you could be using to stretch your subordinates?

On the worksheet on the following page, list the tasks and responsibilities you have identified, then write the name of one of your subordinates at the head of each column.

Stage II

For each task or responsibility listed, decide the *extent* to which you *eventually* want to be able to delegate to a subordinate. Use these symbols:

D: *Delegate* the full responsibility for it. He will act on his own initiative without being asked to do it.

C: *Cover* responsibility to act on his own initiative in your absence.

B: *Brief* him task by task. The task is allocated to him each time — he doesn't do it on his own initiative.

A: *Assisting* you in doing it — taking over certain of the detailed work involved, or understudying the task as part of his development.

Against each task listed in Stage I, note the code letter under the appropriate subordinate in the II column.

Delegation worksheet

Stage I: Tasks and responsibilities	Subordinates:												
	II	III	II	III	II	III	II	III	II	III	II	III	II	III

Stage III

For each task or responsibility, specify how you will *prepare* your subordinate, and how you will *support* him as he begins doing it. Identify the appropriate level in each of the two lists below:

Preparation	*Support*
4 *Training:* attendance at a course and/or extensive on-the-job coaching.	4 *Continuous:* close supervision throughout, helping him with any difficulties.
3 *Demonstration:* show how to do it, explaining purpose and points to observe. Then he practices it himself—you observe and correct him if necessary.	3 *Periodic:* check his progress at intervals and advise or help him as necessary. When completed, review his performance thoroughly with him.
2 *Explanation:* tell him in detail exactly what to do and why. Encourage questions. Use feedback to check he has understood.	2 *On request:* he can ask for help, but you get involved *only* at his request. Review the result with him afterwards.
1 *Instructions:* simply state the requirements. Leave him to work out how to do it.	1 *End check:* you don't expect him to need helm. Check the result only.
0 *No preparation:* he is fully competent to decide what to do, how and when.	0 *Full delegation:* no support needed. You rely on your general controls to maintain accountability.

In the III column for each subordinate note the code numbers against each of the code letters noted in Stage II. For example, '3 4' means that you will give him a demonstration and some practice to prepare, and then provide support by supervising him closely as he does it.

Remember: you are defining how you intend *starting* the delegation. As time goes on, for many of the tasks you might normally expect to be able to reduce the level of support, until eventually he is operating at the 1 or 0 level.

The proper delegation of authority, along with a clear understanding of the accountability that goes with it, is one of the most productive elements of your people-management. It's worth a great deal of time and careful thought to get it right. And it's crucual to the question of striking the right balance in your organisation's pressure system.

Pressure v. stress

There's an important distinction to be drawn here. While a certain amount of pressure is essential to good performance, stress creates mental and physical health hazards, which adversely affect not only the individual but also the organisation. A good deal of research into the cause of stress is still taking place and the picture which is emerging is a complex one. There is considerable evidence that simply working in a large and complex organisation is itself a source of stress. The most extreme effects are obvious to all: physiological symptoms such as ulcers and heart attacks, leading to premature retirement. Less obvious are the tensions which tend to be accepted as the inevitable penalty of certain types of occupation. These are frequently increased in a difficult economic climate or by the organisation's relative lack of success.

It's often assumed that stress is caused primarily by overwork. In fact, it has been shown that equal stress can be created by the opposite: people feeling that they are stagnating, that their jobs are obsolescent, that their skills and abilities are under-used or that they have little or nothing to do. Your problem as a manager is therefore partly what Canadian professor John Howard has called 'managerial rust-prevention'.

Of the two conditions, this 'rusting' may actually be a more serious problem than overwork, both psychologically and in terms of physical health. People in that situation often become depressed, even, in extreme cases, suicidal. The person suffering the stress of overwork often has the protection of enjoying the job. Professor Howard's research shows that the more an individual is satisfied with his job and his career, the fewer stress symptoms he reports. He is convinced that it is better for an individual to run too fast than too slow and that it is better to err on the side of putting too much, rather than too little, pressure on people.

This seems to be a good general guide for the manager, always given the need to interpret it with common sense and sensitivity to individuals' reactions.

In general, as pressure increases, so performance increases — up to a certain point. Beyond that point, where pressure exceeds a reasonable peak, performance declines again in response to new and different stresses. So your task is to try to keep people working at the top of the curve — not too much pressure, not too little. The trouble is, of course, that the shape of the curve differs from one individual to another. You must *know* who reacts well to more pressure, who to less. Getting optimum performance from each individual depends largely on this knowledge.

One final point, about the causes of stress, which reinforces something we said earlier. Medical author Dr Vernon Coleman believes that it is the artificial separation of responsibility and authority which, in his words, 'causes much of the anger, dissatisfaction and jealousy in our society and which, therefore, indirectly causes more stress-induced illness than anything else'.

He cites his own profession, in which a hospital doctor who is morally and legally responsible for the health of the patients in his care does not have the authority to insist that the hospital is kept properly supplied with staff or drugs. He can't even get the heating turned on when he thinks it is necessary. The person more likely in practice to have that authority is the union representative, who has no responsibility for the health of patients. His responsibilities are defined and limited, but his authority may be great. Who can't recognise this situation in hundreds of factories and offices? Foremen and supervisors frequently carry enormous responsibilities, but have far too little authority to make the decisions those responsibilities entail. Equally you will have seen managers who exercise plenty of authority but try to evade any real responsibility for the results of the orders they issue — a perfect recipe for creating stress in their people, rather than productive pressure.

Pressures from organised labour

Dr Coleman's comment on management authority abdicated to union representatives leads us to one other important element in an organisation's pressure system.

Your personal view of this difficult topic, fraught with political overtones, probably depends on the working practices and the kind of relationships with trades unions which exist in your organisation. It may appear to have little relevance if you work in one of those organisations which union power has yet to penetrate. You may be unfortunate enough to have to manage where a climate of poor industrial relations creates major problems in the control and direction of your operation. You may yourself be a member of a trades union, as increasingly many managers and supervisors are. Whatever your personal situation as a manager you shouldn't ignore the fact that union influence over workers in all kinds of organisations and at many different levels is still steadily increasing. Depite any legislation which may be enacted, this kind of pressure is likely to be a factor in the life of most managers for the foreseeable future. Does it *have* to be a negative factor?

It's unfortunate that the greatest media exposure is always given to the worst examples of industrial relations. It's equally unfortunate that in the coverage given by large sections of the press, the unions are usually cast in the role of villain. Although there are obviously many instances of short-sighted and obstructionist behaviour on the part of union officials, such behaviour can often be seen as a response to ineffective management — often over many years. This is illustrated by the views of a maintenance electrician at British Leyland's Speke plant on Merseyside, published a few years ago. 'At Speke, apathy with a capital 'A' is the name of the game. It runs through every level of the workforce, from cleaners to top management. This leads to frustration on the part of an operator. If he has a problem, his only line of communication is through his foreman. If that foreman is indifferent to the man's needs, then his only other outlet is a complaint to the shop steward, who will not be indifferent, and who will know how to cut corners and get things done. Gradually the shop steward becomes the focal point of the shop floor'.

In this instance it would be easy to condemn the formen for their indifference. However, should we perhaps question whether their attitude stems in turn from their experience with their own senior management?

Some other foremen sacked by Plessey for allowing night-shift operators to sleep instead of working felt they had been made scapegoats for senior managers, who knew of these malpractices but ignored them, or who ought to have known, and didn't. The foremen were not made to feel any better by the fact that the workers themselves escaped with written warnings. It is hard to escape the conclusion that a purge on the shop floor might have led to strikes, whereas the sacking of the foremen was acceptable to both workforce and management. Of course, a foreman is (or ought to be) a manager. If he condones wrongdoing on the shop floor the he is as much to blame as his people. But he can only be a manager if his bosses accept him as such. As one of the three sacked Plessey foremen said: 'We are the buffer between management and the workforce. As is always the case with intermediate supervision, we took the kicks from both sides'.

Middle managers also complain that their ability to manage has been eroded, particularly in the nationalised industries. One of the greatest barriers to effective management is seen to be the fact that all conditions of pay and work are laid down nationally. A manager in British Steel asked 'How can I keep my lads motivated, when I am not allowed to do anything for them, because it is all dictated by national agreements and rules? The man who does the minimum all year gets the same as the one who pulls out all the stops'. There is no doubt that in many industries, top management's weakness in union negotiations has made a rod for the backs of junior managers. One of the worst examples is the newspaper industry, with its out-dated work procedures, union power in its most basic and uncontrollable form, poor labour relations, generally bad working conditions, widespread indiscipline, and a history of complacent management. The one national newspaper management which seems to have made inroads into a number of these problems is Rupert Murdoch's *Sun*. Among the reasons for their relative success is that production managers have been given authority to resist sudden union demands (traditionally made in the middle of a vital print run at 3 o'clock in the morning). Equally importantly, a good deal of effort has been put into giving the unions a clear idea of what management wants and the limits within which they can bring pressure to bear. They might not like management's plans, but at least they know what they are.

At the root of so many instances of poor union relationships, this question of communication can be clearly seen to be a major cause. A staff representative at Rolls Royce's aero engine plant is quoted as saying: 'Half my problem as a representative would go away if management would only tell my members what's going on'. This view is backed up over and over again.

A worker in one of the Post Office's major Mail Centres described the atmosphere: 'Supervisors rarely spoke to the men under them, beyond issuing commands, which were sometimes contradicted by other officials. As a result they were often held in contempt by the workers. The upper echelons of management were rarely glimpsed on the sorting floor'. The problem of communication is not an easy one to solve, and we shall have more to say about this in a later chapter. One answer which has been tried with considerable success by a number of organisations is a system of regular briefing meetings. These enable managers and supervisors to communicate with their employees on a regular and systematic basis. If the only meetings people attend are union meetings, then the views put across by deeply sincere, but often militant, representatives will undoubtedly have undue influence on people's behaviour.

The real answer in getting people to accept change, or to exercise restraint in their demands, lies not just in better communication but in good *management*: organising people into teams responsible to a leader at each level, giving that leader a clear understanding of his responsibilities and then communicating regularly through him to his team. Deliberate industrial subversion can only flourish when the seed-bed is right, that is, when labour relations in a particular organisation are allowed to deteriorate, and when those who have a vested interest in fermenting trouble are able to articulate the undefined grievances of the workers. Perhaps the final word on this subject should be that of Roy Gatehouse, who started work on British Leyland's Cowley assembly lines in the 1950s. Writing in the *Oxford Mail* after the end of the notorious 'washing-up' strike, he said: 'Instead of management being motivated by a mixture of arrogance and fear, they should employ natural managerial skills and have more confidence in their ability to handle the vast majority of ordinary people, who don't want to ruin the company or change the political system, but merely want the present system to work in a more manageable way. Only highly incompetent people turn their supporters into enemies'.

As a manager, your responsibility for controlling the pressure of organised labour on your people resolves itself into the problem of creating better industrial relations at the work-place. Part of the problem is to get your own thinking right in the first instance. For example, do you take it for granted that Shop Stewards will have negative attitudes towards the organisation, towards you, and towards their work? A few years ago the British Institute of Management conducted a study of a hundred shop stewards from a variety of occupations and organisations.

This revealed many interesting attitudes, of which the following is only a small sample: 60% rated their managers as below the acceptable level for human relations (many produced specific examples of insensitive managerial behaviour to justify their ratings). Asked whether they thought that supervisors had enough freedom and authority to do their jobs effectively, only 18% said they did (although many considered that supervisors, in their experience, were unwilling to use what freedom and authority they had). The vast majority, 92% believed that 'managers had the right to manage'. Without exception they said they believed in 'strong' management, although one did add that he had never met a strong manager! They all indicated their concern with the way orders are given. They expected to be asked rather than told. Many specific orders were resented, particularly those instructing them to do lower grade work, those relating to personal behaviour or orders that stemmed from management's uncertainty. The survey gave a clear indication that a large percentage of the sample had some loyalty to, and pride in, their organisation (although there were also comments along the lines of 'I have no loyalty, because the management is bad and I don't matter to them'). These and many other similar findings create a picture of the shop steward which is at odds with so many managers' stereotypes.

There is no reason why the pressures on your people from organised labour should conflict with the pressure you apply as a manager — provided your people see you, and not the union representative, as the source of authority and of help with their problems and needs. It can't be denied that in some industries union power is a positive barrier to effective management. But there are far more instances in which the industrial relations climate could be vastly improved by firm, responsible and caring management at the personal level.

Managing the situation

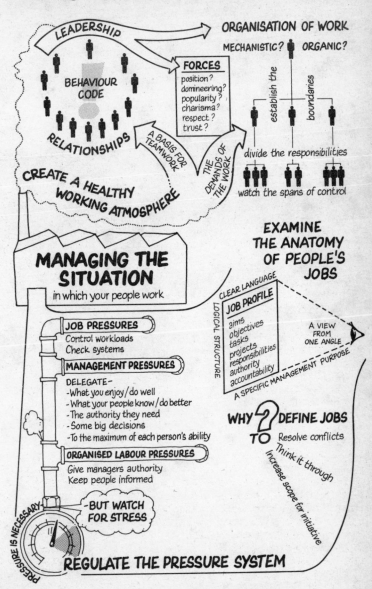

LEADERSHIP

ORGANISATION OF WORK

MECHANISTIC? ORGANIC?

BEHAVIOUR CODE

FORCES
position?
domineering?
popularity?
charisma?
respect?
trust?

establish the boundaries

RELATIONSHIPS

A BASIS FOR TEAMWORK

THE DEMANDS OF THE WORK

divide the responsibilities

watch the spans of control

CREATE A HEALTHY WORKING ATMOSPHERE

EXAMINE THE ANATOMY OF PEOPLE'S JOBS

MANAGING THE SITUATION
in which your people work

CLEAR LANGUAGE

LOGICAL STRUCTURE

JOB PROFILE
aims
objectives
tasks
projects
responsibilities
authority
accountability

A VIEW FROM ONE ANGLE

A SPECIFIC MANAGEMENT PURPOSE

JOB PRESSURES
Control workloads
Check systems

MANAGEMENT PRESSURES
DELEGATE—
- What you enjoy/do well
- What your people know/do better
- The authority they need
- Some big decisions
- To the maximum of each person's ability

ORGANISED LABOUR PRESSURES
Give managers authority
Keep people informed

WHY **?** DEFINE JOBS
TO Resolve conflicts
Think it through
Increase scope for initiative

PRESSURE IS NECESSARY

—BUT WATCH FOR STRESS

REGULATE THE PRESSURE SYSTEM

3. Gauging a person's calibre

In the search for ways of getting consistently high performance from your people we posed the question 'Why do people work well?' The last chapter provided part of the answer. Any individual's performance at work is influenced to a large extent by what we've called his 'situation' — his job, the working atmosphere in which it's done and the various factors that make up your organisation's pressure system.

However, you've no doubt frequently seen that some people in a basically unfavourable situation still perform well, while others whose situation appears to give them every advantage can't seem to deliver the goods. Obviously the reasons lie within the person himself. So what *personal* characteristics determine how well a person performs? We suggested three: a person's calibre, his commitment and his know-how. Each of these needs a good deal more detailed examination.

Now, this is where we have to start to introduce a certain amount of information which originates from the behavioural sciences, particularly from psychology. This shouldn't worry anyone. Although we're well aware of the dictum that a little learning is a dangerous thing, we're also quite certain that in managing people, psychology is too important to be left to the psychologists. If there's one thing you have to be concerned about as a manager, it's the behaviour of the people you manage: what it means, what causes it, how to influence it — and when not even to try! Probably more research has been done and more written in the literature of management on this subject in recent years than on any other, much of it by highly academically-qualified people. Unfortunately its presentation often makes it rather difficult to interpret. The aim of this book is neither to impress nor to win academic plaudits, but to help you, the practising manager. So we shall attempt to offer a simple, practical distillation of what seems to us to be relevant and useful.

When we mention theories we shall be less concerned with their fashionability than with the fact that we've seen them applied with worthwhile (not necessarily earth-shaking) results. And since behavioural scientists are themselves far from unanimous in their conclusions, we shall apply the same test of practical worth to the inclusion of ideas which some may criticize for their lack of scientific proof.

Perhaps one of the most fundamental truths about managing people is that you have no chance of success unless you first understand them. And understanding people means first understanding a few relatively simple and commonsense principles which are too often clouded in academic mystique and jargon.

First, then, calibre. We chose this word because it precisely conveys an idea which we think you as a manager have to accept. Ideally, each of your people should fit his situation, especially his job, as accurately as a bullet fits the internal dimension of a rifle barrel. No matter how well manufactured or how accurately aimed, the rifle is useless without ammunition of the right calibre. And the calibre *can't be changed*. There are only two courses of action open to the marksman: find a weapon which accepts the calibre of ammunition available or replace the ammunition. The analogy holds good for people and jobs. The size and complexity of any job demands certain personal qualities which can't be acquired or improved — except perhaps very slowly, over far too long a period of a person's life to make this a practical proposition. These are the qualities that you have to perceive in people in order to fit them into the right jobs or, if appropriate, to adjust their jobs to fit them. They represent the calibre of the individual.

Let's take a look at one of your people — we'll call him 'Joe'. To get the best out of Joe, you want to put him into a situation where he can perform well — where the degree of responsibility is sufficient to keep him interested and stretch his abilities, but not so great as to demoralize him and endanger your operation. What personal qualities do you have to consider? Probably the most fundamental judgement is one that we sometimes make with far too little real understanding of what is involved. The judgement as to whether Joe has the intelligence for the job.

What is intelligence?

If you say that Joe 'isn't very intelligent', what do you mean? The answer isn't as obvious as we often suppose. Perhaps you mean that Joe can't sort out a problem *you* find easy to solve. Perhaps you mean that Joe has overlooked some obvious factor in a situation he's had to deal with. Perhaps you just don't like something about Joe's accent, Joe's personality, Joe's interests — or event Joe's appearance!

The trouble is that the words 'intelligent' and 'unintelligent' have become mere terms of praise or disapproval. What we see as signs of 'intelligence' in Joe's behaviour often have little to do with his mental machinery. They may be the results of upbringing, experience, interests, common-sense — or even of social skill. But these things are not the same as intelligence.

Ultimately, intelligence is a measure of the mechanics of Joe's brain — the way it was put together. It is defined by psychologists as a physical ability of that brain, an ability to recognise interrelationships and interconnections between things. The higher Joe's intelligence, the greater the range of things he can take into account, the more complex and subtle the interconnections and interrelationships between them that he can recognise and understand — and the more quickly he can do all this.

The speed of understanding is a vital point. A Mini may travel as far as a Ferrari — but it will take longer to get there. Intelligence is the mental horse-power that enables one brain to travel further and faster than a brain of lower intelligence. Given time, a comparatively unintelligent person may come to understand some highly complex and subtle relationships — because of a slow development of his understanding through experience. But he will need time.

This means that Joe's intelligence and his ability to learn are closely connected. He learns whenever he tackles a new kind of mental activity — equally, he learns whenever he undertakes a familiar kind of activity in unfamiliar circumstances. Either kind of learning places demands on his intelligence. As a general rule you can recognize high intelligence by the ability to learn *fast*. But don't confuse this *ability* to learn with the *products* of learning — skill, knowledge, aptitude, judgement or whatever. If Joe knows a lot it doesn't prove he's intelligent. If Joe is intelligent it doesn't prove he knows a lot.

Intelligence stays fairly constant throughout a person's life. Joe's intelligence is basically what he was born with. It follows that he can't do anything to deliberately increase it (and neither can you). Certainly he can learn to use the intelligence he has got to better effect, but he can't actually *make* himself more intelligent. As he grows older he may become wiser, more knowledgeable, more mature, but his intelligence stays the same.

There are of course slight changes in intelligence as one grows older. Just as a car engine improves its efficiency to a peak over the first few thousand miles of its life, so one's intelligence reaches a peak in the middle teens. There it stays for the next ten years or so. Then follows a slow decline — but a decline that is offset by the *results* of learning. Growing experience, increased special skills and aptitudes, improved learning strategies, greater maturity of judgement — all can help develop short cuts in the learning process. These enable us to use our slightly reducing intelligence to far better effect than when we were younger. The net result is that the mental abilities we are really concerned with may be even greater in our mid-forties than they were in our mid-twenties.

Intelligence testing

Now, of course, your problem is to decide objectively how intelligent Joe is. Some organisations think this is important enough to ask their people to undergo some kind of intelligence test. Most of these tests work on the same principle. They define a person's 'mental age' by his ability to solve problems of a certain level of difficulty, and then compare this with his actual age in years. The result is a score — his 'Intelligence Quotient', or IQ.

An IQ of 100 is the norm. Anything above this suggests a higher-than-average intelligence and anything below, a lower order of intelligence. Suppose a fifteen-year-old has solved intelligence test questions that would be appropriate for an eighteen-year-old of average intelligence. His IQ is calculated as:

$$\frac{18 \text{ (his 'mental' age)}}{15 \text{ (his actual age)}} \times \frac{100}{1} = 120$$

Such an IQ suggests the potential to get a good GCE result. IQs of 125–135 suggest the potential to take a university degree. IQs of 135–140 suggest potential for a first class honours degree or some higher qualification.

Such tests attempt to measure what is called 'General Intelligence'. This is the raw ability to 'catch on' — the ability to understand what is happening, to reason, to recognize underlying principles, to make judgements, to see possibilities — irrespective of the *kind* of thinking, whether it involves words, numbers, visual ideas or whatever. But there is a difficulty in measuring this ability.

You can't measure General Intelligence without using some kind of practical problem as a test. And as soon as you produce some test problems, you find you are measuring something more than raw intelligence. You are also measuring aptitudes for different kinds of thinking — and an aptitude doesn't depend solely on what you were born with. It also depends partly on the skill you have learned for using each kind of thinking from your babyhood onwards:

    — the ability to understand words and the ideas they stand for (Verbal Aptitude)

    — the ability to manipulate figures (Numerical Aptitude),

— the ability to think in terms of visual shapes and patterns (Spatial Aptitude).

Intelligence tests try to overcome this difficulty by posing problems with words, numbers and geometric designs that are different from the problems we normally tackle in our day-to-day thinking and reasoning. This means that if you take a test you are unlikely to be able to use skills, knowledge or thinking patterns you have learned beforehand. You have to use your native wit, which is what the test is after.

A more basic criticism of many of the intelligence tests used at present is that they test only one feature of the mental machinery. Each question involves you in a search for the one right answer. But the 'convergent thinking' that this uses is not the only kind of mental ability in intelligence: equally important is the ability to create new and imaginative ideas — 'divergent thinking' as it is sometimes called. To test the one and not the other is about as sensible as testing the forward gears of a car but failing to test reverse. So more recent tests include attempts to measure the ability to think in unconventional, creative ways.

Aptitudes

Besides General Intelligence, a wide variety of aptitudes are important in different jobs. An aptitude is a more specialized ability than General Intelligence. Although it depends partly on intelligence, it is also partly the result of experience and can be developed with practice. (To that extent, you could regard aptitudes more as part of a person's 'know-how', but for practical purposes they are really an aspect of calibre.)

The two things — intelligence and aptitude — are not the same. Suppose you go to a foreign country whose language you can talk, but only with difficulty. Your intelligence stays the same, but to the people you meet you seem dim, slow to catch on, fumbling to express your thinking. Aptitudes provide the channels by which intelligence becomes usable. Broadly speaking, the main kind of aptitudes are

- Verbal aptitude
- Numerical aptitude
- Spatial aptitude
- Perceptual abilities:
  visual
  aural
  verbal
  numerical
- Colour discrimination
- Physical co-ordination and dexterity

— Social aptitude
— Mechanical aptitude

To a certain extent, aptitudes can compensate for a less-than-adequate IQ. The salesman whose intelligence is a little below par may be still effective if he is fluent with words and socially adept. The accountant whose reasoning power is not really as high as the job demands may have a numerical aptitude that enables him to do the job acceptably. The reverse is also true of course — that a high level of raw intelligence can compensate for some initial weaknesses in the aptitudes required.

What use is intelligence?

The cynic might say it is of very little use. And in many modern organisations he is depressingly right. So many jobs could be perfectly well done by a person with subnormal intelligence. As long as he had the right kinds of aptitudes — experience and

skill, he could cope perfectly well with the kinds of problem he is likely to meet. There is no great demand for the ability to reason out new and different problems, to cope with unfamiliar situations, to invent fresh approaches to old tasks. The problem in most jobs is that they place few demands on the intelligence of the people doing them. They don't offer the scope for learning and problem-solving that would tax the brain-power of a ten-year-old, however far they may be beyond his level of knowledge and skill.

Intelligence is of no use unless it is *used*. Of itself it is no guarantee of actual achievement. It simply indicates that the potential is there. And if the intelligence isn't used, the power to use it — the power to learn — becomes stunted. Like a muscle that is never exercised, it wastes away.

The truth is that few of us ever fully use our intelligence. In our youth, we are uncertain how to direct it — perhaps failing to find any brain-stretching issue that arouses our interest and commitment fully enough to fuel our mental horse-power, or perhaps diverted by problems of personality and immaturity from using the potential of our brains to the full. When older we may have settled ourselves to a comfortable maintenance of the status quo, or we may allow ourselves to get out of the habit of learning — even delude ourselves that we no longer have the capacity to learn.

What really decides whether Joe uses his intelligence is a mixture of his external and internal drives. A life in which he experiences too few pressures to think through difficult problems, to understand new and strange situations, to reason out unfamiliar questions, to use his judgement, to be creative — in other words, too few pressures to use his ability to *learn* — all these can cripple his intelligence potential. But so can his personal frustrations and insecurities. Personality and temperament have a lot to do with whether that potential is made usable, or allowed to wither in the bud.

Personality and temperament

When Joe's been working for you for a while you'll find that you can recognise something consistent about Joe's behaviour in different situations, something regular about the way he appears to think and feel at different times, something predictable about the attitudes he shows to different people. It is possible to say 'this is typical of Joe' or 'that is not typical of Joe'. The name we give to these regular, predictable and largely unconscious patterns of feelings, thought and behaviour is personality.

Joe's personality decides his basic attitudes towards the world he lives in — positive or negative, optimistic or pessimistic, altruistic or self-centred. It decides how he sets about influencing others. It decides how well he copes with problems or disappointments. It decides what he learns (and fails to learn) from the situation he finds himself in. It even decides how successful he is likely to be in using and developing his inborn intelligence.

To the extent that these things define the size and complexity of job that Joe can handle, they also define his calibre.

Joe's personality is what his experiences in life have written on his slate of self — his experiences of success and failure, the satisfactions and frustrations he has felt, the attitudes and values of the people who have influenced him, the habits for thought and behaviour he has been encouraged to adopt. But the slate didn't exactly start clean. From birth, the slate of Joe's brain and nerve system had a certain bias, a tendency to take up the writing of experience in one way rather than another. The grain in the slate influenced both what his experiences wrote upon it and the way it was written.

The slate of self

Joe's slate is made up of his basic needs as a human being, and the way his nervous system is constructed to enable him to satisfy those needs. Some are physical: for food, air, warmth, physical comfort and so on. Other needs are psychological: for freedom from anxiety and loneliness, for affection, for personal status, for self-esteem, for freedom from constraint, for psychological and mental growth and development — the opportunity to become a 'better person'. The *psychological* needs have probably played the biggest part in moulding Joe's personality.

To satisfy these needs, Joe has a nervous system with certain special, individual characteristics. Although Joe's nervous system is basically very similar to everyone else's, it will be different on at least three counts. His inborn intelligence potential is one of these; the other two are his placings on the introvert/extrovert scale and the calm/highly-strung scale.

The introvert/extrovert scale

One feature of different people's systems is their degree of introversion or extroversion. But the popular idea of these two words is slightly over-simplified. They are usually thought of as describing different patterns of behaviour with other people — the quiet, shun-the-crowd introvert versus the genial, back-slapping extrovert.

The psychologist accepts this use, but he also uses the words to describe the mechanics of the nervouse system itself that underline these behaviour patterns. In essence, he regards the introvert as someone whose nervous system can tolerate longer periods of concentration on the same thing; the extrovert is for him someone whose nervous system has a lower tolerance for long, intense concentration — he just gets bored more quickly.

Social skill is something different. Introverts can develop it just as extroverts can. It is likely that the extrovert, with a greater need for change and variety in his human encounters, will collect more experience in mixing with different people. But this isn't the only way to develop social skill. Introverts *can* become very persuasive salemen.

Essentially the extrovert is someone who has a greater 'stimulus hunger' than the introvert. The more extrovert Joe is, the more often he needs a change in the sensations he experiences, in his activities, in whatever he is attending to from day to day, hour to hour, even minute to minute; the more often he is inclined to change his preferences for foods, for clothes, for cars, for home or office colour schemes and furnishings; the more often he is likely to want to meet new people, to make new acquaintenceships and friends; the tougher-minded are his attitudes likely to be: pro-flogging, pro-hanging, pro-discipline, pro-militarism, anti-foreigner (although such attitudes are influenced by upbringing too). Broadly speaking he will tend to be an action man rather than a thinking man.

With a highly extrovert Joe, it will be difficult to condition his behaviour, and the effects of attempts at conditioning will fade more quickly (which means that his conscience may be a weaker force than in the introvert). He will find it hard to be vigilant, to be patient with frustrations, to apply his full powers of concentration for long periods.

His learning will need to be done in shorter periods with more frequent rest pauses than in introvert would need. His performance in whatever he turns his hand to is likely to be more variable — ranging widely between very poor and very good.

The more introverted Joe is, on the other hand, the further will his characteristics lie in the opposite direction. He needs less variety, less stimulation, fewer changes in activity and sensations. His attitudes are more tender-minded, less disciplinarian. He conditions easily and can cope with longer periods of concentration and learning. He is likely to be more of a thinking man than an action man.

No one is 100% extrovert — just as no one can be 100% introvert. Each of us has our own degree of extroversion or introversion built into our nervous system around a norm that is neither one thing nor the other. Psychologists measure this degree working from the introvert end of the scale: the degree of extroversion that Joe has is one factor in his personality.

The calm/highly-strung scale

Another feature of different people's nervous systems is how calm or highly-strung they are, the amount of 'emotionality' they have. Again the popular idea is mistaken — that calmness is good, being highly-strung is bad. Extremes of *either* are bad: the very stable person is lethargic, over-placid and unresponsive to any kind of stimulus, which is just as bad as the very nervy restless and compulsive obsessions of the neurotic worrier. Every one of us needs a certain amount of nervous energy stimulating us to respond to the impacts that the world around makes on us.

The psychologist explains the strength or weakness of Joe's emotional reactions by pointing to a part of his nervous system that controls emotion — the 'autonomic nervous system'. This system has two conflicting elements. On the one hand there is a 'fight or flight' element that stimulates emotional feelings, triggering the release of adrenalin in the body: on the other hand there is a 'vegetating' element that reduces emotionality, producing feelings of calm and well-being. The inborn construction of Joe's nervous system decides which of these two elements more easily gets the upper hand.

The more easily the 'fight or flight' element gets control, the more prone is Joe to anxiety and inner tensions, the more often he will need the emotional release of anger, excitement and other strong emotions — and the more situations will tend to cause these feelings in him. The more easily the 'vegetating' element gets control, the more Joe's behaviour will be level-headed, cool — and even apathetic.

But in assessing Joe's placidity or excitability — beware. The more highly-strung Joes may learn how to give an impression of greater calm than they feel inside. The more stable Joes may learn how to suggest greater anxiety or concern than they really have.

No one is 100% highly-strung — just as no one can be 100% calm. Each of us has our own degree of excitability or placidity built into our nervous system, around a norm that is neither one thing nor the other. Psychologists measure this degree working from the stable end of the scale: the degree of neuroticism that Joe has is a second factor in his personality.

To sum up, underlying Joe's outward personality are two characteristics of the nervous system he was born with: his extroversion score and his neuroticism score. The outcome of these two scores is a tendency towards a certain type of *temperament* — a stronger or weaker tendency depending on how far his scores vary from the norms at the centre of the diagram below. The range of personality traits named here have been defined in a great deal of empirical research over the last thirty or forty years (the words towards the centre of the diagram are the names of the classical temperaments defined in the fifteenth century by the philosopher Galen).

Horses for courses

What this might suggest to you as Joe's boss (and to Joe himself) is the kind of work-pattern and control that is likely to enable Joe to give of his best.

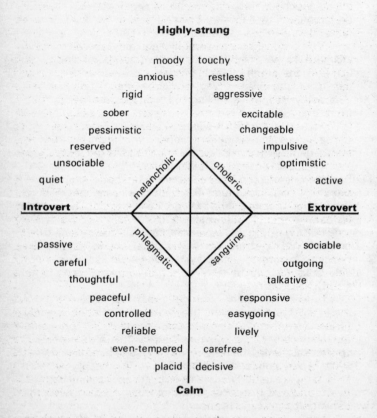

Highly-strung

moody   touchy
anxious   restless
rigid   aggressive
sober   excitable
pessimistic   changeable
reserved   impulsive
unsociable   optimistic
quiet   active

melancholic   *choleric*

Introvert   **Extrovert**

phlegmatic   *sanguine*

passive   sociable
careful   outgoing
thoughtful   talkative
peaceful   responsive
controlled   easygoing
reliable   lively
even-tempered   carefree
placid   decisive

Calm

With a strongly extrovert/highly-strung temperament, he will probably be effective in a job that demands quick but not persistent activity, that gives him a frequent change in the situations he has to cope with (plenty of contact with other people, say) and scope to use his aggressive energy. He may need a good ration of open recognition and public praise. He probably gets impatient with paperwork or with problems that demand a cautious, far-sighted approach.

With a strongly calm/extrovert temperament, he will probably be effective in a job that again gives variety and scope for quick activity. His social and easy-going nature is likely to make him effective with people, but don't expect him to take anything too seriously or to probe problems too deeply. He may need constant reminders about things he has to do — and will probably take them without any ill-feeling. He is likely to be fairly immune to attempts to train or condition him.

With a strongly introvert/highly-strung temperament, he will probably be effective in a job that demands persistence, but does not put a great deal of emotional stress on him. He will need a lot of encouragement, and to be treated with kindliness — a severe telling-off will hurt him deeply and will probably make him ineffective because he takes it so seriously. He may tend to notice the difficulties in a situation before seeing its opportunities. Interaction with others may make him worried, fearful or suspicious. On the other hand he is probably a good learner and may condition rather easily.

With a strongly calm/introvert temperament, he will probably be effective in a job that is both stressful and demanding of long periods of hard concentration. He will tend to warm to people rather slowly, but retain this warmth for longer. He will probably be reasonable in his dealings with them and may often get his own way by persisting in his objectives while appearing to give way to others. He is likely to think deeply about problems, but constructively, and again to be a good learner.

These are extremes of course! One important point to make about them is that very few people will show these characteristics anything like as strongly as described here. But to the extent they *do* show them, they are not likely to change very much. The characteristics are the result of inborn features of their nervous system, not of a conscious decision of will. People can't help their temperament! So you have to *recognise* their temperaments and then *use* those temperaments as effectively as you can in getting your job done.

Nor is Joe's personality totally decided by these characteristics of his slate alone. You also have to take into account the writings that his experiences throughout life have put upon it. What's stressful to you may not be stressful to Joe — and vice versa. What you regard as variety may be same-ness to Joe — and vice versa. You have to find out how *Joe* sees the job.

71

The writing on the slate

Throughout his life, Joe's experiences and his feelings about them have been working on his inborn nervous system to shape the personality he has today. But his experiences and feelings have not all been equally formative. Some have had enormous impact on him, others have had a comparatively mild effect: it is as though some have etched themselves deeply into the slate on which his personality is written — others are lightly chalked upon it.

Almost any experience can etch itself deeply — if it has caused strong emotion or has lasted over a long period. But the mostly deeply etched are almost certainly those that happened very early in Joe's life, in the first few months and years of infancy.

This doesn't mean that Joe is forever what he became in his boyhood. Other things have had there effect: the nature of the slate on which his early experiences were written has decided how sharply he felt those experiences and how long their influence lasted. His later experiences right down to today have also helped to modify his infant personality. The adult is always something more than his childhood history.

But those early experiences of life have had a lot to do with the basic features of Joe's present personality — secure or insecure in his view of the world, optimistic or pessimistic about other people.

The writing of infancy: satisfaction v. frustration

Joe started life with a set of those basic needs we've mentioned very similar to everyone else's. Not only physical needs but also psychological ones — for attention, acceptance, affection, admiration, freedom from constraint, fair shares with brothers and sisters and so on.

As a baby, Joe depended totally on his parents to satisfy those needs. And the extent to which they were satisfied or unsatisfied decided how strongly he developed social feelings or self-centred feelings — wishes for dependence or independence. These feelings and wishes grew first towards his parents who caused them. Later they were directed towards anyone else he encountered in his world.

To the extent that young Joe's dependence on his parents *satisfied* the needs he couldn't satisfy of his own accord, his feelings became positive, friendly, affectionate, grateful and *secure*. To this extent Joe's personality is likely to have developed strong *social* tendencies: to this extent he will have no deep fears of *depending* on other people throughout his life.

To the extent that young Joe's dependence on his parents *frustrated* his needs, his feelings became negative, angry, hostile, suspicious and *insecure*. To this extent Joe's personality is likely to have developed strong *self-centred* tendencies: to this extent he will have a deep wish for *independence* from other people throughout his life.

The social/self-centred scale

No parent can be *entirely* satisfying of course — nor *entirely* frustrating for that matter. So young Joe, like everyone else, developed a *mixture* of plus and minus feelings, of social and self-centred tendencies, of wishes for dependence and wishes for independence.

In forming Joe's infant personality, the working range was somewhere between the extremes of the satisfaction — frustration scale. Accidentally or deliberately, Joe's parents worked predominantly nearer one end of the scale than the other. Whichever end they leant towards and how far they leant that way has probably decided the *broad* lines along which Joe's early personality developed. Teachers, friends, colleagues and bosses working in the same range have finished off this development to give him his adult personality.

For some infants, the world is mostly satisfying, predictable and controllable. They are more likely to grow up well-adjusted, trusting and secure. They have predominantly social needs and only a secondary concern for independence — in their youth anyway (they may learn to like independence later). Such a person likes his associations with other people for the sake of the friendly, co-operative feelings he enjoys in them. He has no hostility towards authority in general. He is concerned for others' happiness, pleased for their success, grateful for their help, protective towards them when they are threatened.

For other infants, the world is mostly non-satisfying, non-predictable, non-controllable from the beginning. They are likely to grow up fearful, aggresive, and insecure. They want autonomy and independence. Such a person likes to have the ability to make others fearful (one kind of power over people). He is ambitious for personal prestige (another kind of power over people), for knowing things that others don't know (yet another kind of power). He feels hostile towards authority just because it *is* authority. He is quick to feel jealous and embittered. In his associations with others, he is mainly out for himself.

The strange thing about a history of frustration is that is seems to make later frustrations *more* difficult to accept, not less. The infantile school of hard psychological knocks does not teach its pupils very successfully how to cope with great psychological pressures later in life. As Joe's boss you should be aware that if Joe has to withstand a lot of stress and responsibility in his job, he will be a safer bet if the world he has grown up in has been, for him, psychologically stable, satisfying and secure. If on the other hand his upbringing has tended to make him insecure and suspicious of others, he will need a lot of proof of your integrity, firmness of decision and good faith before he believes that you really *are* to be trusted.

The read-out from the writing

All that you *know* of Joe's personality and temperament is what you can observe of his habits and behaviour. Physically you notice the characteristic expressions of his face, eyes, voice and hands, the characteristic postures and actions of his body. Mentally you check off the characteristic interests, points of view, ways of thinking and feeling that he reveals when he speaks. You attempt to judge what is going on inside Joe by watching his reactions to the situations he finds himself in. But this is all you know. The rest is guesswork. The act of *accurately* reading and understanding Joe's personality is intensely difficult for anyone to do (including Joe himself). What makes it even harder is that we so often suppose it is easy.

The easy way out is to 'type' Joe's personality. For convenience, or because understanding people is so hard, we mentally shove its subtle complexities into one of a number of roughly-hewn pigeon holes: Joe is 'a typical works manager' or 'a good Rugby type' or 'one of those bloody-minded Union men'. The mental picture is a crude and inaccurate cartoon of Joe's real self. To make matters worse, we then so often react to the cartoon rather than to the real-life Joe.

In the real world there are no 'types'. Real people have a vast range of different personalities, each one vaguely similar to some of the others in a few limited facets of his total complex makeup. Real people can't be pigeon-holed. With all the variables of personality and their possible permutations, there is only one sure thing about Joe's personality. It is absolutely unique. There is not, never has been, and never will be another personality exactly like Joe's.

Yet for you as Joe's boss, it is important to get a better-than-average understanding of Joe's unique personality. If your success depends partly on how effectively you make use of Joe's resources, you had better understand the resources you are trying to use. You can't do that if you don't understand Joe.

In understanding Joe's personality and in managing him effectively to give of his best in the Job, you have to try to understand four things:

— the way Joe sees the situations and events he's involved in,
— the way Joe sees the other people he's involved with (including you)
— the way Joe sees himself and
— the way Joe tries to get others (including you) to see *him*.

How do we see things?

Joe actually notices only a small part of everything he sees and hears. What he watches and listens to is only a small part of all the information his senses feed into his brain. His perceptions are *selective*. This is neither good nor bad. It is a fact of life. If it were not so, his brain could not cope.

Which particular bits of the total information available get Joe's conscious attention? Two kinds. Either those bits that he sees as somehow helpful or satisfying, or those bits that seem to him potential sources of frustration or threat. The bits that seem relevant to doing the things he wants to do, to satisfying the wishes he wants to satisfy, to being the person he wants to be — these bits get enlarged in his thinking. The rest diminish to vanishing point. He will magnify a compliment from his boss and he will also magnify a word of disapproval — but he may hardly notice whether the boss was wearing his blue suit or his grey suit.

This means that you can tell something about Joe's hopes and fears, his values and aspirations, his interests and inhibitions, by noticing what *he* notices about situations and people. His perceptions from a read-out of his personality. (What *you* notice about *Joe* also tells quite a bit about personality — but whether about Joe's or about yours may be a moot point.)

Learning and conditioning play their parts too. The police are trained to notice objective facts to a far greater extent than the public does. A policeman will remember the colour or make of a car, a person's dress, whether a door was open or closed — or any of a variety of static facts about a situation — far more accurately than the average member of the public. But, funnily enough, the average member of the public may remember *dynamic* facts about an event better than the policeman — the expressions on a face or the movement of a hand. Training, in other words, doesn't seem to *increase* the amount you notice: it seems rather to influence the *direction* of your attention.

What Joe remembers depends on the way he has seen things in the first place. Sometimes quite relevant things will slip his mind entirely. He'll forget a dentist's appointment, oversleep when he has a difficult interview to attend first thing in the morning, overlook a report he is supposed to write.

There is a rule governing this: Joe remembers positive, satisfying things better than he remembers negative, unpleasant things. Your biggest problem as Joe's boss is quite likely to be Joe's tendency to forget the little, uncomfortable tasks — like disciplining people, or making cold canvass calls, or digging through reading matter he finds tedious, or replying to unpleasant letters.

If the discomfort is mild, the tasks will be first forgotten. But if the discomfort becomes insistent — if for example you change a mild threat to a major threat to get those things done — Joe will stop defending himself against awareness of the problem and will begin attacking (it may be an open question whether his attack is then on the problem or on you).

What Joe sees as pleasant or unpleasant depends on how secure or insecure he is, and what things he feels secure or insecure about. The more secure he is, the more of his environment he'll see as potentially helpful and satisfying — or harmless at least. The more insecure, the more things he'll see as potentially unpleasant, harmful and dissatisfying.

Your best answer to Joe's tendency to forget uncomfortable things may be to help Joe to find them more comfortable. If you can help Joe to feel more easy about his cold canvass calls, more capable of dealing with disciplinary problems, more purposeful in getting through tedious reading matter, you may well find that the problem resolves itself.

How do we see other people?

This is where so many problems in management begin — in the perceptions a boss has of his subordinates.

Take Joe's boss, Fred. To manage Joe successfully, Fred has to understand how Joe sees things. If Fred doesn't understand Joe, he is quite likely to manage Joe in ways that are guaranteed recipies for disaster.

Fred may assume Joe wants promotion: Joe may be driven to panic because he feels psychologically forced to accept a promotion that no one (perhaps not even Joe himself) bothered to find out he didn't want. Fred may assume Joe wants easier work: Joe may be frustrated, not by the difficulty of his work, but by a job that seems purposeless or parasitic. Fred may assume — correctly — that Joe wants more money: he may fail to understand that the extra money is only acceptable to Joe within a certain framework of independence. So Fred's management of Joe may fail because his own perception of Joe is mistaken or incomplete.

Failures like these usually all spring from the same

unwarranted assumption: that everyone else views the world from the same perspective as I do — or that if they don't they ought to. When Fred the boss wills his own perceptions on to Joe, he is ignoring the difference between his perceptions and Joe's. He is ignoring some important keys to Joe's behaviour. If, on the other hand, he spends time with Joe trying to reach a common view — or at least understanding the difference between their views — he is *not* wasting his time.

How do we see ourselves?

The way each of us perceives ourselves (our 'self-image' as the psychologist calls it) is a fundamental element in our personality — yours, mine, Joe's or anyone else's. It is also extremely difficult to do it accurately. Each of us has a view of himself that is only partly realistic.

Joe has in himself certain real powers, abilities and potentials — his 'real self'. Many of these he will be aware of. But many he won't know or he'll be unsure of. What is more his upbringing will have persuaded him that there are certain abilities he ought to have (whether he has them or not). If he doesn't actually have them, he will try to convince himself he is something that he is not.

Joe's self-image is in many ways the self he subconsciously feels he ought to be. This will overlap with his real self, but won't totally coincide with it.

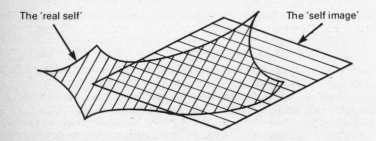

The 'real self'   The 'self image'

Joe's real self is an irregular shape, full of odd corners in the personality that are at best only dimly realised by anyone — perhaps least of all by Joe himself. Joe's self-image is a neater, more sharply defined shape. Like anyone else, he understands things (himself included) in much tidier ways than exist in reality.

To some extent, Joe's self-image must overlap with reality: if there is little overlap we give Joe's ailment a complicated psychiatric name and lock him up in a mental home. But however sane Joe may be, his self-image will inevitably contain some elements of fiction, of Walter Mittyish fantasizing about himself. The important thing is how seriously he takes himself in these fantasy elements of his personality.

This gives us a way of understanding 'maturity'. If Joe is 'immature', his view of himself will contain quite a lot of unreality, private fantasy and wishes of himself that he is unsure of being able to realise in practice. He will take these elements in his make-up seriously. As a defence against his uncertainties about himself and his abilities, he will tend to criticise others harshly for failings that he subconsciously fears in himself.

As Joe grows more and more mature, his understanding of himself fits in better and better with his real powers, abilities and potential. His private fantasies become less and less important to him. Because his picture of what he feels he ought to be is more in line with what he is or could become, he is less easily hurt by criticism or imagined slights. He can think about himself more coolly and objectively. About others he tends to become more tolerant and understanding, less harshly critical of what he sees as their weaknesses — however forceful he may still be in encouraging them to overcome their failings.

Maturity in this sense usually comes with age — but not necessarily so. A cynic subconsciously armour-plates himself against self-knowledge. As he grows older, his cynicism may become more subtle, but his view of himself and others may remain at the same distance from reality. Nevertheless it is true that when we are young, we tend to suffer more than older people from uncertainties about our true potential, from aspirations for ourselves that can never be realised in practice. This may explain both the idealism and the violence of youth.

However maturity develops, of one thing we can be quite certain. Joe *doesn't* develop it because someone tells him a few home truths. That may be satisfying to the teller, but it is counter-productive as far as Joe is concerned. He mentally drops his portcullis on the intruder and prepares to defend himself against the attack. A threat to the self-image is the most dangerous threat known to man — more dangerous even than a threat of physical violence. Martyrs down the ages prove the point.

Your best hope of getting Joe to realise what he is really

made of is to get Joe to test his private view of himself against reality. Give Joe the reality of goals to be won, of problems to be tackled, of responsibilities to be shouldered — and goals, problems and responsibilities that lie at the limits of Joe's true abilities. In the process, Joe will learn something about himself. By slow degrees, he becomes more mature.

How do we try to get others to see us?

The difficulty of understanding Joe is partly the difficulty of seeing through the acts that Joe puts on — more or less continuously, more or less subconsciously.

Psychlogist Erving Goffman puts it like this:

> 'It is probably no mere historical accident that the word "person", in its first meaning, is a mask. It is rather a recognition of the fact that everyone is always and everywhere, more or less consciously, playing a role. It is in these roles that we know each other; it is in these roles that we know ourselves.'

> 'In a sense, and insofar as this mask forms the conception we have formed of ourselves — the role we are striving to live up to — this mask is our inner self, the self we would like to be. In the end, our conception of our role becomes second nature and an integral part of our personality. We come into the world as individuals, achieve character and become persons.'

The self Joe tries to present to other people is his self-image or some part of it — the parts he places high value on, that he is proud to own rather than those aspects of himself that he feels secretly ashamed of. Sometimes his act is a good one. He may be able to convince those he is trying to influence that the front is nothing more or less than the reality. At other times his act may not be so convincing — either because of lack of experience or skill in presenting it, or because of his own self-doubts.

Irrespective of how others view his acts, Joe has his own private beliefs about them. With some acts, he may be conscious of playing a role that he doesn't completely believe in. With others, he may have come to believe they are 'real' — he himself is totally convinced of his own sincerity.

But, however sincere, the acts never become the naked, unvarnished truth. Always Joe is acting in one sense or another, even when his act has become so habitual that he isn't conscious of it as an act any more. As long as he is aware of the presence of an audience he is acting. Indeed he continues to act when no one else is present — when his audience is himself! (What are *you* trying to convince yourself of when you look at yourself in a mirror?).

To make his acts effective, Joe depends on the participation of his 'audience' — the person or people he is with — playing roles that harmonize with his own. They themselves are also engaged in acts at the same time of course — which makes the business of human communication doubly complicated.

Joe will tend to maintain or modify his act depending on the feedback he gets from his audiences. Suppose he goes off to a management course. He will begin the course with an idea of the role he supposes he should play, the role he feels 'suits' him in the situation. Perhaps it is the role of 'the good student', or perhaps the role of 'the practical you-can't-teach-me-anything manager'. Or perhaps he slips back into a role of his schooldays, a role of 'to-hell-with-responsibility-I'll-learn-if-you-make-me'. Or an older Joe might even take up the role of 'don't-know-why-they-sent-me-I'm-too-old-to-learn'.

As the course goes on, Joe may find he can't maintain his first idea. Perhaps the course leader plays a good 'I'm-not-telling-you-what-to-think-just-trying-to-help-you-sort-your-own-ideas-out' role. So Joe changes his role from that of a resentful 'student' to that of a positive-thinking 'problem-solver'. Perhaps on the other hand the course leader is quite happy to play 'teacher' to Joe's 'schoolboy' and so Joe maintains his adolescent role.

One of the problems with roles is the fixed ideas we get about them. The manager thinks of his own role as 'managing' — something he sees as quite different from the trainer's 'low-status' role of 'training'. When taxed with his failures to help his subordinates learn how to do their jobs better, he is quite likely to respond 'But I'm a manager, not a bloody trainer'. So with the accountant who rebuffs any suggestion that he should help line managers develop financial sense: 'They can look after the operations and I'll look after the money'.

Yet logically he would probably agree that you can't really separate 'money' from 'operations' like that.

There is a further problem with roles. Suppose at an office party Joe happens to meet a stranger whom he supposes to be someone at his own level in another department. Joe assumes an appropriate act, joking about Senior Management and offering his 'colleague' far-fetched ideas about how the Company should be run. Joe suddenly discovers that the stranger is the Chief Executive. In that instant, Joe realises that his performance is totally inappropriate and his act is violently disrupted. In the fictional world of films Joe is now offered a senior post on the Board. In the real world there can be three kinds of result:

1. Joe feels embarrassed and confused, resentful of 'losing face' and 'being made to look a fool'.
2. Joe may lose credibility with his audience (the Chief Executive in this case). His reputation may be permanently weakened.
3. If Joe has identified himself deeply with his act, his self-image may be discredited. He may suffer deep humiliation and self-doubt — or violent anger towards the source of his humiliation.

In any personal contact between Joe and others, both Joe and the others take a fair risk of slight embarrassment, and a small risk of being deeply humiliated. Humilation does neither Joe nor his organisation any good of course. It gnaws away at his commitment to doing his job well, and may even divert it into a commitment to 'getting his own back' in one way or another.

As Joe's boss, you can represent a potent source of humiliation for him. So it is as well for you first to consider the roles you try to get Joe to play and Joe's likely reactions:

— Joe resents playing the role of 'slave' — the role you force him into by attempts to *coerce* Joe, making him accept things helplessly. Few of us see a slave in our self-image — and slaves revolt eventually.
— Joe resents playing the role of 'sucker' — the role you force him into by attempts to *manipulate* Joe. If you try to get your way by concealing your own real intentions (your 'real' role), when Joe eventually realises it his reaction is even fiercer. The result may be the permanent loss of Joe's trust.
— Joe resents playing the role of 'sinner' — the role you force him into by attempts to *judge* him. Joe's self-image is unlikely to include a 'prisoner-at-the-bar' element. If you try to play 'God' in an appraisal and so force Joe to play 'sinner', it may be better if the appraisal had never happened. Joe may well continue sinning — but now out of pure devilment.

Don't take this too literally. It *doesn't* mean you must never give your subordinates a direct order, conceal something from them or tell them what you think of their performance. Any manager must do these things. What matters is whether you do them often enough and in a way that suggests you *normally* think of your subordinates as slaves, suckers or sinners. The more often you force Joe to play such roles, the more Joe's resentment will grow until it becomes a normal part of his attitude to you. Once that happens it is most unlikely that Joe will voluntarily change his behaviour for the better.

As a boss you have a variety of other roles to play. Among them, one may be dangerous for different reasons — the role of 'playmate' to your subordinates. It can be difficult to climb back on to the pedestal of respect. But there are plenty of positive, rewarding roles for you, from the decisive captain of the team to the perceptive adjudicator of Joe's successes and counsellor of Joe in his attempts to improve his own performance.

So we've seen that the way each of your people behaves at any point in time is the result of several things interacting: the nervous system he was born with (the slate of self); the characteristic feelings and responses his nervous system has developed from his experiences in life (the writing on the slate); and his ways of viewing the people and situations he meets and their relationship with his view of himself (the read-out from the writing). As a manager you need to understand these things in your people — and in yourself. A manager can hardly be a manager without a practical understanding of human psychology. However, there is nothing you can do actually to change any of these things in your people. They are aspects of their *calibre*. Your job is to employ it in the most productive way possible for both the individual and your organisation.

Gauging a person's calibre

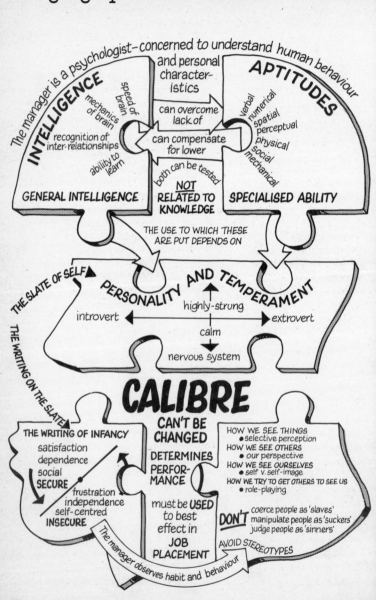

The manager is a psychologist—concerned to understand human behaviour and personal characteristics

INTELLIGENCE

speed of brain

mechanics of brain

recognition of inter-relationships

ability to learn

GENERAL INTELLIGENCE

can overcome lack of

can compensate for lower

both can be tested

NOT RELATED TO KNOWLEDGE

APTITUDES

verbal
numerical
spatial
perceptual
physical
social
mechanical

SPECIALISED ABILITY

THE USE TO WHICH THESE ARE PUT DEPENDS ON

THE SLATE OF SELF

PERSONALITY AND TEMPERAMENT

introvert ← → extrovert

highly-strung

calm

nervous system

THE WRITING ON THE SLATE

CALIBRE

CAN'T BE CHANGED

DETERMINES PERFORMANCE

must be **USED** to best effect in **JOB PLACEMENT**

THE WRITING OF INFANCY

satisfaction
dependence
social
SECURE

frustration
independence
self-centred
INSECURE

HOW WE SEE THINGS
• selective perception
HOW WE SEE OTHERS
• our perspective
HOW WE SEE OURSELVES
• self v. self-image
HOW WE TRY TO GET OTHERS TO SEE US
• role-playing

DON'T
coerce people as 'slaves'
manipulate people as 'suckers'
judge people as 'sinners'

AVOID STEREOTYPES

The manager observes habit and behaviour

4. The capacity for commitment

We've used the word 'calibre' to describe the personal qualities and powers a person brings to his job. These are the things that determine his capacity to cope with responsibility in general and with the demands of the job in particular. Obviously, however, performance in a job depends not only on that capacity but on how well it is used — on the amount of interest and effort any person is willing to put into the job. In other words, as well as appreciating people's basic calibre, as a manager you also have to be concerned with their *commitment*. This is largely a question of people's attitudes to their jobs which, like the elements of calibre, are often deeply entrenched in their characters. Unlike calibre, however, commitment is not fixed within the individual for long periods of time. It may change quite frequently in response to conditions and situations in which the individual finds himself. To that extent, commitment is something that you can endeavour to create in your people — although there are many misconceptions about what this process entails.

The popular term for this aspect of management is of course, *'motivating'*, but it is a term frequently misunderstood and misused in management books and courses. Motivation is what causes someone to act. It is an *inner* force, which exists within every human being. This makes nonsense of statements often heard along the lines of 'these people have no motivation'. What the speaker means is that these people are motivated towards what he considers to be the wrong things: perhaps towards activities outside the job all together, perhaps towards inactivity in pursuit of an easy life, perhaps towards deliberate disruption of the operation for personal reasons of their own. All these actions (or inactions), however, are the result of motivation. Once this is realised you can also see that it is rather pointless to talk in terms of 'motivating' your people. The only person who can motivate anyone is that person himself. What you *can* do, of course, is to manage people and their situation in such a way as to draw out whatever commitment they are capable of and try to get them to motivate *themselves* towards organizational as well as personal objectives.

What is motivation?

If we examine motivation a little more closely we can see that it is in fact an attempt on the part of an individual, often an unconscious attempt, to satisfy certain inner needs — the needs which we referred to in the last chapter as part of the 'slate of self'. Much scientific research has been undertaken in attempts to identify man's basic needs. Most of the thinking in this area stems originally from the work of Abraham Maslow, who produced his well-known hierarchy of needs in 1960.

Self-actualisation needs

Ego-needs

Social needs

Security needs

Physiological needs

In some ways it is unfortunate that Maslow presented his analysis in the form of a hierarchy. This has led over the years to the idea that to have higher level needs is 'good', whereas to have lower level needs is 'bad'. This is not Maslow's point at all. Maslow's research (which was conducted, incidentally, in the sphere of clinical and not industrial psychology) shows that all human beings have all these needs in common. What the hierarchy illustrates is the order in which we are motivated to satisfy these needs. As soon as a lower level of need is satisfied, we have an automatic urge to satisfy the unsatisfied needs at the next highest level. Conversely, when a lower level need remains unsatisfied, we do not devote effort and energy to satisfying the higher level needs until the balance at the lower level has been restored.

Take Joe for instance. At the lowest level of Joe's hierarchy of needs are the *physiological* needs — really the need for self-preservation, the most fundamental of all. If Joe were to be deprived of air to breathe, of food, of warmth, of shelter or of rest, he would become totally preoccupied with his efforts to acquire these things and quite uninterested in the satisfaction of any higher level needs.

There are still millions in the world for whom the satisfaction of physiological needs is still a major preoccupation. But since Joe has a job in an organisation within our Western and relatively affluent society, we may assume that his physiological needs will be comparatively well catered for. So his next concern, consciously or subconsciously, is to satisfy his *security* needs. These include not only the obvious immediate concern for continuity of job and income and for protection from accident or physical danger but also, according to Joe's personality and character, freedom from less obvious anxieties: from the risk of failure, disapproval, even from unfair criticism, which he may see as psychologically damaging.

Assuming that Joe feels relatively safe in this respect and has achieved a level of economic security that satisfies him, these things don't become important. Having reached that position, he wants to ensure that he will stay there. But, if security needs are reasonably well-satisfied, Joe is unlikely to be motivated towards activities aimed at increasing his security still further. A fundamental point about the hierarchy of needs is that *a satisfied need does not motivate*. Once hunger is satisfied we are no longer motivated to seek for food: one we have reached a level of competence in our jobs which satisfies *our* need for achievement, we may no longer be motivated to strive for further advancement.

So the next level of need which Joe, consciously or sub-consciously, will be motivated to satisfy is the level of the *social* needs. In Maslow's original analysis these centre around the need for love. In a work context Joe has a need to associate with others; he needs to be accepted, to belong, to identify with a group; he needs harmonious relationships within that group. It is easy to see that if Joe's work group fails to provide the satisfaction of this need he may well be motivated to seek it in other groups, for example, in trade union membership or in groups engaged in social or domestic activities outside his work altogether.

Next in their effect on Joe's motivation come the *'ego'* needs, the group of needs connected with self-esteem and the esteem of others. Joe needs the good opinion and approval of his colleagues, his superiors and his subordinates if he has any. He needs some king of recognition, prestige, status, or independence. Again the *degree* to which this need is felt will depend on Joe's basic personality.

At the top of the hierarchy comes the term which Maslow used to describe the highest level of human need, *self actualization*. Although this is obviously a bit of psychological jargon, it is nevertheless an accurate term. It means the desire to become an 'actual person'. It is sometimes defined as: 'developing the human potential to the fullest extent possible'.

You can, if you wish, replace it with the term 'self-fulfilment', but to a psychologist that doesn't have the same specific meaning. In this category of need are not only the essentially creative or artistic activities (which may in fact find no place within Joe's work) but also other forms of achievement, competence and progress. They add up to mastery of the job, and being as much as you can be through your work. Joe has the need to feel he is making progress towards a goal which is important to him. He wants to feel that through his endeavours he will reach his full potential. Clearly, into this highest-level category fall the very important needs for growth and learning.

Now, if Maslow's theories are correct, Joe has all these needs — and so do we all. Of course, for many years it was assumed by many managers (and still is, by some) that certain groups or 'classes' of people did not *posess* any 'higher-level' needs! This was the thinking behind the so-called 'Scientific Management' which we mentioned at the beginning of the book. Perhaps you're thinking even now of some of your people who seem to display no evidence of any need, for example, for creativity or even, judging by the standard of their performance, for self-esteem.

Maslow's answer to this is that it doesn't mean they don't have those needs. What it means is that bitter experience has taught them that there is no chance of finding satisfaction of these needs *within their work*. So they have either sought such satisfactions in different activities and relationships outside their work altogether, or in extreme cases have psychologically 'given up' those needs. Often they may compensate by becoming excessively concerned — indeed, militant — about security, money, working conditions, etc. As one psychologist wrote, so often it's assumed that 'all they want is money': it's not all they want — it's all they can get.

When you look at Joe — indeed, at any of your people — it may seem as though many of them are pre-occupied with just one level of need. Joe may seem to be concerned solely with security. His main aim is not to take risks or to do anything which may cause him anxiety. He may try to stop others from 'rocking the boat'. The trouble is, rocking is often equated with rowing! Fred, on the other hand, is socially-orientated. He'll do anything to keep on good terms with everyone. He has to be liked — so he finds it almost impossible to discipline anyone. He has to 'belong' — so he goes along with whatever behaviour code his work-group adopts. This may certainly prevent him from seeking any kind of individual recognition. Dick is (to use the psychological term) egocentric. He has a strong drive towards achievement, independence, dominance, admiration.

This often causes him to take unnecessary risks and to ride rough-shod over the views and feelings of the rest of the group. Again, this doesn't mean that these three people don't *have* the other levels of need. It's just that their experiences and their basic personalities give them a particular emphasis. Each of them requires more satisfaction of one particular need than the others.

An individual's emphasis in his needs may in fact change according to his circumstances. Promotion for Joe *might* mean that he now feels secure enough to place more value on personal achievement. (Of course, if he really feels his promotion wasn't earned or justified he may be terrified of being found wanting in his new job. That would increase his insecurity even more!) The supportive attitude of Fred's colleagues *may* convince him he is so well-accepted that he can now devote more time and interest to developing himself. And redundancy for Dick may mean that he temporarily loses interest in status, and will gladly accept a far less ego-satisfying job in order to restore the feeling of security which is now his major need.

By now you will have realised that this business of motivation is much more complex than it's often assumed to be. It's very difficult to decide which needs are motivating anyone at any particular time. The effect of these needs is rather like the sound of an orchestra. Not all the instruments play all the time. Sometimes one section, say the woodwind, is dominant, while the strings and brass play quietly in the background. Gradually, as the score changes, a different section takes over the melody and fades away in its turn. Sometimes a great crash of the timpani drowns out everything else. And sometimes all the instruments combine smoothly in an almost indistinguishable blend of sound. So, with human beings, any need or any combination of needs may be influencing us at any given moment. The way it seems to happen is through a kind of 'motivational cycle', which looks like this:

When a need remains unsatisfied, it creates within the individual a kind of tension, which in turn provides a driving force or impetus towards certain activities or behaviour. This behaviour is aimed at the attainment of a specific goal which, when it is reached, provides satisfaction of the need and the tension is thereby reduced. The reason for showing this as a cycle is because once the process is complete, it starts all over again in relation to a different need, which has to be satisfied by another goal requiring further (different or similar) behaviour.

From your point of view as Joe's boss, it may be extremely difficult, if not impossible, to decide which needs are motivating Joe at any given moment. It may be a little easier to identify Joe's specific *goals*, which are not quite the same thing. Goals express Joe's individual ways of satisfying his needs for security, for acceptance, for esteem, and for creativity. And Joe's goals will be moulded by the *values* his upbringing has bred into him.

The goals we strive for

There are a number of important things to recognise about Joe's (or anyone else's) goals. First, they are *specific to the individual*. Joe's goals are the result of his own unique mixture of experiences in life. No two people have exactly the same experiences, so no two people will have exactly the same goals. Joe's fear of loneliness may be answered by one or two close friends; Fred's may call for an army of acquaintances and casual friends. Joe's need for significance may be fulfilled by an occasional word of praise from a respected colleague; Fred's may demand a continual chorus of adulation. Joe's creative outlet may lie in the leadership of his team; Fred's may lie in the development of a complex new paperwork system.

Most of us develop our own ideas of what we want early in life. Some children always play to win; others play to be better than average; yet others seem to be quite happy as low man on the totem pole. And as adults, some of us are content to beat our own previous best; others more competitive spirits are never happy until they have beaten everyone else's too. Such goals will not be changed on your say-so as the boss.

Secondly, any goal may be an *integrated response to several different needs*. Joe wants a certain amount of money. That will satisfy his desire for security from the threat of poverty. It may also gain him the status differential he wants from his co-workers. It may buy him possessions that will tell

91

him he is a success — and that might impress his friends and neighbours. It may even offer him freedom to devote time to some creative ambition.

Fred wants to create trouble for management. He gets creative satisfaction from thinking up ways of doing it — and challenge and excitement in putting them to work. Success may give him the personal pleasure of wielding power. It may also give him extra status among his colleagues. And if he can create trouble without drawing management attention to himself, it may help defuse some personal threat — management may be too busy with the fire-hoses to concern themselves with him. To change such goals, you have to help people find other satisfactions for *all* the needs that the goal aims to satisfy.

The third feature of goals is that they are *shorter-term than the needs that motivate them*. Goals depend very much on the information available to us. They are stimulated by the way each of us sees the situation here and now. They *can* change. A new situation can change them. New information can change them. A different emphasis in the information we are already getting can change them. Take Fred's guerilla warfare with management. If Fred begins to see the company's future at risk — or sees that he and his colleagues can reach their goals better by co-operation than by hostility — he may well begin to divert his efforts into fighting alongside management in a common cause.

Goals also depend on the groups we join. Few people are strong enough to stand out against a close-knit group of their fellows. Most of us will adjust our personal goals to conform with those of the group. For the organisation this can be a positive or negative influence — depending on the loyalties of the particular groups we are bounded to most closely, the groups that are most important for the satisfaction of our needs. We'll expand on this point a bit later on.

Goals change as our own inner make-up develops through life. The important goals of our youth, goals on which a lot of our young self-esteem and security may once have seemed to hang, tend to become minor goals for us as adults. As we grow in maturity and self-understanding, our goals become more far-sighted, better adjusted to our real abilities.

The fourth key point is that goals *need not be realistic*. Both for us as individuals and for our organisations, the relationship between the goals we choose for ourselves and our ability to achieve them is important. Joe may have learned to match his aspirations to his abilities — he may be 'well-adjusted'. But if his aspirations exceed his abilities, he has inside himself a potential source of frustration; if you as his boss fail to recognise the gap, the organization too has a potential source of frustration. If, on the other hand, Joe's goals lie below his abilities for achievement, he may realize this too late. And, again the organisation suffers — Joe doesn't contribute what he has the power to contribute.

Lastly, goals are *not always declared openly*. Often it may seem tactically wrong to admit certain goals to other people — if they are declared, perhaps others will want to find out ways of blocking them. Often it may seem psychologically dangerous to admit them — they may seem ridiculous to others. Some goals may be admitted only to close, intimate friends. So as a manager you can't rely on the answers you get to the question 'What are your goals?' Better perhaps to look at what people do, the kinds of things that get emphasised in their conversations, the ways they react in different situations. These are likely to provide better clues to the real goals of the individual.

All of this places a big responsibility on you as a manager. You have to enable your people to harmonise their private goals with their working objectives. You must keep them informed of what is going on, of aims and plans being made for the group as a whole. You have to know your people's real potential — often more accurately than they themselves do.

You have to understand their personal goals for themselves, to help them adjust their sights to the furthest goals they have the potential to achieve. You have to involve them as far as you can in defining their roles within the group and organizing their objectives among themselves. You have to help them develop pride in their achievements and confidence in their true capabilities. And you do have to do all this with a genuine concern for their success as individuals as well as for your organization's success.

The frustration of blocks

Many people seem to have a deep-rooted dissatisfaction with life. They seem to find it difficult to achieve the security, the acceptance, the sense of significance and creativity they need. Or, at least, to achieve these things in ways that are positive and constructive — for themselves individually, for their organisations, for society itself. Their self-destructive apathy can't be explained simply by national and international crises. Their resentment of ability and corroding envy of others' success isn't totally accounted for by poor schools and bad housing. Their grasping after money can't be due solely to rising prices and the falling value of money. Nor do 'sloth' 'envy' or 'greed' help as explanations. These are symptoms, not causes.

The explanation is frustration. The willingness to opt out, the desire for unprovoked revenge, sinister bids for power, the materialistic amassing of more and more possessions — all become a kind of compensation for feelings of unfulfilment in life itself. And there is no point in telling those who suffer from the malady that they *oughtn't* to feel frustrated. The causes have to be tackled.

Frustration is the normal response to the *blocks* that bar progress to our goals, that prevent us from satisfying our needs. Many — but not all — of the blocks are external. Many indeed lie in the occupations in which we spend the greater part of our mature lives. The need for significance and creativity should be largely satisfied through daily work. But if work is non-creative, deadly boring or of doubtful social value, it is made bearable only if the monetary or material rewards are high. And these rewards provide compensation — not satisfaction. (Since taking your present management job, what have *you* done to develop the interest of your people's work, or the scope for creativity and sense of personal significance that it offers them? What have you done to develop these things in your *own* job?).

There are also many *internal* blocks, the battlegrounds pf psychological conflict. Joe wants to free himself from some intolerable pressure, but his conscience bars the way. Or he has an urge to let himself go, but cannot risk letting himself down. Or he wants to make something of himself but doesn't know how — or even isn't sure what it is he wants to become. And the conflicts go on not just in Joe's guts but also in his brain (what we conventionally call 'decision-making'). We can better understand many an irrational business decision when we understand the different issues, objective *and* subjective, that were involved in making it.

When Joe does meet a block, he may react in one of three different ways:

— He gets aggressive. This is the reaction of a secure, self-confident person. Physically he attacks the external block. Psychologically he slashes through the internal inhibitions.

— He gets demoralised. He feels ashamed and nervous. This is the reation of an insecure anxious person, pessimistic about his abilities. Psychologically he withdraws from the conflict and accuses himself of failure.

— He feels neither anger nor fear. He coolly and rationally thinks out his next move. This is the (rare) reaction of the very mature person. He sees the block not as being a thing to get frustrated about but as something that has deprived him (temporarily perhaps) or a particular goal. The difference between these three reactions is the difference we've already described in personality and perception. We don't all see the same world. The secure, self-confident person sees most of his world as potentially harmless or satisfying. He is less likely to meet serious blocks (serious, that is, for him), but more likely to blow up when he does meet them. The insecure, anxious person sees more of his world as potentially harmful or hurtful. He meets many serious blocks — so many that he has had to 'internalize' his anger, turning it habitually against himself in the form of anxiety, shame and self-doubt.

Industry prefers secure, solid optimists to shy, withdrawn, insecure people. But there are usually strong taboos on their expressing anger openly. The result is to force them to stifle their feelings of anger — which is psychologically, even physically, bad for them. If Joe does get angry, it is probably better for him to have his explosion and get it off his chest.

This leaves the third person — the one whose reaction was cool and rational. What kind of world does he live in? He probably sees a 'bigger' world, a world that has already satisfied most of his needs for personal significance in other ways, a world that provides a broad base for his needs for security, a world in which his own goals are better adjusted to reality. It is also a world in which he can see many different paths to his goals. He has few goals that are vitally important to his security and self-esteem (since his inner stability is so solid that few things can threaten it). He meets few insurmountable blocks (since he has ways around most of them). This gives him a high tolerance for things that are threatening or frustrating for others. He does not keep his temper through any effort — it is kept for him by his own secure self-knowledge, and by his broader understanding of his goals with the people and situations he meets.

Tactics and strategies

To cope with the things that frustrate his inner needs, that block his goals, Joe can either *do* various things, or try to *think* and *feel* about the problem differently. The first possibility is any one of a variety of tactical 'games' he can play with you, or anyone else who seems likely to provide the block:

— He can try to divert attention from his main concern (for instance, making an 'obvious' mistake in a report in the hope that it will cause you to ignore something else he wants to get past unaltered).

95

- He can suggest, subtly or crudely, that you must have some disreputable motive in blocking.
- He can try to rally support among a group (which usually has greater psychological power than the solitary individual).
- He can try to use some element in your argument as a way of 'proving' his own point.
- He can use a show of outrage, amazement or complete unconcern as a way of knocking you off balance psychologically.
- He can try to get through by simple insistence and perseverance.
- He can even ignore the block and go ahead as if it didn't exist, hoping to get away with it — or even trusting that his pudding will be proved in the eating.
- In the last resort he can play 'tit for tat', getting his revenge by creating some block or frustration in turn for you.

Such tactics are common in most organisations — in most families even. To some extent they are the inevitable result of different people with different personalities seeing things from different viewpoints and having different goals — both declared goals and secret goals. There is a big danger for you here: you may prohibit one tactic, thinking you have also prohibited the goal. Not so. Subordinates will just invent more subtle (and perhaps more damaging) tactics to achieve that goal. It may be more sensible for you to try to learn what your subordinates' personal goals are so that you can try to harmonize their goals with your own. Perhaps this will take the form of some broader, more far-reaching goals for the team as a whole.

But more crucial for the individual are the strategies he uses for dealing with his inner conflicts and the blocks they cause. How does Joe cope when he has two goals — and can satisfy either one only by frustrating the other? How does he cope when he has made a bad descision — but cannot accept the loss of face involved in reversing it? How does he cope when he has an impossibly boring job — and commitments for his family that prevent him leaving it?

Joe will try to cope through some psychological defence. If he can see no way to cure the problem, his strategy will be one that at least holds his personality together in the face of forces that threaten to disintegrate it:

- He may simply forget the problem. This is not a deliberate ploy. Joe's subconscious self denies from his conscious thoughts memories that could injure or destroy his idea of himself. Dreams are a clue to this unconscious mental activity.

— He may transfer the problem to others. He may blame them for the faults he subconsciously fears are his (this is common enough to cast serious doubts on the validity of the conventional 'judgement' type of appraisal: are the boss's criticisms of his subordinates always objectively valid, or do they sometimes represent his unconscious attempts to find a scape-goat for his own hidden feelings of guilt?).

— He may take refuge in a more comforting private world of imagination and self-delusion. Fantasies about himself and his world may be a perfectly normal defence against threatening realities.

— He may freeze his feelings, subconsciously refusing to let himself respond emotionally to the problem. If the crisis is severe, this emotional freezing may extend far beyond the original problem, affecting almost all his contacts with other people. He may become inwardly numb and unresponsive.

These are not 'peculiar' reactions. They are perfectly common strategies for handling common problems within our complex human personalities. The first three happen quite often in the everyday lives of perfectly sane people. All of us have some bits of memory uncomfortable enough to be relegated to the subconscious, some personal fears unpleasant enough to wish them on to other people, some private fantasies that help us cope with the harsher realities of life.

But there are other more constructive strategies available.

With these strategies we do not simply push the problem elsewhere. Instead we find a way to resolve the conflict altogether:

- We may realize there is a way we hadn't seen before of satisfying both of the conflicting goals. We manage to find a way of harmonising them. Perhaps Joe can learn to accept the boring job as a price he is prepared to pay for his family's happiness.
- We may be able to change our minds about one of the goals so that we are no longer interested in it. Perhaps Joe can *find* some interest in the job and so maintain both his self-respect and his pay-packet. Perhaps he can overcome his fear of unemployment and find himself other more congenial employment!
- We may be able to change our view of the world to put the conflict into a new, less significant perspective. Perhaps Joe can start to view his job as less important to him psychologically (however important it may be financially) and find other interests outside work that give him the self-respect his job denies him. To see the practical effect of this strategy, think back to the fears and anxieties of your 'teens' — and then ask yourself what has happened to make them as unimportant to you as they are today.

Values and attitudes

In addition to being directed towards his personal goals, Joe's behaviour will be determined to a large extent by what his upbringing has taught him. As a young child, Joe was sometimes prevented from doing things by his parents — throwing his food on the floor, or wandering off by himself, or pulling his baby brother's hair. In his successive attempts to do these things, he found he could not outsmart his parents. Eventually his parents no longer had to apply pressure to stop him. He developed inhibitions against doing these prohibited things, *internally* taking the part of his parents and feeling guilty about even thinking of doing them. He had become socially conditioned.

Just how strong Joe's feelings of inhibition and guilt are depends largely on where his personality lies on the social self centred scale. It also depends partly on his degree of inborn introversion or extroversion. Conscience will be a stronger force if he tends to be introverted and if his upbringing has emphasized his social tendencies. It will be a weaker force if he tends to be extroverted and if his upbringing has emphasized his self-centred tendencies. With an over-developed conscience he will suffer perpetual feelings of guilt and inner tension. With an under-developed conscience he may suffer few pangs of remorse about anything at all. He may even be classed as a psychotic — he will feel fine, but society will suffer.

What Joe regards as questions of conscience depends on what his parents prohibited or punished him for. Perhaps they gave him inhibitions against being self-seeking. Perhaps inhibitions against being inconsiderate. Perhaps against being dishonest or distrustful. Perhaps against being 'lazy' or 'untidy'. Perhaps against acting independently. Perhaps against any of a variety of inner impulses — against expressing feelings openly, against breaking the accepted moral code, against enjoying sex. The *pattern* of whatever inhibitions Joe has is what we call Joe's 'conscience'.

For you as Joe's boss, the point of all this is that Joe's conscience may make it difficult for him to do some things effectively — or at any rate to do them without severe psychological after-effects. He may find it difficult to be less than frank in talking to his subordinates, or to act in self-seeking ways in his relationships with his colleagues, or to be inconsiderate of his customers' true interests. And if you find a Joe who *can* do these things without any soul-searching, perhaps you shouldn't be too surprised if you also find that he's untrustworthy in his relationship with you, his boss.

Values and attitudes have a certain similarity. For Joe, both are questions of the *way* he views the people and situations he comes across in his day-to-day experience. The difference is that attitudes are mainly conscious things — Joe knows what his attitudes are and can talk about them: values are largely subconscious — Joe will hardly realize that he holds them unless he is put into a situation where his values are in conflict with the values of other people. Even then he may find it hard to explain what his values are or rationally why he holds them. It may also be very difficult for him to accept that other people can *really* have different values. He can understand attitudes that differ from his own, but values that differ from his he is likely to regard as misguided or dishonest.

For example, Joe will be quite conscious of his attitudes towards the people he meets and towards *their* attitudes, towards politicians and their policies, towards questions of the day — marriage, the family, education, leisure, his job, the people he works with, the nature of business, the Common Market and so on. His underlying values that tend to mould his attitudes will be less easy to put into words — his personal angle on conforming or non-conforming, on the relationship between money and success, on the balance between concern for self and concern for others, on the rights and wrongs of 'making the most of your own potential' versus 'being a good member of your team', or whatever.

Compare Joe's values with Jack's. Joe was brought up in a middle class home. Jack was brought up in a working class environment. Joe is a manager, Jack an operative.

Throughout Joe's young life the pressure was on him to be 'different', to 'succeed' — to be liked by his teachers, to do well in exams, to get ahead of his classmates, to equip himself for 'a good job'. Joe went to university. Success was still measured in the same terms — by his individual ability to 'get ahead'. So for Joe the manager, one of his key unquestioned assumptions is that people *ought* to be motivated by a desire to do well for themselves.

Throughout Jack's young life, the pressure was on him *not* to be different — to conform with the rest of his social group, to be accepted and trusted by his fellows, to be at one with his classmates. Jack started a job. And still the pressure was on him to conform to group attitudes and values, not to be a rate-buster or blackleg, not to try to get ahead. So for Jack the operative, one of his key unquestioned assumptions is that people *ought* to be motivated by a concern for equality with their mates, for supporting their own kind, for remaining at one with their particular group.

Attitudes and values *can* change later in life — attitudes rather more easily than values. New information can change attitudes — Joe's discovery that an old attitude was based on incomplete evidence for example. This can depend on the source of the new information: if Joe doesn't trust it, it won't have much effect. It can also depend on Joe's deeper values: if Joe subconsiously places a high value on *not* changing his mind, it may be difficult for him to accept a change even in his conscious attitudes. New friends and associates can also change Joe's attitudes — and even modify his sense of values.

But it is difficult to predict how far anyone can change Joe's attitudes and values. It depends on a number of questions. How deeply are the old values etched into his brain? How important do they seem to Joe for his success and happiness? How great is the psychological pressure on Joe to modify them? How long term is that pressure? What are the characteristics of Joe's slate — his brain and nervous system? Someone who's highly-strung may change his attitudes more readily than a stable personality. An introvert will accept conditioning more readily than an extrovert — and so is likely to start with a more strongly held set of values. For the extrovert, values are likely to be less of a key determinant of behaviour.

If you are bent on changing Joe, one important thing to recognise is that his attitude, values and aspirations are not totally rational things. True, he can argue logically for his attitudes — and perhaps for those values that he is conscious of too. But supporting them in the background will be strong emotional factors. So it may be next to impossible to get Joe to change them by rational argument. He is more likely to change if *he* discovers facts that make his present attitudes and opinions difficult for him to justify to himself — or if he finds himself out of step with *groups* of people (not just individuals) whose influence and esteem matter to him.

Another important thing to recognize is that Joe will try to keep his attitudes, values and beliefs broadly consistent with each other. In most people there are more or less clear *patterns* of attitudes and values: if you know some of Joe's attitudes you can usually guess others. But this isn't a perfectly safe bet. The pacifist student can still attack a policeman. Most of us can do balancing tricks that allow us to feel comfortable with patterns that look inconsistent to outsiders. The important thing is that Joe will try to find in his attitudes and values what he can *feel* as harmony. He will try to reduce 'dissonance'. The verbal justification comes later.

To understand and predict Joe's attitudes and behaviour, you will do better to try to understand Joe's internal make-up than to look at the rational facts of the situations that Joe meets. And if you do so, you will have a far better chance of changing Joe's attitudes than if you try to convince Joe by rational, logical arguments. You have a chance of changing the *situation* as Joe sees it (including changing your own behaviour towards Joe) so that Joe changes his attitudes for himself.

A final point. While you can sometimes change Joe's behaviour by first changing his attitudes, the reverse is also true: to change Joe's attitudes, first change his relevant behaviour. If you can get Joe the sales clerk to change his manner of talking to customers on the telephone, you may also change Joe's attitudes to customers. If you can get Joe the shop steward to argue an issue from the management's point of view, you may get a little more understanding from Joe for the problems of management. If you can get Joe the tough-minded foreman to explain a grievance from his operatives' point of view, you may develop a little sympathy in Joe for the frustrations fo his subordinates.

The capacity for commitment

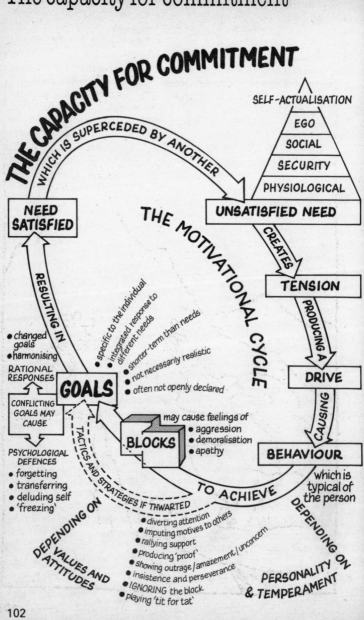

THE CAPACITY FOR COMMITMENT

WHICH IS SUPERCEDED BY ANOTHER

SELF-ACTUALISATION

EGO
SOCIAL
SECURITY
PHYSIOLOGICAL

NEED SATISFIED

UNSATISFIED NEED

THE MOTIVATIONAL CYCLE

CREATES

TENSION

PRODUCING A

RESULTING IN

- changed goals
- harmonising

RATIONAL RESPONSES

- specific to the individual
- integrated response to different needs
- shorter-term than needs
- not necessarily realistic
- often not openly declared

GOALS

DRIVE

CONFLICTING GOALS MAY CAUSE

may cause feelings of
- aggression
- demoralisation
- apathy

BLOCKS

CAUSING

PSYCHOLOGICAL DEFENCES

- forgetting
- transferring
- deluding self
- 'freezing'

TACTICS AND STRATEGIES IF THWARTED

BEHAVIOUR

which is typical of the person

TO ACHIEVE

DEPENDING ON

DEPENDING ON

VALUES AND ATTITUDES

- diverting attention
- imputing motives to others
- rallying support
- producing 'proof'
- showing outrage/amazement/unconcern
- insistence and perseverance
- IGNORING the block
- playing 'tit for tat'

PERSONALITY & TEMPERAMENT

5. Managing for motivation

The commitment which any one of your people gives to his job is mainly the product of all his internal influences. Firstly, his pattern of basic psychological needs and the goals they drive him towards; secondly, the blocks which he experiences in striving to reach those goals, and the tactics and strategies which he employs to overcome them; and lastly, the values and attitudes which he has built up over a great many years, and which largely condition the behaviour he displays. These are the things which are at the root of anyone's motivation, not only within their work situation but in their approach to life in general: what they want out of it and how they go about achieving their ambitions. This knowledge is vital to you as a manager because it enables you to understand your people better, and understanding is the first essential step in managing. However, so far we haven't given very much specific advice on how to *use* this knowledge in your day-to-day management.

We *have* pointed out the fallacy of the approach to motivation which consists of trying to manipulate people, by means of rewards on the one hand and sanctions on the other. This 'stick-and-carrot' approach to motivation has by now been well tried, and shown to be very limited in its effect, in a wide variety of industrial situations. Actually, as a manager you are probably not short of advice on how to handle the motivation of your people. Numerous books, films and training courses, have been produced over the past decade, most of them based on one particular theory, probably the outcome of a specific behavioural science research project. Indeed, one American writer on the subject refers to the field of motivation as a 'jungle of theories', which is not too far from the truth. The purpose of this chapter is to help you find a path through the jungle, by appreciating the key points of each of the major motivational theories and by giving you the opportunity to distil from them an approach which will work for you in your situation.

One of the first academics to recognise the need for a new look at motivation in the workplace was Douglas McGregor, who published his book *The Human Side of Enterprise* in 1960. His contention was that: 'under the proper conditions, unimagined resources of creative human energy could become available within the organizational setting'.

McGregor's investigation of management methods at that time revealed that a great many managers appeared to be operating on a particular set of assumptions, which he called 'Theory X'. These assumptions were based on the belief that the average man has an inherent dislike of work and will avoid it if he can; that because of this supposedly human characteristic, people must be coerced, controlled, directed and threatened in order to get effort from them; and that, in fact, they prefer being directed, want to avoid responsibility, have relatively little ambition and are primarily concerned with security. These assumptions naturally led managers to try to control their people's behaviour by external means — the promise of rewards and the threat of punishment.

In contrast with this Theory X, McGregor suggested a different theory of managing people, based on more adequate knowledge of human nature and motivation. He referred to it as 'Theory Y'. It takes a completely different view of the nature of man. It believes that it is as natural for him to expend physical and mental effort in work as in recreation or leisure; it recognises that he is capable of exercising self-direction and self-control in order to reach objectives to which he is committed; and that he will become committed to those objectives according to the rewards he perceives for reaching them. It also asserts that, under the proper conditions, the average human being will not merely accept but actively seek responsibility, that he has the capacity to use imagination, ingenuity and creativity — in fact, that he has considerable intellectual potential, which in most industrial jobs is very little used.

McGregor's contention is that Theory Y represents a much more accurate view of human nature. He says that these assumptions 'point up the fact that the limits on human collaboration in the organization setting are not limits of human nature, but of management's igenuity in discovering how to realize the potential represented by its human resources'. He also observed the interesting phenomenon of the 'self-fulfilling prophesy'. A manager who assumes his people are lazy and unco-operative often ends up with lazy and unco-operative employees, while a manager who assumes his staff are ambitious and co-operative frequently finds himself managing ambitious and co-operative people. Managers' assumptions about their people tend to condition the way they approach their own role. In turn, the way managers *behave* towards their subordinates clearly determines the kind of reaction which they receive.

As a result of these observations, McGregor put forward the idea that 'the essential task of management is to arrange organisational conditions and methods of operation so that people can achieve their own goals best, by directing their own efforts towards organisational objectives'. The management approach which he suggested consists primarily of creating opportunities, releasing potential, removing obstacles, encouraging growth, and providing guidance. He referred to it as 'management by objectives' (long before John Humble adopted the phrase and turned it into a system) and contrasted it with a Theory X approach which he called 'management by controls'.

As the number of such studies increased and the literature generated by them proliferated, so the jungle of theories grew thicker. Two people who attempted to put together a number of different theories and produce a model for management behaviour were Robert Blake and Jane Mouton. They carried out extensive research to develop their 'managerial Grid'. This is really an analysis of managerial style. As you will see from the illustration below, it combines the manager's concern for people with his concern for production. It produces five different styles of approach.

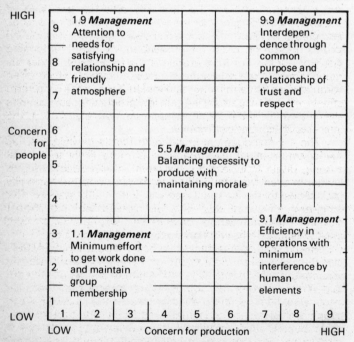

Blake's researches showed that every manager has a *dominant* style, that is, one which is most characteristic of him as an individual and with which he normally approaches any situation. It also showed that each manager has what Blake referred to as 'a back-up' style, which came into play when his dominant style was not getting him the results he wanted.

The back-up style was particularly evident in managers under stress. Of course, the five positions described on the Grid are extremes and an individual's style could in fact be located in any of the 81 squares.

The 9.1 management style measures success solely in terms of production: output is the watchword. The 9.1 manager clearly subscribes to McGregor's 'Theory X'. The effect on the workforce is often the suppression of creativity, which may then be devoted to activities aimed at 'beating the system'. The long-term effects of a 9.1 management style, contrary to the manager's intention, are usually that commitment and productivity *both* tend to decrease.

The 1.9 style is adopted by the manager who believes strongly in the 'human relations' school of management which we mentioned earlier. (He probably also has the kind of personality which gives him a very strong social need to be accepted and liked.) To win acceptance from his people he avoids pressuring them for production. He avoids imposing goals or quotas. For him, morale is the focal issue. Under his management, creativity suffers because conflict, which often stimulates creative thinking, is avoided. One of the long-term effects of his management is again low production, as decisions are made in the interests of maintaining morale and not in the interests of economic efficiency.

The 1.1 management style could hardly be described as management at all. The manager is more likely to be lost among, rather than leading, his people. He probably tries to isolate himself from both his subordinates and his boss. His goal tends to be personal survival within the system. The long-term effects of this style of management are almost certainly communication breakdown, disorganisation and general failure of the work-group to reach its objectives.

The 5.5 manager balances his concerns between the people and the production dimensions of his job. He works on the assumption that people will work willingly and do as they are told if the reasons for doing so are clearly explained. He 'motivates' by mild reprimands or pats on the back. He keeps people well-informed and handles conflict by compromise, but tends to gloss over problems to maintain an acceptable rate of production. The longer-term effects of his management may well be the maintenance of the 'status quo' and a gradual slipping behind, as other work groups recognize and take advantage of the opportunities.

9.9 management is the style which Blacke suggests should be strived for. Here the focus is neither wholly on production nor on people, but on achievement of goals through the effective collaboration of an involved group. It differs from 5.5 mainly in that it assumes no inherent conflict between the purpose of the organisation and the needs of the people. Compromise is not necessary. Through participation of his people and proper delegation of authority, the 9.9 manager attempts to merge the goals of the individual and the objectives of the organisation. He attempts to channel the needs of individual people for creativity into useful activities from the organisation's view point. In this sense he acts in the direction suggested by both McGregor and Maslow. The long-term consequences of 9.9 management are improved relationships within the group, effective use of individual talents and greater productivity and success generally.

A further and very widely-quoted contribution to the theory jungle was the work of Dr Frederick Herzberg. In this research project, nearly 2,000 people at different levels in different organisations were asked to describe two events in their jobs: one that had created high morale and one that had caused a sense of grievance. A professionally-designed questionnaire was used to discover not only the events themselves but also the underlying *causes* of the feelings they produced. It also revealed additional information, such as the length of time for which those feelings continued to influence the people concerned. Herzberg then ranked the answers which he received. At one end of the scale he put those events which had *most often* been mentioned as creating a sense of *high morale*. He concluded that these were the factors most likely to gain people's commitment. He called them *'motivators'*. At the other end of the scale were the factors *most often* mentioned as causing a sense of *grievance*, but far less frequently mentioned as a cause for high morale. Herzberg's conclusion was that these factors caused *dissatisfaction* when they were absent or inadequate in people's jobs, and therefore led to lack of motivation and commitment. However, once they were perceived by the individual as having reached a satisfactory level, he was unlikely to be motivated by improving those factors still further. To identify these factors in people's jobs Herzberg used the term 'hygiene'.

It is extremely important to realise that in separating these things Herzberg was *not* indicating that the hygiene factors were unimportant. Their effect on people is, if you like, something similar to the nature of a sewer. When it fails to function properly it becomes extremely important for everyone in the vicinity that it should be put in satisfactory working order as quickly as possible! Once this is done, however, it quickly fades from the memory of the people concerned and no longer has any effect on them. As long as the sewer continues to work properly, improving its efficiency still further will have no beneficial effect on those living around it.

The following table summarises the motivators and hygiene factors identified in Herzberg's survey, the length of each bar showing the comparative frequency with which that factor was mentioned, as either a positive or negative force. The *depth* of each bar indicates the length of time for which the feeling of high morale of grievance lasted.

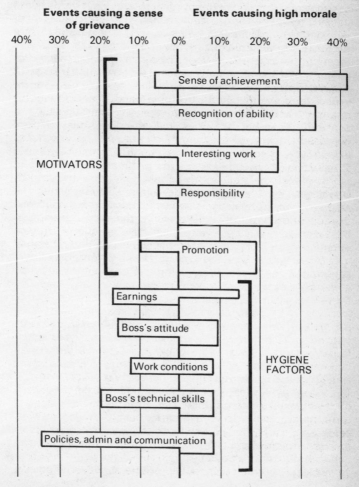

One of the most controversial conclusions of this study is that earnings are shown as a hygiene factor. This led to Herzberg being widely quoted, after publication of his book, as saying that 'money does not motivate'. In fact, in his later writings he agrees that money acts as both a hygiene factor *and* a motivator, mainly because in our materialistic, present day society we tend to use earnings as a *symbol* of such things as achievement and progress, and also as a yardstick by which to measure the recognition of our ability. The whole question of the effect of money on people's motivation is therefore a complex one, but Herzberg's original contention is partly borne out by our experience. Most of us would willingly accept greater monetary rewards for whatever it is we do. The question is, are we really prepared to work harder or better in order to receive them? In other words, if your people's pay is inadequate or unfair, that will undoubtedly cause resentment and a sense of grievance which, until it is put right, will be a permanent thorn in your side as a manager. On the other hand, once your people see their pay as being sufficient for their immediate needs, and fair and reasonable for the job they are doing, they will not necessarily give any *more* commitment to the job in order to increase it further (although their commitment may be reduced if they don't get an increase they reckon they deserve!).

Another interesting and important point from the research is that, as the table shows, where earnings were mentioned as a source of high morale, the *duration* of that feeling is the shortest of any of the ten factors. In other words, the evidence seems to be that when monetary rewards increase, they quickly become accepted as the 'norm' and lose whatever motivating effect they may initially have had. Just as there is no food which will perpetually keep you from being hungry, so there is no monetary incentive that will perpetually satisfy people's financial wants.

This same principle applies to the other hygiene facets. Being nice to people may be worthwhile for all sorts of reasons, but will have only a relatively short-term *motivational* effect. Once your people's working conditions are at a level which they find acceptable and satisfactory, improving them still further won't necessarily get you any additional effort or commitment. And so on. While these things are of great importance because of the negative effects they can have on your people's commitment, they are no substitute for the positive factors such as the opportunity to gain a sense of achievement, recognition of ability, more interesting work, greater responsibility and opportunities for promotion.

Incidentally, we have checked out Herzberg's findings (in

our own less scientific way) with literally thousands of people we've trained over many years, and have found them to be consistently confirmed. Also, it's fairly clear that the various theories we've outlined have the benefit of being mutually supportive. Herzberg's 'motivators' obviously relate to the satisfaction of the 'higher-level' needs in Maslow's hierarchy. Blake's 9.9 style of management is most likely to create these motivators and also corresponds with the thinking implicit in McGregor's 'Theory Y'.

This doesn't mean that we offer you these theories as a blueprint for success in managing your people. What we do suggest is that the evidence of the behavioural scientists needs to be carefully considered by any manager. As we've said before, as a manager you can hardly help being a practical psychologist. How well you 'get things done by other people' depends very much on the skill with which you handle your contacts with them. You can't avoid tangling with questions of human personality and behaviour day by day, even moment by moment.

Many managers still regard psychology with suspicion or derision — perhaps understandably. Psychology in the past has been more concerned with probing people's inner states than with influencing their outward actions. You might perhaps be more impressed with psychology if it gave you some tools to use in your day-to-day dealings with others. Before we leave the subject, therefore, let's introduce you to at least one set of such tools, developed by the psychologist Eric Berne, probably best known as the author of 'Games People Play'. He called it Transactional Analysis. It's a method of explaining what happens when 'I do something to you and you do something back' — in other words the basic transaction between two people of stroke and counter-stroke. It's value is in showing you how you can deliberately adjust your *own* behaviour to get the reactions you need from others.

More than one personality?

In an earlier chapter we spent quite a bit of time describing the elements of personality. But it is common experience that none of us has a single consistent personality. Each person's thoughts, feelings, and actions seem at different times to stem from different parts of his total make-up. 'I recognise that I am made up of several personalities' said Somerset Maugham, 'and that the person that at the moment has the upper hand will inevitably give place to another. But which is the real one?' All of them or none? Sir Desmond Morton, a close friend of Winston Churchill, described him as:

'the brilliant, great, imaginative, ever-dreaming child, whom no one ever taught to control his imagination or to be disciplined or to think of others. . . . When he was out of power in the Thirties he ran to anyone for comfort, as would the child with its broken toy. If the passer-by helped him to mend his toy, he ran off happily to play with it, with no sense of gratitude to the kindly stranger.'

'Of course this is not the whole story. No man can be dissected into a single object. Every man is intensely complicated. But I think the dissection has indicated a very important part of the watch. Perhaps the main spring.'

Transactional Analysis shows that such ideas about human nature are not mistaken. Each of us has in our make-up three distinct kinds of personality — a 'Child', a 'Parent', and an 'Adult'. In our behaviour moment by moment, each one takes the centre of the stage by turns. Usually the change of actor is involuntary. But it doesn't have to be. For the mature person it *can* be a conscious decision.

Where the personalities come from

From birth, the human brain acts as a high-fidelity tape-recorder, making an exact recording of every experience of its owner and of the feelings it aroused. The experiences are unique for every individual, giving him his unique character and personality. The most powerful are the experiences of early childhood, so the recordings from birth to the age of about five have a huge influence in the mature personality.

These tapes are not usually available to our conscious memory — although they can be consciously replayed under hypnosis. But in the subconscious mind they are continually re-running to create three alternative types of feeling, thought and behaviour:

The 'Child' personality is esentially a set of *feelings* towards life, created by past experiences.

This role grows out of the recordings of childhood experiences as a small, wonder-filled but inept and dependent youngster. There is a positive side to these experiences — the child's sense of carefree fun; his creativity and curiosity; his urge to touch and feel and experiment; his love of happy companionship; the glorious pristine feelings of first discoveries. But there is an overwhelming negative side too, however happy one's childhood — the child's sense of being weak, helpless and totally at the mercy of parental whims; his emotions of fear, anxiety and frustration; his feelings of being incompetent, misunderstood, never able to do things right.

Whenever something happens to the grown person that recreates for him the situations of his childhood, he relives the feelings he felt in those situations and behaves accordingly. Point-scoring, boasting, teasing, daydreaming, worried looks, evasion of responsibility, expression of delight, curiosity, boredom, nervousness, embarrassment or anger are all aspects of his Child personality. (Do you recognise them in your own behaviour?)

Parent

The 'Parent' personality is essentially a set of *teachings* about life, created by past experience.

This role is created from memories of mother's and father's behaviour, pronouncements and edicts. The recording contains all the admonitions, rules and laws that the child heard from his parents and saw in their behaviour: the thousands of 'nos' directed at the toddler, the repeated 'don'ts' that bombarded him, the looks of horror caused by his misdemenours or carelessness, the 'always' and 'nevers' that ruled his childish world. In fact everything the child had to accept without opportunity to question or explore for himself is recorded in his Parent — all the inconsistencies of parents' behaviour, the occasions when they said one thing but did another, their behaviour towards each other.

When occasion offers, the grown person reproduces his parents' behaviour. He attempts to restrict or mould others in the same way as he has recorded his own parents once doing to him. He accepts responsibility. He is concerned about 'good manners'. He is self-righteous and correct. He judges and praises and criticizes. He knows all the answers, adopts 'superior' postures and mannerisms — all aspects of his Parent personality. (Do any of these strike a chord?)

Adult

The 'Adult' personality is essentially a process of logical *thinking* about life, based on its present realities.

This role starts to develop as soon as the young child becomes mobile and can explore and test his environment for himself. Basically it is a rational rather than an emotional approach to life. Its development in the youngster enables him to begin to tell the difference between life as he felt it, wished it or fantasized it (Child), life as it was taught and demonstrated to him (Parent), and life as he figures it out for himself (Adult). Rather like an internal computer, the Adult receives valid information from the world outside, processes it, estimates probabilities and makes decisions appropriate to the circumstances. The computer doesn't get angry, nor does it have any habits. As time goes on, it builds a data-bank of tested, updated information on which the Adult can base his behaviour.

When his Adult personality is to the fore, the person's behaviour is calm and straightforward. He probes problems coolly and objectively, and makes rational estimates of consequences. He questions and listens for the facts, not for others' attitudes towards him (unless they are relevant facts for the matter in hand). He considers whether the standards of his 'Parent' or the feelings of his 'Child' are appropriate to present circumstances. Hopefully you can recall times when you've behaved like this!

In every mature, well-balanced person, all three personalities are present as distinct and separate modes of feelings and behaviour. All three are needed in the complete person: if his Child is blocked out by distressing memories or inner tensions, he cannot play or have fun — he is duty-dominated,

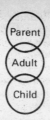

over-serious, rigidly conformist in his attitudes. If his Parent is blocked out, his conscience or social self-control may be defective — in estimating consequences he is likely to be more concerned about the chances of getting caught than about fair play or justice for others. If his Adult is blocked out, he is out of touch with reality.

But granted that all three personalities are available, at any moment only one of them will be in control. Now the Child is uppermost, now the Parent, now the Adult. In each interaction with another person, one and only one of the personalities will dominate. Now the actor and the action is decided depends on the person's basic view of his own position versus other people.

To make the decision a conscious one, we have to understand one further basic idea about human nature: a person's entire outlook on life grows out of a fundamental conclusion he has arrived at, usually in childhood, about his own position versus other people. For most of us, even the most successful, that conclusion is 'I'm not OK' — a deep-laid sense of personal inadequacy. For an unlucky few it may also include a basic disbelief in other people: 'You're not OK'. For the fortunate minority the decision is positive on both sides: 'I'm OK — You're OK'.

Self versus others

Very early in life, every child concludes 'I'm NOT OK'. He makes a conclusion about his parents too: 'You're OK'. This is the first thing he figures out in his life-long attempt to make sense of himself and the world in which he lives. This conclusion, 'I'm NOT OK — You're OK', is permanently recorded and will influence everything he does, all his contacts with other people. The you of his parents will eventually be generalized to include everyone else he has contact with.

Because this is a conclusion, it can be changed by a new conclusion. It is the first of four possible conclusions each of us can come to about ourselves versus other people:

1 I'M NOT OK — You're OK.
2 I'm NOT OK — You're NOT OK.

3 I'm OK — You're NOT OK.
4 I'm OK — You're OK.

The first conclusion is a tentative one based on the child's experiences in his first year. By the end of the second year it will be confirmed for him, or he might have changed his mind in favour of the second or third conclusion. But once the conclusion is settled, it will stay with him for the rest of his life, governing everything he does — unless he consciously replaces it later by the fourth possibility. People do not shift back and fourth between these viewpoints. For each person, his conclusion makes a kind of life-style for him.

I'm NOT OK — you're OK: To survive the baby needs bodily contact and stroking from his parents. The source of the stroking is something pleasurable and good — his parents are OK. His view of himself is based on his position of subordination to his parents and of defenceless inferiority — he is 'not OK'. For most people this first conclusion remains unchanged throughout life.

If this is the final conclusion, the grown person has a variety of ways in which he can accommodate himself to it, none of them entirely happy. He may try to escape the 'NOT OK' burden through personal fantasies. He may play 'games' with other people, usually of the 'Mine Is Better Than Yours' type — and aggressive defence against the deep fear that yours is really better than mine. Nearly all such games are designed to bring some momentary relief from the 'NOT OK' feeling. He may read the 'I'm NOT OK' as 'I might become OK': if this might mean he constantly seeks approval from the Parent in other peopls through being eager, willing and compliant to their demands. Or it might mean he tries to appease the Parent in himself by continual striving after success. But he commits himself to a life of mountain climbing — at the top of each cliff he confronts yet another cliff. However successful he may become in the eyes of the world, his Child maintains: 'No matter what I do I'm still not OK'.

I'm NOT OK — you're NOT OK: this is likely to be the conclusion arrived at by the child of cold and undemonstrative parents. Deprived as a toddler of the stroking he received in infancy, the child concludes that his parents are basicaly 'not OK'. He gives up. Even though people offer him affection in later life, he rejects their stroking. He may get some masochistic satisfaction from confirming his 'not OK' conclusion — perhaps by withdrawing emotionally from others, perhaps by provoking them to the point where they turn on him: 'If I'm bad then I'll show you're bad too'.

I'm OK — you're NOT OK: the child who is brutalized long enough by the parents he originally saw as OK will switch his conclusion to this — basically an anti-social, even criminal view of life. He has survived of his own accord despite the brutality, so I'm O.K. But he has learned to hate and distrust his parents: 'You're NOT OK'. In later life, hatred sustains him, although his Adult may learn to conceal it behind a mask of measured politeness. But his Parent gives him permission to be tough and cruel. He may acquire a retinue of yes-men who praise and stroke him to excess. Yet the more they praise him the more despicable they become, until he rejects them in favour of a new group of yes-men: 'come close so that I can let you have it'.

I'm OK — you're OK: this is different from the other three. Those were conclusions drawn spontaneously by the Child, based on his feelings early in life. This is a deliberate decision by the Adult, based on conscious thought and repeated opportunities to prove to himself his own worth and the worth of others. There the Child was still at the wheel; here the Adult has taken over.

The essential thing about 'I'm OK — you're OK' is that it is a view of life, not a feeling. The decision to adopt it doesn't erase the 'not OK' recordings in one's Child. The Child still resents criticisms and rebuffs from others and wants to respond in kind. The Child still wants instant victories, instant approval, instant results — and feels hurt or angry if they are not immediately forthcoming.

The Adult cannot wipe those tapes clean, but he *can* choose not to play them. He can recognise the negative Child response in other people and refuse to play tit for tat. He can understand the need for patience and persistence in working towards his objectives. He can also recognise the positive aspects of his own Child and Parent personalities and give them constructive outlet in his contacts with others.

Transactions

Now that we have developed a language, we can use it to analyse 'transactions' between people. A transaction is the basic unit of behaviour between two people — a stroke and a counter-stroke. 'I do something to you' and 'you do something back'. Transactional Analysis identifies which of the different personalities in the two people are involved:

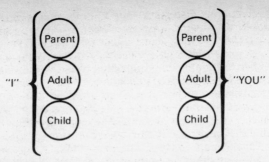

Imagine that the 'I' and 'you' are a boss and subordinate talking together. The boss says 'Two days ago I told you to write that report' and the subordinate replies 'Sorry but I just haven't had a chance'. The boss's Parent scolds the subordinate's Child, who responds with an excuse he might have used in childhood to his real parents:

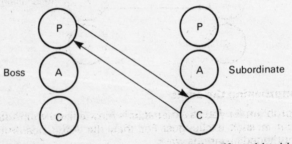

But suppose the subordinate instead replies 'If you'd told me more clearly what you wanted, I'd have done it for you'. Refusing to accept the Child role in which his boss has cast him, he brings out his Parent to scold back:

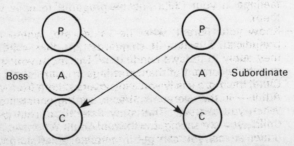

These two different transactions are likely to lead to very different results. The first, a 'parallel transaction' will probably lead to further exchanges — so long as the subordinate continues to play Child to his boss's Parent. As long as the lines remain parallel, the transactions can go on indefinitely. The second, a 'crossed transaction' leads to trouble: 'How dare you speak to me like that!' Communication stops. There follows a series of noisy exchanges that end up with a bang somewhere in the purple outer reaches of slammed doors and angry faces.

It's true of course that even in the first transaction, further exchanges on the same lines probably won't lead to any very practical conclusion. A different transaction might get better results: 'That report really is urgent' — 'Yes, I'll get it done today'. This is an Adult-Adult transaction:

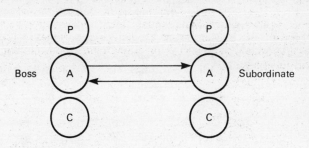

Strengthening the adult

The problem for you as a manager is how to keep your Adult in control in such exchanges. For that, the Adult needs to be strengthened in various ways:

- Know your Child, what its fears are, where it is vulnerable. Aroused feelings are a sign that your Child has been hooked. To help your rational-thinking Adult maintain control, you have to be aware of the 'NOT OK' feelings in your Child and be prepared to cope with them.
- Know your Parent, what its values are, where it is prejudiced. Question its standards: are they valid? Do they apply to today's conditions? The more you know about the content of the recordings in your Parent and Child, the more easily you can separate them from your Adult — in the everyday phrase, 'sorting yourself out'. When you can say 'That is my Parent' or 'That is my Child', you are saying it with your Adult. When you feel under stress, you can get immediate relief simply by asking 'Who's reacting?'.
- Be sensitive to the Child in others. Talk to that Child with

understanding. Appreciate its need for creative expression as well as help with its burden of 'not OK'.

— When you feel anger rising, count to ten. Delay your Child's and Parent's emotional response while you give time for your Adult to think. You may still decide to let your anger explode, but now it will be for effect, not just for relief.

— When in doubt, leave it out. You can't be attacked for what you didn't say.

— You can't learn navigation in the middle of a storm. Take the time to make big decisions about your values and objectives, which will make a lot of smaller decisions easier or unnecessary. By your big decisions, your priorities are shaped to answer the moment-to-moment questions of what to do.

Building your people's commitment is a far from simple task. In the end it probably comes down to a process of intelligent trial-and-error — finding out what influences each individual and trying to create the circumstances in which those influences have a positive effect. All we've said about understanding people and their motivation is no more than useful background knowledge. Because of the many subtle differences between individuals, no one set of rigid rules will help you in managing them. What is needed is a flexible, creative approach, based on interested concern for the individual, as well as for your organization. But that approach can be far more effectively worked out in practice if it is founded also on a thorough understanding of the principles of human behaviour — including your own!

What makes you a leader?

Your attempts to build your people's commitment to their work and to the organisation are really attempts to fulfil one of your most crucial management roles — the role of leader. In discussing earlier the effect of the working atmosphere on people's performance, you'll recall we listed what we called the forces of leadership.

Formal leaders adopt different relationships with their subordinates. Some few still seek to evoke fear and anxiety in their subordinates. Many (perhaps the majority) seem to regard their formal hierarchic position as sufficient to establish their role. Some better ones try to build their team's respect. A very few manage to develop a relationship of mutual trust. Any of these might produce reasonably effective results given the right conditions, even though the first two hardly merit the term leadership.

— *Fear* can be effective with a low calibre group with a tendency to irresponsible behaviour — if the boss is continually present. But with intelligent people it is likely to cause a high loss of capable staff (leaving only the yes-men and the masochists), and eventually perhaps the growth of strong anti-management groupings. It is not likely to encourage team members to use the initiative needed to cope with situations of change and uncertainty (which are likely to increase in organisations in the future).

— *Conventional position* work as long as convention rules the work-force. When this fails, the typical management reaction seems to be one of helplessness ('you'll never do anything with those bloody Union people').

— *Respect* doesn't necessarily carry trust with it. Many an effective leader is disliked personally, but respected. The members know he will fight for his team, however much he might ride roughshod over their personal interests.

— *Trust* is a belief in the leader's *long term* view of his team's interests — not necessarily giving the members what they want at the time. They believe he can be trusted to understand them and their intrests, and to play fair. Though perhaps the rarest of leader-led relationships, it is the most effective for team-building.

What leadership is *not* is trying to be '*popular*' — a mistake that many, many managers and supervisors make in their relationships with their subordinates. Perhaps this is a basic personality problem — they are strong on affiliation needs but weak on the need to establish authority.

'Traditional' ideas on leadership have tended to concentrate on the personal qualities of the leader. These ideas, especially in the early part of this century, were linked to the assumption that there existed a special 'leader-type' or class — the so-called 'born leader'. Before we dismiss that idea altogether, surely we can't deny that there are some people who have an advantage over the rest of us when it comes to leadership? They have an indefinable but recognisable quality which seems naturally to attract followers — perhaps it's what we mean by that difficult word, 'charisma'. Perhaps we've said enough about personality and temperament by now for you to be able to work out for yourself the roots of this remarkable quality.

But where does that leave *us*? If we don't happen to be so gifted, have we no hope of becoming a leader? If not, then many thousands of otherwise well-qualified managers will always lack an essential ingredient of their management ability.

Leadership style

In recent years the direction of research into leadership has shifted away from the personality traits or qualities of successful leaders and towards analysis of their actual behaviour in leadership situations. One of the most significant of these, identified by Robert Tannenbaum and Warren Schmidt, is the way *decisions* are reached in the working group.

As the leader of a group you may decide to take all the decisions yourself, relying on your authority to get those decisions implemented — a 'style' which has often been categorised as the 'autocratic'. On the other hand, you may decide (for a variety of reasons) to involve the members of your group in the decision-making process. To the extent that you do this, your style is moving closer to the 'democratic'. These two extremes have been better described as the 'controlling' and 'participative' styles of leadership.

As a leader therefore, you are faced with several questions: Is it a simple choice between controlling and a participative role? Are these the only two kinds of leadership style? Faced with evidence which shows that sometimes a controlling, and sometimes a participative style is most effective, what are you to do? Should you behave in a controlling or a participative way?

Tannenbaum and Schmidt suggested that the highly-controlling and the highly- participative styles were the two extremes of a *continuous scale* of leadership style. They identified seven points along this scale, which are shown below.

Amount of direction by the boss

The boss gives orders: you alone decide what to do. You may or may not consider your subordinates' feelings about the order. They are expected to obey.

The boss 'sells' his decision: you alone decide what to do. Besides giving orders, you persuade your subordinates to accept them — recognising they may resist.

The boss explains his decision: you alone decide what to do. But you give your subordinates the opportunity to discuss your thinking and your intentions. This allows you to explore the implications of your decision and to develop fuller instructions for carrying it out.

The boss's decision is open to change: You still take the initiative in deciding, but are willing to hear your subordinates' ideas before finally making up your mind. You will change it if they come up with a better idea.

The boss chooses between his subordinates' ideas: you define the problem or need. Your subordinates suggest ways of tackling it — giving you a range of alternatives. You select the most promising.

The boss states the problem — the group decides: you define the problem and the limits within which the decision must be made. Your subordinates work out their ideas and decide as a group what to do.

The boss defines the limits within which the group has total freedom: within the limits you specify (or *your* boss specifies for you), your subordinates define and analyse problems as they seem them and decide as a group what to do. You commit yourself in advance to helping implement whatever they decide.

Amount of involvement for subordinates

In fact, of course, the seven point on the scale are in themselves an over-simplification. Because it is a continuous scale you could logically adopt a mixture of direction and involvement at virtually *any* point along it. The important thing is to realise that as one increases, the other decreases.

Research shows that you will have a 'natural' style, that is, one which corresponds with your personal make-up. That is the way you will tend 'normally' to behave as a leader. However, it is also clear that you can, if you wish, modify your behaviour and adopt a style which you think is more likely to help you reach your objectives. To make the conscious choice of a leadership style, you must recognise and consider three kinds of force:

Forces in you yourself

Your own leadership beliefs and inclinations. Some managers operate more comfortably as directive leaders. They may argue that they are paid to take the responsibility for making decisions and for getting work out. Others operate more naturally as 'first among equals', sharing many of their functions with their subordinates. Their view may be that people should have a say in the planning and decision-making that affect their work, and that this contributes to their growth and development.

Your confidence in your subordinates. Managers differ greatly in the amount of trust they have in other people generally. This colours their views of their subordinates, and affects their willingness to trust their people's competence and good intentions.

Your tolerance of uncertainty. The manager who involves his subordinates has to accept that the outcome is less predictable than if he himself took the decisions. Some managers have low tolerance levels for such uncertainty. Others seem to enjoy a less stable environment, regarding the risks involved perhaps as a challenge to their nerve and judgement.

Forces in your subordinates

The strength of their need for independence. People vary widely in the amount of independence they need. Some prefer a strong leader, seeing delegated responsibility as 'passing the buck'. Others prefer greater freedom, seeing it perhaps as a tribute to their competence and sense of responsibility.

Their tolerance of uncertainty. Like some managers, some

subordinates have low tolerance levels for the uncertainty they feel when they have freedom to decide things for themselves. They prefer clear-cut directives. Others enjoy accepting the risks of greater self-direction.

Their expectations about leadership style. If the subordinates are used to strong leadership, they are likely to be un-nerved when you attempt to involve them in decision-making. If on the other hand they are used to greater involvement, they will resent it if you begin to make all the decisions yourself.

Their ability to tackle the problem. Your subordinates cannot participate effectively if the problem is beyond them. Do they have an interest in the problem and feel it is important to solve it? Do they have the knowledge and judgement to deal with it? Do they understand the aims of the organisation and have a commitment to them? The answers will suggest the kinds and sizes of decision you can successfully delegate.

Their effectiveness as a group. A group that is a well-knit team, used to working together, will have developed habits of co-operation that pay off in joint planning and decision-making. A new group, or a group without this cohesiveness and confidence in each other, will be less effective with a highly participative leadership style.

Forces in the situation

The organisational climate. The values and traditions of the organisation are important influences. Some organisations expect their managers to be dynamic, decisive and persuasive. Other put more value on their managers' human relation skills. Such factors tend to push you in the direction of either authoritarian or democratic leadership. There may also be practical influences — and size and stability of the working units, their geographical spread, the power and militancy of unions, the organization's current economic or marketing position. These may narrow the range of leadership styles you can use.

The pressures in the manager's job. A manager's leadership style is only partly due to the sort of person he is. It is also heavily influenced by the position in which he is placed. Many of the failings attributed to a manager's personality may really be caused by his job and the pressures it imposes on him.

The problem itself. A problem that calls for judgement and experience rather than highly specialised knowledge may be tackled more successfully by participative leadership. Groups are more likely than individuals to take risky but necessary decisions. But where the facts are involved and the solution is likely to be complex, it may be better tackled by one person. The key question for you is 'have I heard the views of everyone who can contribute useful knowledge or ideas?'.

Pressure of time. This is perhaps the greatest pressure you feel (although it is often less than you imagine). The more urgent the need for action, the more difficult it is to involve subordinates. In an organisation that is in a constant state of crisis and 'crash planning', you are not likely to develop habits of involving your subordinates in decision-making.

Making the right choices

There is no single 'best' style for all situations. To be an able leader you are not likely to be *consistently* autocratic or *consistently* democratic. You use a range of leadership styles depending on the situation, the problem and the subordinates. On each issue, you accurately assess your own needs and those of others in the organisation likely to be affected by your methods of leadership — superiors, colleagues, people in other departments. You also understand your subordinates and can assess their readiness for growth and development. If direction is in order, you direct. If involvement is called for, you involve.

The amount of freedom that subordinates have is not measured by the sheer *number* of decisions they help make. More important is the *significance* of the decision. Several minor decisions will not given them any particular sense of involvement, however much freedom they are given in taking them. A big decision, even within narrow limits, demonstrates to a far greater extent your confidence in them.

In any decision-making, the subordinates must be clear about what authority you plan to use. If you intend to decide something yourself but the group get the impression you have delegated it, they are likely to be confused and resentful. And to try to 'make them think it was their idea in the first place' is risky. Far better to be honest and clear about what is being delegated and what is not. Once you've decided to give your team freedom to decide, you must consider what part you will play. Sometimes you should leave them to decide for themselves — particularly if your involvement would inhibit them. At other times you may be able to help as an extra member of the group, so long as they can genuinely accept you in that role rather than as a higher authority.

In any case, remember you cannot disclaim responsibility for your subordinates' decisions. You have to accept whatever risks are involved whenever you delegate to them freedom for decision-making. Delegation is not a way of passing the buck!

The effect of the situation

A practical way to analyse whether a controlling or a participative style is more effective has been put forward by Fred Fiedler in his book 'A Theory of Leadership Effectiveness'. He examined many work-groups in different situations. In each work-group he measured the group effectiveness, the leader's style, and what he called three 'situational factors': group atmosphere, task structure and position power. The result showed convincingly that different situations, as measured by these three factors, requird different leadership styles if the group was to be highly effective.

1. *Group atmosphere*
Group atmosphere is a measure of the extent to which members have feelings of trust, respect, loyalty, admiration, and liking towards the leader and each other.

The stronger these feelings are, the more favourably situated the leader is to exert a strong influence on the members. The trusted, respected and well-liked leader does not have to rely on rank or power over his members; they follow his lead because of their feelings of trust, respect, loyalty, admiration and liking.

Fielder's research found that group atmosphere was the most important of the three situational factors. It is clear also that group atmosphere is the factor which the leader has the greatest power to affect.

2. *Task structure*
Fielder found task structure to be second most important of the three situational factors.

The tasks of some groups are clearly more structured than those of others — for example, the tasks of a typing-pool are more structured than those of an advertising copy-writing team. Further, different tasks a leader has to perform are different in structure from each other. For example, a sales manager's task in planning his territories is more structured than his task of training his salesmen.

A group's tasks can be analysed by answering the following questions:
    — Can the task and its end result be measured in terms of the correctness of the decision or the rightness of the

solution? There may be a correct mathematical answer, or an authoritative solution as with a legal problem, but many decisions or solutions will be arrived at by conjecture, opinion, assumption or hunch, and are thus low in structure.

— Are the aims of the task clear? 'Reduce the scrap rate from 8% to 4% is a clear aim', whereas 'improve the profitability of Product Group Y' is much less clear and explicit and is a less structured task.

— How flexible is the task in terms of method? There may be a range of alternative methods of strategies that could be pursued. For example there are only a limited number of ways of funding the advertising appropriation, but a very much wider range of ways of spending it, which is a less structured task.

— In carrying out the task, what degree of interpersonal co-operation is required? Some tasks may be carried out in virtual isolation — certain types of research for example — while others will require a very high degree of co-operation, for example determining a set of delivery priorities, which is low in structure.

3. *Position power*

This means the extent to which group members feel the leader has power over them — power stemming from the leaders' position in the hierarchy and the authority granted to him by the organisation.

It is a measure of the power members believe the leader to have over them in terms of praise and blame, reward and punishment, the allocation of work and of resources, and so on. It is also, therefore, a measure of the degree to which the members are dependent on the leader, and he independent of them.

The greater their dependence on the leader, the more influence he has over members. However, Fiedler's research shows that, although it *is* a factor in the situation which relates style to effectiveness, it is third in importance after group atmosphere and task structure.

Fiedler's leadership model

By measuring many groups, Fiedler obtained average scores for group atmosphere, task structure and position power. He divided each scale of scores in two — above average and below average — giving a breakdown as follows:

Group atmosphere	Task structure	Position power	Strength of evidence in favour of:		Octant
			Controlling style	Participative style	
good	structured	strong	◯		I
good	structured	weak	◯		II
good	unstructured	strong	◯		III
good	unstructured	weak		◯	IV
poor	structured	strong		◯	V
poor	structured	weak		◯	VI
poor	unstructured	strong		◯	VII
poor	unstructured	weak	◯		VIII

— Group atmosphere — better than average (Good), and worse than average (Poor).
— Task Structure — above average (Structured), and below average (Unstructured).
— Position Power — above average (Strong), and below average (Weak).

Three variables, each of which can be in one of two conditions, gives a total permutation of eight leadership situations, which Fiedler called 'octants'. The octants are ranked 1–8 in order of favourableness for the leader — in octant 1 the leader has everything in his favour to exercise influence, a good group atmosphere, a structured task, and strong position power — and so on down to octant 8, where the leader has little in his favour, a poor group atmosphere, an unstructured task, and weak position power.

A simple division of each factor into above and below average is, of course, pretty abitrary. Fiedler's model would be more discriminating if instead of dividing each scale into two, he had divided it into three or four. But a leader would then, however, have 27 or 64 situations to recognise and adapt to. In practice, this would be quite unworkable.

For each octant, Fiedler then showed the extent to which the style and the effectiveness of the many groups he had studied correlated with each other. The results are shown in the diagram below. Note that the distance from the centre line does *not* indicate how participative or controlling the effective leaders were, *nor* does it indicate how effective the participative or controlling leaders were; it indicates the *strength* of the evidence that a controlling or participative style is effective in that situation.

You will note that the evidence is fairly conclusive in all octants except two. In octants III and VII the evidence is inconclusive — participative and controlling leaders are almost equally effective in these two situations. The model shows, by and large, that the controlling style is effective in highly favourable or highly unfavourable situations, whereas the participative style is effective in situations of 'intermediate' favourableness.

Using the model in practice

According to Fiedler, what determines your effectiveness as a leader is not your style alone, nor the situation alone, but the matching of style and situation. The first step is to attempt to measure the leadership situations you face in terms of the three situational factors. The second is to try to adopt a style appropriate to that situation. There is, of course, another alternative, which is to try to change one or more of the situational factors, to put the situation into an octant to which your natural style is more suited. You may well have several roles in your organization, and several tasks in each role. You will probably find that your various tasks have a different degree of structure; you may also lead various work-groups who have different preceptions of their group atmosphere and your position power. In total, therefore, your job may face you with leadership situations which are in different octants.

To be effective in all octants facing you in your job as a whole, you must above all be *flexible*, in order to get a good match between style and situation in each octant. To do this, you must be able to recognise and analyse the different leadership situations you face, have a good idea of your own natural style, learn which style is most effective in each situation and decide (where your natural style and the situation do not match) what leadership strategy to adopt in each situation.

You may be able to change both task structure and position power to some extent. To do this you have to be flexible about the way you organise, issue instructions, allocate resources, and so on. Group atmosphere is much more difficult to change. It depends mostly on your interpersonal skills and the way you interact with members of your group. In the research into leadership behaviour, three things stand out as having a significant effect on group atmosphere. In suggesting these to you we run the risk that you'll think we're stating the obvious. Or even that you'll feel insulted by the idea that you'd behave in any other way. All we can say in our defence is that it is precisely these sorts of behaviour which we are told over and over again by people we train that they fail to see in their managers. So what are they?

Being considerate

The manager who wants to be a leader is not only considerate to his people, but encourages them to be considerate to each other. (Actually, if you are considerate they will tend to be so too anyway, because subordinates tend to model their behaviour on that of the leader).

Considerate behaviour means treating people with courtesy and making them feel they have importance, dignity, and self-respect. Easily said, not quite so easily done. In practice, it means you must:
— *Communicate:* talk to your people often; make them aware of your own positive attitudes to the job; get to

131

know them as people, and let them get to know you; get them to talk to you, and listen patiently and attentively.
— *Be courteous:* treat your people with respect and good manners.

— *Be tactful:* do nothing hurtful or spiteful; always let the subordinate save his face; never nag or show impatience; never pass the buck; always admit your own mistakes and accept more than your fair share of the blame.
— *Be tolerant:* suffer mistakes not gladly but with forbearance. They will happen — but the leader's job is to ensure they don't recur. Accept your subordinates as they are (it is the leader's job to improve them, but this is a gradual process).
— *Keep your temper:* recognise that losing your temper may hurt a subordinate and will certainly damage his feelings towards you; keep your emotions and those of your subordinates calm and cool.
— *Praise and criticism:* always express approval, appreciation, congratulations, and thanks whenever they're deserved; always give praise where due, but avoid flattery; soften the harshness of criticism, and try to make criticism constructive; criticise the idea or the mistake, not the person.
— *Be sincere:* always mean what you say; always keep any promises you make; never make promises you have no intention of keeping.
— *Be loyal:* to individuals, by never criticising a person

132

behind his back or in front of others and by always defending individuals when necessary. To the group as a whole, by not criticising the group to other people, by defending the group against the criticism of others, and by fighting for the group when necessary (and by making it obvious you fought). To the organisation, by not criticising policies to the group (if you criticise your superiors behind their backs, the group will suspect you do the same to them).

In short, behave towards your people as you would wish them to behave towards you.

Incidentally, being considerate (the way you treat your subordinates as people) has nothing to do with being participative (the way decisions are reached). You can be a controlling leader — that is, take decisions and issue instructions in a highly controlling way — but still behave considerately and create feelings of trust and loyalty in your people. As a controlling leader you will exercise more influence, and find it easier to lead, if you are considerate. It is perhaps even more important for a controlling leader to behave considerately than for a participative leader — considerate behaviour is a way of getting subordinates to accept a controlling style, whereas they might resist or reject a controlling leader who behaved towards them very inconsiderately and made them feel small, stupid, without self-esteem and unworthy of respect.

Considerate behaviour towards your people will tend to cause them to behave considerately to each other — and vice versa. Subordinates tend to emulate their leader's behaviour.

Because considerate behaviour feeds people's needs for security, belonging, acceptance and esteem, and causes feelings of trust, loyalty, and liking towards others who behave considerately, it clearly improves some elements of group atmosphere.

Being task-centred

Other elements of group atmosphere (people's feelings of respect and admiration) are improved when the leader is seen to be highly task-centred. This means being highly concerned about doing the job in the best possible way; a task-centred leader tends to work hard and consistently, strives to keep to deadlines, always tries to find the best solution to a problem however much work or inconvenience it involves him in, places the task before his own desires, feelings or status, and sets high quality standards for himself and his subordinates.

Unlike considerateness, which is concerned with attitudes and behaviour towards people, task-centredness is concerned with attitudes and behaviour towards the job. Nearly all subordinates say (this has been researched many times) that one of the things they expect a leader to do it 'to show a good example'. Part of what they mean is that they expect a leader to be what we have described as task-centred. It is also clear (by both research and common-sense) that they respect a leader who is highly task-centred and that they also tend to reflect his attitudes and behaviour to the job in their own. There is also a deal of evidence to show that the influence a leader's task-centredness has on his subordinates increases with the frequency and depth of his contact with them. It is no use being task-centred if your contacts with your people are too infrequent for them to notice.

So, being highly tasked-centred increases your people's feelings of respect and even admiration for you and thus improves the group atmosphere; but your task-centredness only affects your people if you have sufficient contact with them for some of your attitudes to 'rub-off'; where your people see you as highly task-centred they will tend to become more highly task-centred themselves, which is likely to improve their performance.

Being proficient

It is also common-sense (confirmed by research) that a manager who is good at his own job is respected and even admired by his people. There is some evidence to show that a proficient leader generally has proficient subordinates (though this may be due to the way he has selected or trained them). So his group performs well.

As a proficient leader you gain not only your people's respect, but also their trust in your judgement — 'he knows what he's doing'. Because of that, subordinates will do as you say, irrespective of your style or their other feelings towards you.

Subordinates expect you to be proficient at your own job — this is another part of what they mean by 'setting a good example'. If you are proficient in your job, they will often emulate you by trying to become more proficient at their own jobs. Although subordinates don't usually expect you to be proficient in *their* jobs, their respect and trust will be increased if you are. But there's a snag in this: it may tempt you to interfere in their work and to contol things too tightly. This is more damaging than productive.

So to summarise: the way to improve group atmosphere is to behave considerately towards your people; to be highly task-centred; to be proficient in your own job, and reasonably proficient in as many of your subordinates' jobs as possible; to cultivate the maximum job-related contact (not social contact) with your subordinates, so that your considerateness, task-centredness and proficiency have the maximum effect.

Group atmosphere is the most difficult factor in a situation to change, but it also has the greatest effect on making that situation more favourable for you as a leader. In being considerate, task-centred and proficient you are feeding the needs of your individual subordinates and the needs of the group — as well as achieving the task.

The motivation of groups

These three elements are the basis of yet another leadership model, developed by Dr John Adair initially for leadership training in the armed forces, but widely applied by the Industrial Society under the name 'Action-Centred Leadership'. In this model the three sets of needs overlap and support each other.

The leader's role is to see that these three sets of needs are met by balancing the amount of attention given to each. In this book we've already discussed pretty thoroughly the task and individual needs. Perhaps we need to take a slightly closer look at the question of group needs.

Firstly, people who work in a team — and who belong to it willingly, rather than by complusion — usually want that team to succeed. This is partly because the team's success will affect them personally. It helps to meet their individual needs for

achievement. This desire to reach team goals may be a strong influence on your people's commitment and their reaction to your leadership.

Secondly, when people have worked in a team for any length of time, they develop a desire for what is known as 'group cohesiveness'. They want the team to stick together — partly again because this meets their individual needs for acceptance and belonging. This in fact may cause you problems of leadership, especially since quite strong pressures can be brought to bear to resist changes in the group's make-up or to make members toe the group's line. Constructively and intelligently used, however, these group motivations can work for you as a leader in helping to increase the effectiveness and the performance of your people as a team.

Teams and team-building

One of the ways to get higher performance from your people is to make sure that they work together as a team. Groups that work as teams have strengths that are missing from collections of individuals. They usually make better use of the different talents of their members. Nearly always morale is higher, particularly in changing or unpredictable situations. When facing a difficult challenge, a team of only moderately able people often achieve far more than a number of talented individuals working independently. But how do you tell when the group that you are managing has become a team? It doesn't happen simply because organisationally they all report to you, or because they happen to work near each other, or are friendly in their relationship. Team-sense requires more than organisation structure, or personal proximity, or good social relationships.

Features of a team

If you think about any group of people with whom you have

worked, or that you have been able to observe, which you regard as being an effective team, you will probably find that it demonstrated seven characteristic features:

1. Its members share a strong sense of *common purpose*. They are linked by their commitment to team goals and they work as much for their team's success as for their own. But the team's idea of its goals develop within the team as a whole: it can't be imposed by you or altered by outsiders.

2. The members of the team *interact* to achieve their purpose. No one regards his job as something he can do in isolation. All the members feel a need to collaborate. They discuss ideas with each other, offer and accept suggestions about each others' work, and take decisions together on anything that is important to the team's success. In a sense, they learn how to be self-organising.

3. Each member has a strong sense of the team's *identity*. They are very aware of themselves as a group. Over time they develop a feeling of belonging together, as they get to know each other and learn about each other's capabilities and foibles. They think in terms of 'insiders' and 'outsiders', of 'us' and 'them'. This sense of group identity includes the team's leader. In fact he is very much at the centre of it. A formal boss who is not 'one of us' becomes just another part of the team's external environment rather than a source of internal influence. This strong group identity means that the team is more likely to compete than to collaborate with other teams. Properly managed this attitude can result in fruitful inter-team competition and constructive rivalry. Badly managed, or not managed at all, it can cause inter-team hostility and destructive 'one-upmanship' games.

4. A team is *small enough* to be self-coordinating. Each member has to be able to maintain a continuous awareness of how his actions affect the other members, and vice-versa. This really limits the group's size to between three and twelve members. Fewer than three lack strength as a group, but with more than a dozen the group begins to fragment: either smaller cliques develop within it, or team sense is lost altogether and co-ordination has to fall back on formal organisation links.

5. A team has its own internal *code of behaviour* (an important part of the working atmosphere that we've seen affects the performance of each of its members). They not only

conform to this code but act as a group to enforce it upon any out-of-line members. A variety of disciplinary sanctions may be applied, not just by the team's leader but by the team as a whole. They may range from a raised eyebrow to a Kangaroo court; from a certain quality of laughter in the group to outright expulsion (a member being 'sent to Coventry'). The team's behaviour code doesn't necessarily match the ethics of the world outside — nor even the personal ethics of every individual member. Sometimes it may fly in the face of external realities, although here the leader can play a key role in getting the group to adjust its code for the sake of its self-respect or self-preservation. The team's effectiveness within the organisation will depend very much on whether this behaviour code is positive, neutral or negative toward the organisation's general interests.

6. Members of a team afford each other a high level of *mutual support*. There is a bond of loyalty within a team — the members are more concerned for the team's interests than for those of the wider organisation, or for their own personal interests. Frequently they will set aside private advantage for what they see as the team's advantage. In return, the team protects its members from external pressures or threats. It closes ranks against anything the members regard as an attack on an individual member or on the group as a whole. Whether it is a workforce group or a management group, it practices 'solidarity'.

7. The team has an *internal structure* which has little to do with the organisation chart. The members adopt roles that are quite different in nature from the formal functions described by their job titles or job descriptions. These roles evolve out of the different personalities, temperaments and aptitudes of the members, and the way they relate to one another. Usually these roles are not consciously adopted, although objective analysis woul reveal that members are in fact operating within them. The seem to be intuitively perceived rather than openly declared. The key role is that of the leader. This is the individual member who is recognised by the team as having the greatest influence on their opinions, attitudes and behaviour. He is the member accepted by the others as best able to guide an integrate the team's efforts. This is a practical working role, not a status position. The leader doesn't stand on his authority. he doesn't need to, in fact. The rest accept him instinctively as the natural leader. He may *not* be the formally appointed head of the team! This

role can in fact be shared by more than one team member. Although it is a crucial role, it by no means the only one which is important to the team's success.

Team roles

Recent research has shown that members of a management team can contribute in two ways: in functional roles defined by their technical or professional abilities, and in team roles defined by the kind of contribution each member makes to the internal working of the team. It also appears that certain roles recur time and again in different teams. They seem to be necessary components of effective teamwork. These team roles define for each member his most effective way to contribute. Most people have a natural primary role, one they usually play in whatever teams they join. Many also have secondary roles they can play if these roles are not filled by other team members, or if their own primary role is more effectively filled by another member. In a small team they may play a combination of roles.

The role that each person finds it most natural to adopt will depend on a number of psychological traits: the degree to which he is introvert or extrovert, the degree to which he is calm or highly-strung, the degree to which he is dominant or submissive, and his level of intelligence. Other aspects of the individual will also have an influence: his maturity, his instinct to trust or suspect others, his tolerance of uncertainty, and so on.

The long-term research project which has identified these team role has been run at the Administrative Staff College at Henley by Dr Melville Belbin. As his test-bed he used teams formed during the Henley courses to work on management exercises. He used psychometric tests to establish individuals' traits and formed teams accordingly. The following are the eight most typical roles identified, under the titles Dr Belbin gave them. Neither the roles nor the personal traits that go with them are rigid; no-one is likely to be completely typecast. You may see yourself in more than one of these descriptions, but it is likely that one will approximate closely to your 'preferred role' — the one in which you are most effective as a team member.

The *'chairman'* is the team's *natural leader* — whether he is its formal head or not.

His concern is for purposeful, effective teamwork. He clarifies team aims and priorities and co-ordinates its resources to achieve external goals. He has a clear perception of members' strengths and limitations and focuses each on what he does best. He establishes roles, work boundaries and communication channels, sees gaps and takes steps to fill them.

He tends to be extrovert and calm. He has 'character' and integrity; possesses common-sense rather than a brilliant or creative intelligence; is dominant but not domineering. His natural authority is expressed in a relaxed unassertive way. He is trusting unless someone is proved untrustworthy, singularly free from jealousy, talks easily and is easy to talk to. In discussions he asks questions, listens and sums up group feelings or verdicts. He takes decisions firmly after all have had their say.

The *'shaper'* is the team's *action man* — and often its formal head.

His concern is for action and results. He shapes team effort towards specific task aims. In discussions, his compulsive drive is directed to objectives: he tries to unite ideas, needs and practical considerations into a single feasible project — which he pushes forward urgently to decision and action.

He tends to be extrovert and outgoing, highly-strung, nervily energetic, impulsive and impatient. He seems confident but is easily frustrated: only results reassure him. He is dominant — sees the team as an extension of his own ego, is competitive and quick to offer or accept a challenge. He may steamroller discussions. He is short-tempered but rows are quickly over without grudges. He is quick to sense a slight or suspect a conspiracy; intolerant of woolly thinking; may seem arrogant or abrasive. He can make the team uncomfortable, but he makes things happen.

The *'plant'* is the team's *ideas man* — the type to 'plant' in an ineffective team.

His concern is for major issues and fundamentals. He provides the most original suggestions and proposals, radical approaches to problems and obstacles and creative insights into existing lines of action. But he may miss detail or make careless mistakes. He can waste energy on irrelevancies and over-theoretical ideas.

He tends to be introvert, yet thrustful and uninhibited. Dominant and highly-strung, he can be prickly if his ideas are criticised. The most imaginative and intelligent member of the team, he criticises others' ideas to clear the ground for his own counter-proposals. He may do this tactlessly and cause offence. He may sulk if his own ideas are rejected. To get the best from him may required judicious flattery and careful handling — usually best provided by th 'Chairman'.

The *'resource investigator'* is the team's *contact man* — its diplomat, salesman and liaison officer.

His concern is for exploring possibilities in the world outside. He keeps the team from stagnating or losing touch with reality. He lacks original ideas himself, but encourages innovation — is quick to see the relevance of new ideas. Within the team he is a good improviser, but he can waste time on irrelevancies that catch his fancy.

He tends to be extrovert, sociable, gregarious and dominant. He has an easily-aroused interest. His response is enthusiastic but short-lived: he fails to follow through. The most active external communicator, he makes friends easily and has many contacts outside the team. He's in his office rarely — and then is probably on the 'phone. Without the stimulus of other people he becomes bored, demoralized, ineffective. Not someone for a solitary job.

The *'company worker'* is the team's *practical organiser*.

His concern is for feasible action plans. He turns decisions and strategies into defined tasks that people can get on with. Give him a decision — he'll make a schedule; give him a group of people — he'll make an organization chart. He needs settled plans with which to operate. He flounders in uncertain or rapidly-changing situations.

He tends to be controlled and calm. He has 'character', integrity, and a disciplined approach, is not easily deflated or discouraged. He's efficient and methodical, but a bit inflexible. He is sincere and trusting towards others and will trim and adapt his schedules to fit agreed lines of action, but is unresponsive to ideas if not immediately practicable. He can be negative and unconstructive towards others' ideas, but is their best informant on what has been agreed and what each is to do.

The *'finisher'* is the team's *checker* — a compulsive meeter of deadlines and fulfiller of schedules.

His concern is for what might go wrong. He's never at ease unless he has personally checked every detail to ensure everything has been done, nothing overlooked. He's pre-occupied with order, can get bogged down in detail and lose sight of objectives. His great asset to the team is his relentless follow-through.

He tends to be introvert, highly-strung, anxious, obsessive and impatient. He has strength of character and self-control, low dominance and is rather unassertive. He keeps the team constantly aware of the need for urgency and attention to detail. He is intolerant of the more casual and slapdash members. This can be morale-lowering and depressing for the rest of the team.

The *'Monitor evaluator'* is the team's *judge* — its most objective, uninvolved member.

His concern is for cool, sound judgements. He provides

dispassionate analysis, unclouded by ego-involvement, inter-preting and evaluating large volumes of complex information; in analysing problems; in assessing others' contributions. He protects the team from committing itself to misguided projects or ideas. He likes time to mull things over.

He tends to be introvert and lack jollity, warmth, spon-taneity. He has little enthusiasm or euphoria but is calm and dependable. He has a high IQ but low drive, is unambitious. He has a serious and unexciting manner — a bit of a 'cold fish'. He may be fairminded and open to change, but is often depressingly negative and unreceptive. He may be tactless and disparaging, and can lower team morale by damping at the wrong time.

The *'team worker'* is the team's *harmoniser* — the 'cement' of the team.

His concern is for team unity and good spirit. He's aware of others' needs and worries, knows most about their private lives and family affairs, has the clearest preception of the emotional undercurrents in the team. Normally his contibution isn't very visible. But when pressures threaten to disrupt the team, his loyalty, sympathy and support is invaluable.

He tends to be extrovert and calm. He has low dominance, is uncompetitive, soft and indecisive. He is the most sensitive of member of the feelings of others. He is the most active internal communicator. Likeable, popular and unassertive, a good listener, he builds on others' ideas rather than producing his own rival ideas. He dislikes confrontation and tries to avoid or defuse it. He's loyal to the team as a unit and supportive to all its members.

From all this, Belbin concludes that the effectiveness of a team depends on how far its members recognize each others' abilities in specific team roles and adjust their own con-tributions to suit. Personal characteristics fit each member for some team roles, and make it less likely he will succeed in others. About 70% of people seem to be capable of playing an effective role in a team. The rest tend to perform as make-weights, or to be non-team people.

A team can deploy its members' technical or professional abilities to best effect only when its membership provides an appropriate balance of team roles. There is no single 'best' pattern of roles within a team. The ideal pattern differs from team to team, depending on the team's purpose and its environment. To create and effective team for a particular task, the required team roles have to be selected from a common inventory (i.e. the eight roles described), and the people who can play these roles have then to be drawn into the team. Most people's repertoire of roles can be extended through counselling and training.

This may be rather sophisticated stuff for the average middle manager or supervisor. Certainly, if you're managing a team of shop-floor operatives or clerical workers it has a limited application. However, apart from the fact that it's one of the most interesting pieces of new thinking about the human factors in management in recent years, it may be of value to you in recognising and fulfilling your role as a *member* of your management team, rather than as a leader. As you rise in the management hierarchy, so this kind of thinking will become progressively more relevant and necessary.

How teams are built

With a clear understanding of the features of a team and of the roles which may have to be filled within it, you are now better equipped to turn your group of subordinates into a cohesive, effective team. Probably the first place to start is with a hard look at the organisation structure.

You have to develop, as far as you can, structures that satisfy both the needs of the work and the requirements of team-groupings. This is often difficult in industries where people customarily work in large numbers without any identification in small work groups, such as production-line work or large administrative offices. The problems are not only in how to divide the work, although this is a considerable task in itself. You may also have to overcome suspicion in the work-force and resentment by the shop-floor leaders, who have *already* created their own groupings — union-interest groups rather than task groups. Rightly, they will see the motivational power of work teams as competition to that of their own groupings. Many managers also misunderstand the nature of team groupings. Applying the principles we outlined in the section on organisation of work, they may come up with an organisation chart that looks not unlike this:

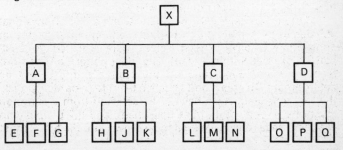

Many a manager in X's position sees this as *one* team rather than as four — and himself as having sixteen subordinates rather than being the leader of a team of five (the X-A-B-C-D) team. As a result he fails to create clearly differentiated responsibilities for his four subordinates and to delegate full authority to them. So *they* are not able to play effective leadership roles, and *he* is likely to play an 'external boss' role than that of a leader integrated with his team.

Organising for co-operation

Organisation charts serve a useful purpose by showing the formal relationship of jobs and responsibilities. What they do not necessarily create, however, is the sense of purposeful teamwork, without which the organisation structure remains sterile and lifeless. This can't be illustrated by means of a chart. The *idea* of organisation would be far better represented by a very different sort of picture — one which turns the impersonal structure of jobs into a series of teams, bound together by co-ordinated aims.

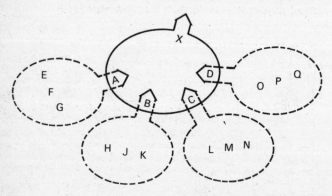

Each team has 'players' and a 'captain'. The players in the higher-level team are captains of their own teams: they are both leaders and followers.

The arrows show the co-ordination of *aims*. X's aim is not just for himself but for his team, comprising himself plus A, B, C and D. It is made up of the aims of A, B, C and D, each of which is the aim of his team (A-E-F-G, B-H-J-K, and so on). Aims are for *teams*, not just for individual managers.

The same principle applies when an aim is made specific and given a deadline for completion, in which case we call it an objective.

Joint objective-setting

The concept of *'Management by Objectives'* so popular only a few years ago suggests that objectives are for individuals to achieve, by their own ability and wit. This in fact destroys a sense of leadership and team achievement. And it wasn't what the originator of the phrase meant by it at all.

For effective team-building, objectives are objectives for the whole team. They have to be discussed within the team and jointly clarified and agreed. As leader you play a prime role in doing this, but you recognise (and get your team to recognise) that the objectives are the team's, not just yours: you also get them to recognise that their objectives must interlock with the objectives of other teams in the organisation (both the lateral teams and the 'superior' team, of which you are one of the members).

The clearer your aims, the better the start you have in working out where your priorities lie, how you can best use your time and other resources, which particular skills and abilities you need to develop, what you need *not* concern yourself with. And similarly for your people. You may be efficient without clear, constructive aims, but you can't be *effective*.

The more closely your aims are identified with those personal skills and abilities you and your people can take a pride in, the greater the human stimulus they provide. In striving towards them, your people develop high morale, a sense of commitment and the spirit of comradeship that welds the individuals into a team.

Many MbO exercises fail to get commitment — perhaps because the objectives are thought of as being 'put in'. They ignore the fact that the members of the team already *have* some sense of aims — possibly vague and uncoordinated and never sharpened into words, but nevertheless there. In identifying your aims you should try to draw out these hazy ideas and feelings and crystallise them. You realise what your aims are, you don't create them.

Other failures in MbO exercises can be put down to shallow thinking. The objectives given are unimaginative statements of the obvious — so obvious indeed that they serve little useful puspose in improving the way the job is run. (Anyway the obvious is often wrong: profit objectives for example. For anyone but a shareholder, profit is a convenient yardstick of progress, not the progress itself.) The act of thinking through the aims should give your team a *better* understanding of what their job is essentially about. The result should be a set of constructive ideas on improvement, and this must cost you some hard but stimulating mental effort. Good aims are never easy to realise in words.

Yet another reason for the failure of MbO — perhaps the key reason — is that the objectives are not thought of as the aims of *people*. Instead we have aims of 'positions', 'functions', or 'departments' — all abstractions. The reality is people. Ultimately an aim is a self-guidance mechanism in a human brain. If it is to influence human behaviour, it must become the personal property of the team members.

Team membership

The selection of people in a team is also important. A team benefits from variety in its membership: a variety of temperaments and personalities, of types of ability and skill, perhaps of age and experience. It is a mistake for managers to try to put 'like with like' in forming their working teams.

But some people do *not* seem to make effective team members — they are better perhaps in roles where team-work is unimportant. Among them are the self-centred and ambitious 'superstar'. He may in fact damage team sense. He may stand too far apart from the other members for them to feel that the *team* benefits from his ability, and his attitude towards them may cause demoralisation. The other generally ineffective team-member is the highly aggressive 'loner'. He finds it difficult to place any trust in his colleague's intentions and goodwill. The reactions his aggressive attacks evoke outside the team may also rebound on the team itself.

Visible leadership of the team

Team meetings are often given a low priority by managers — perhaps because they find them too difficult to organise and run effectively — we'll say more about that a bit later on. Certainly bad, unproductive meetings which waste everybody's time are no help in team-building — or in any other way, for that matter. But if your people never actually meet *as* a working team (not just socially), they never really get the chance to *see* themselves as a team — or you as the leader of it, rather than the 'boss' of each individual.

Regular team meetings help to develop your people's sense of common purpose and co-operative effort. The meetings need not be long — perhaps half-an-hour once a fortnight or so. Each member reports briefly on what is happening in his part of the operation: progress, problems and intentions for the future. Any questions of co-ordination are noted (to be sorted out later between the people directly involved). A short discussion follows about your own concerns, plans and ideas for the team over the next period. Minutes are brief, prepared promptly, and circulated to all team members.

Such meetings serve several important purposes. They prompt each of your people to think of himself as one of a team, not as an isolated individual narrowly concerned with his own job alone. They enable each of your people to understand what his colleagues are doing and why, and to see how his own actions affect the others for better or worse. They convert the individual member's problems from a private burden into a team responsibility, calling for the team's ideas and abilities to help solve. And they persuade your people to see you as the team leader, thinking not only of individual's needs and problems but also of the interests and demands of the whole team. In some situations, for example in a widely-spread sales team, meetings may be the *only* way to accomplish these purposes.

Successes and failures

A team needs to have it successes if its members are to feel it worth allying themselves with their colleagues. It needs some failures and frustrations too, perhaps — the too-successful team may be too involved in mutual self-congratulation to achieve what it *could* achieve. It becomes complacent. But too many failures can destroy the interest of the members in belonging to the group.

As an effective team-leader you should try whenever you can to create the conditions (perhaps with your influence on objective-setting) where the team has to stretch — with a mixture of successes and failures. For team-building, you should also use team meetings to review both kinds of result; the successes, so that the team can recognise and repeat the group interactions that helped it succeed; the failures, so that members can see why they failed as a group (not for appraisals of individuals) and so what *not* to do in the future.

Team incentives

If your organisation operates a system of bonuses or other kinds of incentive, team-building will benefit from a group-bonus element as well as individual awards. A good example is the field of selling. Many salesmen tend to think and act as soloists, yet most kinds of selling also require co-operation between salesmen in different territories or areas. An incentive related to team achievement will encourage them to contribute to each other's success and build their commitment to team-work. We once saw an office full of forty telephone salespeople, all hard at work at 7pm on a Friday evening, striving to reach their *group* target for a week.

Implications for the organisation

One word of warning about team-building. In developing team structures, you need to think of the implications for co-ordination *across* the organisation. Teams do tend to get self-centred. So managers have to create the mechanisms that ensure that teams do not hamper each other by the side-effects of their internal loyalties and objectives, their methods of working and decision-making. Inter-team committees to look at inter-team problems are one sort of useful mechanism. They do not usually need frequent meetings, but do need to work as inter-team problem-solving, action-planning or system-development working parties.

If the sense of working teams is weak in the organisation, this gives more power to the informal or union groupings among its workforce. Effective team-building does *not* necessarily increase *output*, though it frequently does improve the *quality* of performance. But one of its main effects is in reducing the disruptive power of other types of groupings.

True team-work and team-sense is only possible with a more participative style of management than is customary in British organisations. Many old-style foremen and supervisors (and managers too) find the change of role and attitude too hard to accept. Even when they can accept it, they need a considerable amount of training and development to accustom themselves to working in a different kind of way, as leaders of their subordinates rather than as bosses.

There is a related issue of supervisor and management selection. For effective team-building, selection of leaders is crucial. The common style of 'the best worker becomes the next supervisor' just won't do. Industry will have to pay much more attention to new, more objective methods of supervisor and manager selection, such as multiple assessment, or the 'assessment centre' approach. At present there is virtually no other reliable way of picking managers with the potential to be leaders.

A practical step towards leadership

In all that we've written on this subject it must be evident that the key to leadership and team-building is the way you develop and use your people. The first step in putting the various ideas into practical use is to clarify your present understanding and knowledge of your team. Here's a fairly simple exercise to help you. We call it a Team Analysis.

First decide who to include. It should be everyone who report *directly* to you, but no others. If you have more people than the seven allowed for in the worksheet, perhaps they operate in two or three semi-independent groups — if so, take each of these groups as a 'team'. The alternative is, of course, to extend the worksheet. But don't pick people at random, otherwise parts of the jigsaw will be missing. Now start to complete the columns.

Team analysis

A *The jobs*
 1 *Job titles:* give the particular title for each job. If the job doesn't have one, what would you call it in a recruitment advertisement?
 2 *Responsibilities/tasks:* a short list of the things *done* in each job. If the same things apply to several jobs, write them across as many columns as your need.
 3 *Specifics of each job:* the special features that make each person's job different from the others. The area in which it's done, the results required, the particular problems it presents, etc.
 4 *Communication links:* between which of the jobs must work or information be passed? Who must liaise with whom within the team?

B *The people*

1 *'Name':* give Christian names if you normally use them, or just write in your people's initials.

2 *Age and personal circumstances:* this is just background to fill out the picture a little. A rough figure will do for each person's age. An 'M' or 'S' for married or single. 'CH 2' for two children living at home, etc.

3 *Temperament and attitudes:* a thumbnail sketch of what each team member is like as a person. How do you place him in the range of extrovert/introvert? calm/highly strung? mentally bright/dim? mature/immature? open/closed minded? trusting/suspicious? etc. This asks you to be fairly perceptive.

4 *Time in job:* a figure for the years the person has been in this job.

5 *Performance strengths and limitations:* what things *in the job* is the person good at? In what areas are his abilities limited? Put a '+' or '−' in front of each note to identify it as a strength or limitation.

6 *Team role and relationships:* who is close to whom within the team? Where are relationships lacking or bad? Who gives a lead and who follows? Can you define the team role of each person?

Now you've completed the worksheet you may already have identified some interesting facts. One may be how much you *don't* know about some of your people. Some things may now have become immediately obvious which before were only dimly-recognised. Some may suggest immediate action. Others may imply the need for action that would be difficult or impossible in the short term. At least you may now have clarified the cause of a problem.

If you're *not* in any way surprised by the results of your analysis, or if it seems not to have revealed anything of significance, try these questions:

What sorts of abilities do the different jobs require?
Are people's experience, skills and temperaments well matched to their jobs? Could any moves between jobs or changes in the jobs themselves make better use of their talents? Is the total workload fairly divided?

Are there clear performance standards against which strengths and limitations are assessed? Do standards exist for any management or supervisory responsibilities within the team? Do people understand and have commitment to high standards?

Is the team membership well-integrated? No over-weighting towards extremes of youth or age? A good blend of different temperaments and abilities? Any 'bad apples' in the team? What planning is being done for future changes in its membership — the effects of people leaving, the needs of people joining?

How is the team's sense of team-work being built? Through regular team meetings? Through involving people in joint tasks or activities? Through drawing on the abilities of the more able members to help the weaker members' development? Through building the need for co-operation into the team's organisation?

Do the placings of people in jobs take account of personal relationships within the team — good, bad or indifferent? Could any moves be made to take advantage of good relationships or to discount the effects of poor relationships?

Are people with potential for growth being identified? How are decisions made about the directions in which to guide them? What scope is there within the team to give them the experience and coaching they need for their development? What opportunities exist outside the team for activities that could contribute to their growth?

What is being done about any 'problem people'? Do they recognize their problems? Have they been told? Are they being given training, coaching or guidance? Or are their problems more fundamental one of calibre or attitude? Could they be given other jobs where their limitations would matter less? Or are they really not suited to the team at all?

Sporting analogies in management are not always very helpful. The manager of, say, a football team has, in fact, very little team-building to do. The team's objectives are crystal clear — to win the game, the cup, promotion, or whatever. The members are (usually) highly committed. The team is very cohesive (they're even wearing the same colours — perhaps the Japanese have something with their company 'uniforms'). Everybody's responsibilities are clearly defined and well co-ordinated. This is not to say that the league soccer manager doesn't have problems of *motivation* — some of them are expert motivators. But team-building is a different ball-game (if you'll forgive the pun) in commerce and industry.

Nevertheless, team games provide you with a model of sorts for the kind of co-operation and 'togetherness' you need to

Team analysis

A. The jobs

1 Job titles						
2 Responsibilities/ tasks						
3 Specifics of each job						
4 Communication links						

B. The people

1 'Name'					
2 Age and personal circumstances					
3 Temperament and attitudes					
4 Time in job					
5 Performance strengths and limitations					
6 Team role and relationships					

create in your working group. The more they see themselves as a winning side, with you as the successful captain (or perhaps player-manager), the more commitment and the better performance they'll be willing to contribute to the common cause.

Managing for motivation

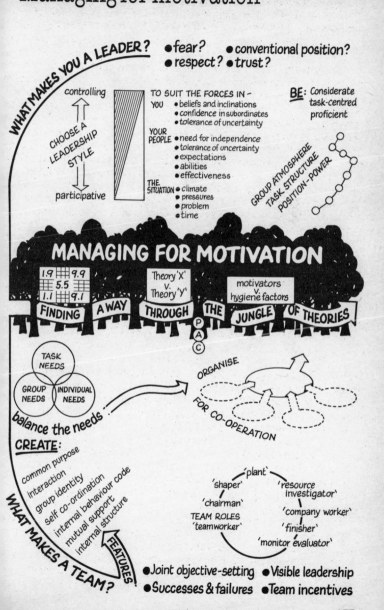

WHAT MAKES YOU A LEADER?
- fear?
- respect?
- conventional position?
- trust?

CHOOSE A LEADERSHIP STYLE

controlling ⇅ participative

TO SUIT THE FORCES IN –

YOU
- beliefs and inclinations
- confidence in subordinates
- tolerance of uncertainty

YOUR PEOPLE
- need for independence
- tolerance of uncertainty
- expectations
- abilities
- effectiveness

THE SITUATION
- climate
- pressures
- problem
- time

BE: Considerate
task-centred
proficient

GROUP ATMOSPHERE
TASK STRUCTURE
POSITION-POWER

MANAGING FOR MOTIVATION

1.9	9.9
5.5	
1.1	9.1

Theory 'X' v. Theory 'Y'

motivators v. hygiene factors

FINDING **A WAY** **THROUGH** **THE** **JUNGLE** **OF THEORIES**

P A C

TASK NEEDS
GROUP NEEDS
INDIVIDUAL NEEDS

balance the needs

ORGANISE FOR CO-OPERATION

CREATE:

common purpose
interaction
group identity
self co-ordination
internal behaviour code
mutual support
internal structure

'plant'
'shaper'
'chairman'
'resource investigator'
TEAM ROLES
'teamworker'
'company worker'
'finisher'
'monitor evaluator'

WHAT MAKES A TEAM? **FEATURES**

- Joint objective-setting
- Successes & failures
- Visible leadership
- Team incentives

6. The essential skill

Winning your people's commitment through motivation and leadership demands the application of both knowledge and skill. Some of the specific skills are implicit in what we've already written, but there's one that has to be made explicit. Its effect on every aspect of management can't be over-estimated. If you can't *communicate*, you can't manage people in any sense at all.

Yes, of course you can communicate. How have you managed to exist all these years, otherwise? But what about the people all around you, up and down the organisation? Does your boss keep you fully in the picture? does he always understand your point of view? Does he even seem interested in it? Your colleagues — do they realise what you need to know in order to dovetail your work with theirs? Do they really understand how their inefficiencies affect your responsibilities? And your subordinates — do they easily grasp what you want them to do? Are they able to explain their difficulties? Do they seem to appreciate *your* problems? How do you rate the communicative ability of all these people? Not too high? Then do you really think their view of you is significantly different?

As consultants over the years we've worked with hundreds of organisations of all sizes and in many diverse industries — in the States and in the Far East as well as in Europe and the UK. We can't recall a single one where, sooner or later, from someone or other, we didn't hear the complaint: 'communication in this outfit is really bad'. What did these people mean? Sometimes they meant 'I'm the last one to be told'. Sometimes they meant 'our management isn't interested in us'. Sometimes they meant 'I don't really know what I'm supposed to be doing'. And always, when these comments were discussed at a higher level, we were met with vehement denials that any such thing could be happening.

One of the great difficulties in dealing with communication is that it has so many *different* meanings, on so many different levels. To clarify it a bit we can perhaps reduce these to two principle concepts: Communication can be regarded firstly as a set of *skills* — the skills of speaking, writing, and of choosing and using all the appropriate mechanics and methods of communication. On the other hand, perhaps more importantly, communication can be seen as an *attitude of mind*. If managers don't *want* to communicate (fully), or don't see *why* people should expect to have information or understand what's going on, then all the skills in the world won't create a satisfactory standard of communication in an organisation.

The way you behave as a manager actually communicates far more loudly that what you say. And too many organizations positively encourage managers — especially at exalted levels — in a belief in their own innate superiority, which effectively relieves them of any concern for their subordinates' opinions. If you think this is another bleat about our British class-ridden society, our favourite example actually occurred in a West German company. It was decided that one of four badly-needed car parks should remain permanently empty — because it was overlooked by the offices of the directors, who couldn't be disturbed by the slamming of car doors! To be fair, it's not clear whether this was in fact a board decree or an example of the sort of sycophantic deference on the part of subordinates which is equally common in this country. While respect for seniors (when it is earned) is a healthy component of a management relationship, undue and sometimes unwanted deference nearly always inhibits the chance of genuine leadership from the top. The point is that management *behaviour* communicates; management *attitudes* often destroy the basis of good communication.

One of the newer facets of our industrial scene which is muddying the waters of corporate communication is the spectre of worker-participation, the involvement of various quasi-governmental bodies and such statutory requirements as 'disclosure of information'. Some managements' fears of the possible consequences have tended to retard — rather than promote — progress towards genuine corporate communication. In other cases there has been a surge of activity in making available to employees a wealth of information about such things as company results. In two organisations at least that we know, this has been taken to the extent of a 'dial-a-fact' telephone service. It is also now quite common to see a company's Report and Accounts presented in a 'popular' version for employees.

Unfortunately, much of this activity is still interpreted by workforces as propaganda or 'window-dressing'. It's no substitute for a genuine desire and will to communicate on the part of line managers at all levels. Innis Macbeath, Professor of Industrial Relations at the London Business School, quotes a manager speaking at a conference: 'Can we be sure that methodologies of this character' (they were talking about ways of improving communication with subordinates) 'do not involve an excessive input of managerial talent in relation to any likely pay-off'. Quite apart from that as a sample of the gentleman's personal communication ability, the real significance of the remark is in the *attitude* that says 'is it worth it?'.

One way for an organisation to check on its employees' views about communication is the kind of internal survey carried out by professional agencies such as MORI (Market and Opinion Research International). One such report revealed that 45% of the workforce in a particular company felt they got most of their information from the 'grapevine', but only 2% said they actually *preferred* this as the main source. On the other hand, only 29% said most of their information came from their manager or supervisor, while 75% said they would prefer this to be the main source. Individual comments included such remarks as: 'I dislike hearing information on the grapevine before it is announced by the company' and 'a lot of changes and decisions that go on at management level only rach the majority of employees through the grapevine'. True, this is only one piece of evidence: nevertheless, it implies that giving your people full and timely information will help win their respect and trust.

Many managers — and, more importantly, *managements* — resist the idea of sharing information. Alan Cooper, director of personnel policy for the Imperial Group, found that many managers 'guarded information like money, rather than treating it like air, available in the atmosphere to anyone who wants to breathe it in'. He found many familiar reasons: 'On the face of it some of them seemed reasonable, but they too often turned out to be fear of loss of authority by those who had the information over those who did not'. His company has since spent a good deal of time and effort getting its managers, instead of asking what *harm* might be done by disclosing this item or that, to explore the *benefits*, not just of doling it out, but of helping employees to understand and interpret information on the basis of their own experience.

Keeping your people in the picture

There can be little doubt that your people like to be in the know about what is happening in your organisation, and why. Their morale and interest in the organisation is damaged by comments such as 'there's no reason for it — it's just company policy'. Failure to communicate suggests 'you are not worthy to be told'. It breeds couldn't-care-less attitudes and insecurity. It helps the trouble-maker who implies 'they dare not tell you'. It also breeds rumour: if you do not give a good reason for a decision, a plan, a resolution, someone may invent — and publicise — a bad one. Increasingly in the future, you will have to keep your people in the picture about things that used to be thought of as private 'management information'.

As a manager, you should talk with your people at regular intervals about the things that might affect them, interest them or influence the way they do their work:

— organisational progress, difficulties and successes.
— relevant events and trends in the world outside.
— the problems, opportunities and changes they will create in the organisation.
— the ways that management generally is thinking about the future.
— plans and policies and the reasons for them.
— union negotiations and their implications for the organisation.
— the organisation's personalities.
— how you see the future of your operation against this background.

Supervising the operation

How do you keep *yourself* in the picture? Good communication means knowing as well as telling. It is knowing about the progress of your subordinates' work and the results they are achieving, as individuals and as a team. It is keeping yourself regularly informed about these things — and ensuring that your people know you do so:

— *About the work:* how it is progressing in terms of quality, quantity, time and cost; the problems and difficulties that impede it; where plans have to be modified to cope with changing conditions, altered needs, unforeseen events and accidents.
— *About the people:* the efforts they are putting into the work; who the able performers are and who needs help;

161

the level of morale and commitment down through the department.

But the main reason for being on the shopfloor, in the general office, out in the sales field is not simply to check up on the work or the people — what many managers regard as 'supervising'. Certainly it provides you with the grass-roots knowledge you need for realistic planning and decision-making. And it's the *only* way you can really keep your finger on the pulse of morale and discipline in your operation. But properly done it also provides your people with evidence of positive, interested leadership.

What does 'properly done' mean? Well, it *doesn't* mean running around like crazy, trying to watch everybody all the time and operating a kind of 'shirt-sleeve management'. Most people don't work efficiently if they're constantly watched. Nor will they acquire much enthusiasm for using their initiative if you insist on trying to handle every problem yourself.

It means seeing, and being seen, and being seen to see. It means reading signals. It means *noticing*:
— the things that are happening that shouldn't be happening
— the things that are not happening that in the normal way of things *should* be happening
— changes in people's manner or behaviour
— changes in the way people do things
— changes in the relationships between them
— the things that *don't* change when perhaps they should
— the things that have been happening the same way for so long that everyone else has stopped noticing them.

Then take the time to find out why — don't jump to conclusions.

Supervising properly means no only reading signals but also *giving* the right signals to your people. For instance, stand alongside them — don't confront them across their work. Ask them how *they* do things. Ask for *their* views on the methods and systems used in your operation. And show interest — genuine interest — in your voice, your eyes, your expression. The more interested *you* are, the more you'll engage their interest. Don't cross-examine people — ask for help. Get them to explain things in their own words, then they'll be more likely to say what they really mean, more freely. And make notes of what *they* want you to remember. If you have points of your own to note, do it afterwards.

Above all — follow through. If someone has an idea you can act on, do so and tell them how it's going. If you can't act on it, tell them why not. This is what 'supervising properly' means. If you fail to recognize or accept this responsibility you can't disclaim responsibility for the foul-ups, crises and failures that follow.

Communicating an attitude

So the first essential for a good manager-communicator is not to develop the silver tongue. It is to demonstrate an attitude that *places value* on communication. In the management context, what you say is more important than how you say it. Saul Gellerman, well-known consultant pschologist and management author, cites two managers' talks to the salesmen of an agricultural machinery manufacturer: 'The first manager gave a bravura performance. He failed, because it was the wrong performance. He had misjudged his audience or, more precisely, hadn't bothered to judge its members at all. He was content to treat them as sterotypes. The second manager was brief, colourless and almost perfunctory. He succeeded, because he had correctly diagnosed the anxieties and misdirected energies of his audience and was able to deal with them promptly and directly'.

If what you say is more important that how you say it, it is often also true that, to your people, what you say is less important than *why* you're saying it. It isn't enough for them to *understand* what you mean. If you are to get reaction, they also have to *feel* the right way about it. Communication has to work on people's feelings as well as on their brains.

It's your responsibility as a communicator to develop the right feelings in your 'audience': holding their interest, generating enthusiasm, gaining their approval and willing co-operation. So you have to communicate the right attitudes as well as the right information. This means finding the most effective blend in your personal approach of two elements: positive thinking and the 'You' attitude.

1. *Positive thinking*
People tend to go along with the manager who transmits a sense of self-confident drive and energy. A cautious approach may be all very well in deciding what can or can't be done, what should and shouldn't be said — but once a decision is made, you need to communicate it with conviction.

If positive thinking is overdone, it suggests this sort of approach:
'I am right. My beliefs and ideas cannot be questioned. You

must listen to and accept them just because I am personally convinced they are right (and because anyway I have the authority to force my ideas on you).'

That is exaggerated, but it gives the flavour of positive thinking. It's the approach in which you come to the point quickly. You put it over briefly, acting on the assumption that if others don't agree they must be either fools or villains. You tend to ignore their negative attitudes of doubts, suspicion or lack of interest, assuming that they will be carried by your own conviction. You don't worry about doing the expected thing, so your approach is often striking and original. In marshalling your arguments you concentrate on those that favour your case, and finish on a strong note. You are single-minded about getting the action you think is needed.

In manner, you speak forcefully and with emphasis, probably rather loudly and fairly quickly. You look others in the eye, stand erect and use firm decisive gestures. Your writing is very vigorous and direct, showing little concern with smoothness or gracious cliches, but using many personal expressions ('I', 'we', 'you') and short sentences. You have no fear of using pithy conversational phrases on paper. There is no suggestion that you regard others as your superior in human terms, whatever your levels may be in the organisation.

The total impression is one of enthusiastic certainty about what you are saying.

2. The 'You' attitude

People tend also to go along with the manager who transmits a sense of concern for their own views and feelings. As Abraham Lincoln once wrote: 'a drop of honey catches more flies than a gallon of gall'. Personal conviction in one's own ideas has to be balanced be sensitivity to the views of others. It is what the psychologists call 'empathy'.

If the 'You' attitude is overdone, it suggests this sort of approach:

'You are all-important. I want to understand your interests and motives, your likes and dislikes so that I can allow you to decide for yourself whether to accept my point or reject it. You must not be upset whatever happens (so I must not allow my authority to influence your thinking)'.

Again, an exaggerated form, but the flavour is there: taking the 'you' attitude, you show you have a genuine respect for others as human beings — whoever they may be. You start by putting them in the picture, or stating what you believe to be their point of view. You show concern for their troubles, sympathy for their difficulties, pleasure for their successes, appreciation of *anything* they have done which you can construe as helpful: but above all you show interest in them, their beliefs and views, their welfare. You tend to talk to them in terms of how things affect them for good or ill. If your proposition has real disadvantages for them you probably advise them not to accept it. If the disadvantages are only apparent ones, you explain why they should not be too concerned about them. You are prepared to speak or write at length to gain their approval and understanding.

Your manner shows a desire to be friendly. In speaking to others you show a keen interest in their reactions — and adapt your manner to suit. In conversation you listen to them a lot of the time, and ask many questions about their experiences, views and attitudes to make sure you have understood them properly. You look for his reactions. You tend to talk fairly slowly and to use pauses to give your listener thinking time. You use his name often and the word 'you' constantly. You probably smile a great deal to help encourage an easy, relaxed atmosphere. On paper you use a simple natural style to avoid any suggestion that you feel distant from your readers. The word 'you' will tend to be emphasized in your correspondence, and you probably start most of your letters 'Dear Mr. . .'. Whatever others levels in the organization, you show that you regard them first and foremost as other human beings.

The total impression is one of enthusiastic concern for their understanding and approval.

These two elements — positive thinking and the 'You' attitude — have to be blended together. You can't just take one or the other — *both* are important. After all, both elements speak of a sense of relationship with other people. Both are enthusiastic for something. It is lack of this sense of enthusiasm which cripples communication, which causes the grey tide of dull unconcern that oozes over so much of the writing and talking done in organizations. Effectively personal communication demands that you show an enthusiastic interest in what you are doing. It also depends on your displaying an equal interest in your 'audience'.

The process of communication

It has become one of the great clichés of communication to say that effective communication must be two-way. But the late Joe Whitton, Head of Training at the Tack Organisation and one of the best personal communicators of his day, used to define a cliché as 'yesterday's truth'. And the truth is no less true today for having been so often repeated.

The true meaning of communication is not merely (as the dictionary first defines it) to impart or transmit, but to *share*. Perhaps an even better definition for practical purposes is 'to ensure understanding'. And understanding not only the *words* that are used, but also all the subtle nuances of meaning which may be conveyed by tone, expression, gesture, style, intention and selection (or omission) of what is communicated.

A popular analogy to help understanding the process of communication is the working of electrical circuitry. In this analogy you, the manager, become the *transmitter* (Tx). The individual or group with whom you're communicating at any given moment the *receiver* (Rx). And between you there has to exist a *channel* of communication.

If you are speaking to someone, the channel is no more than the air which carries sound waves from your mouth to their ear — sounds which must then be conveyed to the brain and processed (interpreted and understood). If you write, the channel is represented by the internal postal system or the notice-board. If you're not communicating directly with an individual or a small group but, say, with the entire workforce of your organisation, the choice of a communication channel (or channels) may be crucial. Practitioners of mass communication (your company's advertising and public relations people, for instance) have an even more difficult choice from among the multiplicity of possible channels (or, as they would no doubt call them, media) for communication.

But let's stick to the most common (and sometimes the most difficult) communication task — talking face-to-face with your people. The first pre-requisite is that you have something to say — a 'message'. If that seems too obvious, think back to all those meetings you've attended which were a dismal failure because there wasn't really anything to discuss.

As the transmitter you now have the task of putting your message — which at this stage may be no more than a set of ideas in your mind — into a form in which the receiver can understand it. You have to *'encode'* it. Most often this simply means putting it into words, although there may be other 'codes', many of them highly complex, by which information can be transmitted.

The choice of words is no easy task for most communicators. So often it is governed by the wrong criteria: will the words I use convey the right impression of *me* — of my education, experience, authority, maturity, etc. to my listeners or readers? Will they be impressed by my superior knowledge or my deep grasp of the technicalities involved? Whereas, in fact, the choice should be governed by two simple considerations: what is my *aim* in communicating, and will the words I use achieve it effectively *with this specific receiver*? Will my words be understandable to him or them, in the way I intend them to be understood, and will they convey my message clearly and without ambiguity?

Many communication failures lie with the transmitter at this encoding stage. He is unable to see the message through his readers eyes, hear it through *their* understanding. In fact his message passes through a number of *'filters'*: his feelings about his position, his technical or professional bias, his emotional attitude, his limited facility with language or capacity for clear, logical thinking — any of which may make it difficult for him to encode the message in the most appropriate way for the receiver.

So, recognising this danger, you do your best to encode your message clearly and you despatch it (as a 'signal') along the chosen channel. In the example we're using, you simply say what you want your people to know. You make it as clear and simple as you can and you don't forget to include whatever background information you feel is necessary. You try to say it in the tone of voice and in the manner that you think they'll find most acceptable. You've fulfilled *your* responsibility for communicating. It's now up to them, the receivers. They have to *'decode'* the message.

The trouble is, they have to cope with filters too: their inability (or unwillingness) to concentrate and absorb your message, their low attention-level, their lack of interest in the subject, their preoccupation with other things. And some of the *same* filters you experience: special viewpoints based on emotional responses, their technical disciplines, their own personalities and temperaments. And to make things worse, the message may not even reach them in the same form in which it left you. Somewhere along your chosen channel of communication there may be 'noise' — anything which distorts the message in transmission (even a simple spoken instruction may be distorted if delivered in conditions which provide too many distractions for the listener).

The problem is not that the message completely fails to reach the receiver. When that happens it's usually fairly obvious (even with written messages) from the lack of response, and something can be done about it right away. The worse problem is with the message you *think* has been correctly received, but which in fact ends up looking significantly differet from what you intended in the minds of your listeners.

Because of the effect of filters (at either the encoding or decoding stages) and noise, one of two things may have happened: part of the message may have been missed altogether; but, equally dangerously, something may have been *added* to the message, by interpretation or assumption, which wasn't there in the first place. Either way you have communication failure, with potentially dangerous consequences, and neither you nor your people realise it. (The field of industrial relations is littered with classic examples of total misunderstanding, leading to catastrophic confrontation). Diagramatically, the process look like this.

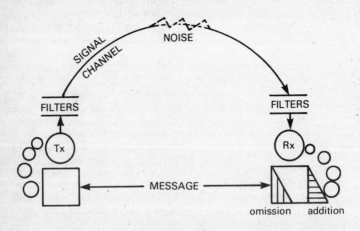

Now the answer to this problem is probably only too clear to you. It's so blindingly obvious that we're baffled as to why we continually find it being missed by managers and supervisors. It lies in that cliché we mentioned — the need for communication to be two-way. But perhaps its not quite as simple as that.

To follow our electrcal analogy, what the transmitter has now to do is to *close the circuit* — to set up a further channel along which he receives *'feedback'* which enables him to judge how completely his message has been received. However, bear in mind that this feedback, like the original message, has to be encoded (this time by the original receiver) and decoded (by the transmitter). It is also subject to the same risk of filters and noise. So getting accurate feedback also requires effort. Too many managers accept a nod of the head or an 'OK boss' as proof of reception. You may have to go round the circuit a number of times before communication is complete:

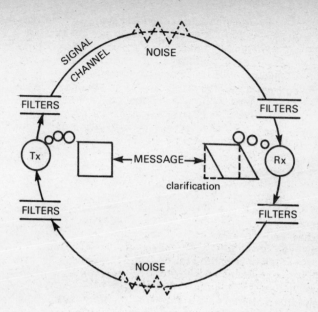

SIGNAL CHANNEL NOISE

FILTERS

FILTERS

Tx ○○○ [ ] ←MESSAGE→ [ ] ○ ○ ○ Rx

clarification

FILTERS

FILTERS

NOISE

The *most certain* form of feedback is to ask someone to repeat what you have just told him. Most of us have an inbuilt resistance to this — it seems almost insulting. If you've given someone some complex instructions, however, it may be the only way to ensure they've been completely understood. But get him to re-phrase whatever you're checking in *his* words. If he only repeats parrot-fashion the words *you* used, that doesn't give you any idea of the interpretation he's placed on them.

The *quality* of feedback will depend largely on how you ask for it. If you end your instructions by saying sternly, 'now, does everyone understand what I've said?', you shouldn't be surprised if no-one owns up to being the dummy. What you're doing here is putting the burden of understanding on the listener. A simple re-phrasing can give you a better chance of getting feedback: 'Have I explained that well enough?' shifts the burden to you. Now they can speak up without testifying to their own inadequacy — the point at issue is your ability to explain, not theirs to understand. Of course, manner and tone of voice are especially important here — said in a certain way, the words 'have I made that clear?' can convey the very opposite of a desire for feedback!

Actually, the standard of feedback you get from your team will not really depend on the phrasing of your request. It will depend more on their belief, built up over a period of time, as to whether you're really interested in hearing it or not. A climate of communication which is generally anti-discussion is hard to break down on specific occasions. A climate of open exchange of ideas and views will lead to feedback being freely offered as a matter of course. This also depends very largely on your ability to use one of the most neglected yet most influential communication skills for a manager.

Is anybody listening?

At least half of all this communicating involves *listening*. It is not only a matter of getting people to listen to you, to understand you, to do your bidding. You also need skill in listening to *them*. The lack of this skill causes many failures in management and supervision.

When you don't listen properly to your subordinates, it is often because you assume that the only things that matter are the facts of the operation as *you* see them: the units of work completed, your superiors' pressure for results, the behaviour of your subordinates. True, these facts are often enough for you to get results from your people in the short term. But there are costs in the longer term — costs in their apathy and in your own ignorance of the weaknesses developing in your operation.

A lot of the information you need for your management thinking and planning is in your people. They know far better than you exactly what they are doing and the problems that prevent them from doing it better. Their attitudes and feelings influence their commitment and will to perform well. Their ideas about the operation may well be more practical than yours. You'll never get this information if you are forever talking at them. As the old Irish saying goes, if God had intended us to talk twice as much as you listen, he would have given you two mouths and one ear!

Numerous research projects have shown that most people are poor listeners. One of the fundamental reaons is suggested by Ralph Nichols and Leonard Stevens in their book 'Are You Listening?'. It is that we think faster than we speak. Although the brain doesn't function solely through the medium of language, thoughts and ideas race through it at many times the average speed of speech. As there is no known way to slow down the thinking process, we continue to think at high speed while words arrive at low speed. This means in effect, that while listening we have some spare, unused thinking capacity which we automatically fill with other material. This reduces the effectiveness of listening and makes us vulnerable to a lot of bad listening habits.

A second problem is a misconception that most of us have about listening. We equate it with simply *not talking*. As long as we keep quiet and allow our ear-drums to vibrate we are 'listening'. But, of course, listening is an *active* and not a passive process. It demands hard work (if you've ever tried to listen to a lecture in a stuffy room at about half-past three in the afternoon you know just how hard it can be!)

Unfortunately our education doesn't teach us to listen. We learn to write and (with varying degrees of success) to talk, but no-one teaches us *how* to listen. They only *tell* us to listen ('pay attention!'). Listening is a skill and *can* be learned. The first step is to appreciate the difference between good and bad listening.

The bad listener:

- — 'switches off' dry or uninteresting subjects
- — resists 'heavy' material — seeks 'entertainment'
- — is put off by poor delivery
- — tends to judge, evaluate, agree or disagree *before* the speaker has finished
- — reacts to emotional words
- — listens only for facts, not implications
- — fakes attention, puts no effort into listening
- — is easily distracted
- — employs 'spare' brain capacity by 'day-dreaming'
- — takes copious notes, using only one system.

The good listener:

- — tries to find interest in every subject
- — uses 'heavy' material for mental exercise
- — judges content, not delivery
- — doesn't judge until his comprehension is complete
- — interprets emotional words rationally
- — listens for themes, not just for facts
- — works hard at maintaining real attention
- — concentrates — fights or avoids distractions
- — uses 'spare' brain capacity to summarise, weigh the evidence, anticipate
- — takes fewer notes, suiting the system to the speaker or the subject.

Each of these ten points encapsulates a 'key to effective listening':

```
1  Find areas of interest
2  Exercise your mind
3  Judge content not delivery
4  Withhold evaluation
5  Keep your mind open
6  Listen for ideas
7  Work at listening
8  Resist distractions
9  Capitalise on your brain-power
10 Be flexible
```

For practical purposes such lists are not much help in your everyday management. You can't run through a checklist every time you have to listen. These things have to become habits if they're to be of any real use to you. But habits have to be built, and this list provides useful guidelines for self-development.

Listening in practice

Real listening has four stages: hearing, interpreting, evaluating and responding. One of the Xerox Corporation's management training programmes stresses this by calling this subject not just 'Listening' but *'Listening and responding'*. Responding is the key to *active* listening. The only way a subordinate can tell whether his manager is listening to him is by the response the manager makes. The importance of this is in its effect on motivation. When you listen to someone you fulfil some of his important needs, so it's necessary not only to listen but to rspond in a way that makes it clear.

As a manager there are two situations where it's especially important for you to listen: firstly, where your *natural* impulse is to disagree with, ignore or reject what a subordinate has said; and secondly, when you have to make a decision based on it. In either case, you have to be sure you understand not only what was said but also the subordinate's *reason* for saying it. If you think you do understand both, it's still a good idea to check your understanding, by putting into your own words and asking the subordinate to confirm that that's what he meant. In this way you're providing the necessary feedback to complete the circuit. If you *don't* understand either what was said *or* why it was said, you need to clarify. Having clarified, you may *still* need to confirm your understanding.

Effective, active listening, *including* clarifying and confirming your understanding, is an absolute pre-requisite for most of your everyday management communication tasks, such as maintaining discipline and dealing with grievances.

What price discipline?

Some years ago, the Director of Labour Relations at General Motors wrote:

'Most people prefer an orderly and efficient atmosphere within which to work. They will readily conform to rules of conduct and obey reasonable orders as long as they clearly understand what is expected of them. Over 95% of employees behave in a perfectly responsible way. So the manager's disciplinary problem reduces itself in the main to dealing *promptly* and *firmly* with the few who will not comply — those who resent authority, who have little respect for the rights of others, and who ignore or defy the normal rules of conduct'.

We could argue with the percentage, perhaps, but the underlying contention rings true. If, like many managers, you'd rather not think about specific disciplinary action, you should really ask yourself:

If rule-breakers are allowed to get away with it, what results can you expect? If you *have* to take action, what resources do you have for dealing with infringements of rules and regulations? Better still, what can you do to maintain good discipline — to *prevent* infringements?

Your organisation will have its own disciplinary procedures, usually agreed with the unions involved. You have to *know* these procedures as well as the rules themselves. But there are some general principles in dealing with offences against the rules:

- *Act promptly:* delay means that evidence will disappear or distort. Inaction will lead to further indiscipline.
- *Get the facts:* you may have to report on them and produce proof, so keep records. But do stick to facts — no judgements at this stage.
- *Listen to the subordinate's side of the story:* ask him to explain the reason for the offence. Investigate what he says, however unlikely it sounds. Otherwise he may later have grounds for complaint.
- *Decide action: was* there an offence? If so, how serious? What is your aim now — to improve his future behaviour or to punish? (If he is not to be sacked, you will still have to live with him in your team.) What is his record? Are there any mitigating or aggravating circumstances? *Can* you act? Or do you have to refer to your boss for the sort of action you think is due? Should you suspend the offender from duty meanwhile? Ought you to involve the union representative?
- *Announce your decision:* restate the facts and tell him what action you're taking. See that he knows what is expected of him in the future. Don't nag. Don't get involved in argument. Afterwards, reinstate your previous relationship with him. Don't bear a grudge.

The best kind of discipline is the self-discipline exercised by people who are committed to the aims of their team and respond to the lead of a manager they respect. In any team of people, however, inevitably some dissatisfactions will occur from time to time. These have to be recognised and dealt with if morale is to be maintained.

Handling your people's grievances

It's pointless to argue the toss over whether a grievance is genuine or trivial. If any of your subordinates *feels* aggrieved, you have to deal with the problem — whatever you feel about it personally.

A grievance is more than a complaint. It can grow from a complaint that has not been dealt with in a way that satisfies the complainant. Some organisations hold that no one can have a grievance until he is dissatisfied with the way his boss has dealt with a complaint. The trouble with this view is that the boss may have had nothing to do with the complaint. Indeed, no actual complaint may ever have been made. Yet a grievance may still exist, and a grievance of the most difficult kind — one the boss does not know about directly.

Who should deal with a grievance? You, the immediate boss, are the first choice. You may be able to settle it promptly and with full knowledge of the personalities involved. But there are risks: on the one hand you may be tempted to make concessions that have troublesome side-effects in other parts of the organisation — even concessions that are beyond your authority to make. On the other hand, if you yourself stand at the centre of the grievance, you may be incapable of being fair and just in dealing with it. The subordinate must have a right of appeal to others in the organisation.

Such problems should be answered by the organisation's *grievance procedure*. You must of course know what it is yourself. Equally you must see that *everyone* in your subordinate organisation knows what it is, both your direct subordinates and *their* subordinates at lower levels. No one must feel he is 100% under the thumb of his immediate boss. Although this may seem to undermine the boss's authority, it in fact strengthens the relationship of a good manager with his people. They know as well as he does that he cannot act towards them arbitrarily.

So how should you handle a grievance? In the first place, once again, *listen*. Take time to find out what really troubles the complainant — remembering that people take time to open up. Doctors are familiar with the patient who only reveals the real cause of his worry in a parting remark as he goes out of the surgery door. Many grievances are, anyway, based primarily on the *absence* of anyone who will listen!

—*Analyse* the problem. Don't rush to a solution before you know what you are trying to solve. Even though grievances may be more matters of feelings than of facts, get whatever facts you can. Try to assess the extent of the grievance. Is it held by just this one person or do others share his feelings? Is it based on an isolated incident or does it have a history of dissatisfaction behind it?

—*Decide action*. Don't be too quick to assume that your recognising the grievance is enough to resolve it. What can be done to reassure the complainant? Is this action practical from the organisation's point of view? If it were generalised or made permanent, would you be happy to live with it? And once you have made up your mind, explain it to the complainant — whether or not it is likely to satisfy him fully.

Disciplinary problems and grievances are severe tests of leadership and require especially the exercise of good communication skills. There are many other everyday events in your relationship with your people which place equal demands on your ability to listen and respond.

Criticising constructively

No-one likes criticism. Mature people learn to accept and even profit from it, but most of us really want only to be told how good our work or our ideas are. Criticism, however, properly handled, may be a necessary and positive step in improving performance. The trick is in getting a subordinate to see what is lacking in his performance or his thinking, while *maintaining his commitment to the task*.

Because of our task-centredness as leaders we often tend to focus initially on what is wrong with a subordinate's work or ideas, without giving enough consideration to what is commendable. Stating the merits you see in someone's suggestion or idea, *before* pointing out the faults, will help you in getting constructive criticism accepted as a form of feedback. Also, make both merits and faults clearly task-related, avoiding personal aspects where possible. When faults in performance have to be pointed out, being constructive means that you make a positive suggestion for overcoming them *without* completely distorting or discarding the original contribution of the subordinate.

Build on people's ideas

To maintain a subordinate's commitment, he should be able to see suggestions for improving his work or ideas as increasing the value of his *own* contribution, rather than replacing his idea by a 'better' idea of yours. To do this you have to make the *connection* between your constructive feedback and the contribution originally made by the subordinate. Having suggested a modification, improvement or change, *check* with the subordinate to be sure that his 'ownership' of the idea or approach is retained. Then invite his comments on the suggested change.

Resolving differences by discussion

Providing constructive feedback and building on people's ideas may not be sufficient to get their willing acceptance and commitment to a different course of action. Differences of opinion or of attitude between you and the subordinate may still exist. If a good group atmosphere and individual motivation are not to be jeopardized, it's essential that you discuss and resolve these.

Many managers tend to supress differences. They use various devices, ranging from pretending differences don't exist to resorting to threats if the subordinate persists in the difference. A difference suppressed unresolved is a permanent barrier to good relations and a threat to motivation. You must be prepared to spend time suggesting, inviting and discussing alternatives which will satisfy both your priorities and the subordinate's needs.

If the process proves especially difficult, thinking can sometimes be cristallised by stating what is for you the most important principle or aim involved and inviting the subordinate to do the same. In this way you can often isolate the real root of the difference and find ways of dealing with it.

Ultimately, if a resolution *can't* be found, you may have to insist on your view being accepted, while acknowledging that the subordinate has a right to feel differently. In this case, however, the fact that you've spent time discussing the difference will make the subordinate more likely to be committed to the decision, even if he still can't agree with it.

Offering justifiable praise

As we know, people's need for recognition is seldom fully satisfied. You can do a lot, however, by making justifiable praise part of your regular communication. The key here is the word 'justifiable'. Unless your people perceive praise as having been *earned* it becomes flattery. Insincerity is easily detected and disliked. Give credit only where credit is due.

For praise to have a motivational effect it must not only be perceived as real and justifiable but must also identify exactly what aspect of performance is praiseworthy. Make it as specific as possible.

You probably remember to praise when *outstanding* performance occurs. However, don't forget that praise may also be appropriate when someone *consistently* performs to an acceptable standard. It is even worthwhile to offer praise for a job well done by a person whose performance is usually *not* up to standard. In this way the improvement is rewarded and will hopefully be repeated or maintained. If no one notices, he'll probably revert to his former standard.

In general, British managers seem to find it difficult to praise. There's something in our national character which gives us a horror of appearing fulsome. Many managers work on the principle that 'as long as my people don't hear from me, they know they're doing a good job'. All we can ask you to do is to examine your own feelings the last time you accomplished something worthwhile and your boss actually said 'well done'. On the surface, slight embarrassment, perhaps. But deep down, a real sense of satisfaction, unless you're very different from the rest of us. And while you're at it, think back also to the last time you put a lot of effort into something which was totally ignored! How did that feel?

One point we must make clear. There's little evidence that praise itself actually *improves* performance. You have to do that in other ways. What is clear is that the continual *absence* of praise, when it is justified, ultimately has a damaging effect on people's respect for and relationship with their manager. The dangers of *not* praising people's achievements are greater than those of being thought 'soft'!

Maintaining discipline, sorting out grievances, criticizing constructively, building on people's ideas, resolving differences and praising achievements: these specific applications of your communication skills constitute a kind of 'care and maintenance' programme for your relationships with your people. But a working relationship often gets off to a poor start. Communication with a subordinate is seldom more important than on the *first* occasion he meets you as his boss.

Welcome, stranger

A new recruit is joining you. So far he has had a few limited chances, during the interview, to find out about your organisation and the job he'll be expected to do in it. He has probably tried to put the clues together to form a mental picture of what it will be like to work for you — quite possibly a vague and distorted picture.

He arrives feeling insecure and perhaps apprehensive. He has just a bare idea of what the job actually involves, how you expect him to tackle it. What kinds of new knowledge and skill he has to develop, what sort of results you expect. He knows nothing of the problems he'll have to cope with, which ones you'll expect him to solve for himself, whom he can turn to for help. He wonders about his new colleagues' attitudes to him. He wouldn't recognize any senior manager who walked through the door. He knows next to nothing about the geography of the place, what happens where, who does what and why. He has yet to find out about the organisation's style, about its disciplines,

rules and traditions, about its personalities, politics and pressures, about the kind of behaviour that's expected of him. He has a lot to learn before he can become a confident, competent member of your team.

So you get him into your office. You quickly run through what he has to do, and tell him what he should get on with today. You take him over to his working area, introduce him to a few people who happen to be around — and leave him to get on with it.

A few months later he comes to tell you he is leaving. Well! — he was a bit of a disappointment in that job in any case.

Of course you'd never knowingly allow that sort of thing to happen in *your* department. Or would you? Does this cautionary tale have just a slight ring of truth, in the light of your own experience?

The learning load

Managers often under-estimate how much a new recruit to their organisation has to learn. So much of it is second nature to an old hand it is difficult to realise it *does* have to be learned by a newcomer. But if you put together all the many, many questions he has to find answers for, you begin to see how heavy is the learning load on him in his first few weeks and months:

1. *About the job*
   — What are all the various situations I have to deal with? What am I to do in each of them and how am I to do it? How far do I have to work out my own days of doing

things? In what order must I do things? How much time will I have to do them? How do I know if I'm doing them properly?

— Why do I have to do each of these things? How do they fit in with what other people are doing? Which do I have to give priority to? Which aren't so important? What sort of results will I be expected to produce?

— What problems will I meet? How should I tackle them? When should I seek help, and whom do I go to for it?

— What systems and procedures must I follow? How do they work? What do they apply to? What exactly have I go to do?

— What skills do I need to develop? What do I have to know about equipment and its capabilities? What kinds of judgement do I have to learn to make? What decisions do I have to take? Whom do I go to for what other decisions?

— How might the job change in the future? What scope will it give me to develop new abilities? How should I prepare myself for these things?

— What goes on in the department? What has been happening in it up to now? How do things stand at present? How does all this affect what I'm supposed to do?

2. *About the people:*

— What sort of person is my boss? How does he operate as a manager? What does he expect of me? How easy is he to talk to? How do I address him?

— Who are the people I'm working with? What are they like? What things do they do? How good are they at doing them? What kind of interests do they have? What are their attitudes to each other? What are their attitudes to me? How will they expect me to behave?

— Who else will I have to contact? Who of the other more senior people? Who in other departments? What do they do? How does my work affect them? What am I expected to contact them about and when? How should I act towards them?

— Who are the top managers in the organisation? What are their names and positions? How will I recognise them? How am I expected to address them?

— What is the union set-up? Who are the union representatives? What sort of issues are they interested in? How powerful are they? What relationships do they have with their members? With the managers? When and about what do I have to contact them?

3. *About the organisation:*

— What does it do? What things does it make or provide? How is it organised to do this? How did it get to where it is today? What other organisations does it deal with? What is it trying to achieve?

— What is its standing with customers and suppliers? With its competitors? With the public? What is happening in the country and the economy that will affect it? How successful is it? How secure is the employment it offers?

— What sort of an outfit is it? What are its policies and ethics? How is it run? Who are the powerful people in it? How are decisions taken in it? How does one find out what is going on in it? How do people get promotion?

— What are its rules and traditions? How am I supposed to behave as a member of it? What could I get disciplined for? How would I be disciplined? What if I have any complaints? What are my rights as an employee?

— What is its geography? Where are the different people, operations and offices sited? How do I find my way around them? Where is the canteen? The medical section? The personnel department? The cashier's office? The transport office? How does one use them?

Most of these things have to be learned on the job — they aren't things you can 'teach' the newcomer in any meaningful way. But what allowances do you make for the fact he has to learn them? What help do you give him? Learning by accident isn't good enough. It's a poor manager who expects newcomers to pick things up for themselves. His staff take an excessive time to learn the ropes, and make many needless mistakes as they do so. Often they learn wrong lessons, negative attitudes — and even fail to learn some things at all. Induction needs a systematic, planned approach.

Whatever formal induction programmes your organisation may have, *you*, the boss, personally carry the main responsibility for your new subordinate's induction.

The initial briefing: be selective. Don't give the newcomer too much to absorb. Let him read the job description and question you about it, but concentrate on the key features of the job. Explain how they fit into the pattern of work in the department. Introduce him to the people's he'll work most closely with and see there is someone to help him find his way around the department's ropes (someone who won't try to confuse him with subtleties or pass on negative or cynical attitudes).

The first fortnight: keep him in the picture on what he is to do day by day — whom he is to see and what he is to learn. Involve him fairly quickly in some practical tasks so that he begins to feel involved and productive, but keep them simple and straightforward. After each one, check back with him on how it has gone.

The learning plan: work out a programme for him to follow for however long it takes him to achieve basic competence in the job (three months? six months?). Plan it in stages so that he doesn't become overloaded with things to learn: observing others at work, interviewing contacts in other departments, studying the system and procedures he will have to use, reading files, manuals, background documents etc. Stage by stage, monitor his progress by getting him to tell you what he has learned and discussing with him its implications for his job.

When he begins to tackle parts of the job that demand skill and judgement, delegate them properly. Demonstrate them first. Then when he makes his first attempts, don't hover at his shoulder and cripple his nerve. Let him do them by himself. Run your post-mortems afterwards — and tailor your standards to his inexperience. Let him build some self-confidence before you start sitting in on his efforts.

If you haven't the time to do all this yourself, then you'll have to delegate it (or parts of it) to subordinates of yours who have the time — *and* the ability — to do it properly.

Perhaps your Personnel Department runs formal Induction Courses at intervals. They can give useful background, with talks about the organisation's history and structure, presentations on its products and services, visits to different departments, briefings by other managers. Booklets may be available describing the organisation and what it does, who's who in senior management, and so on.

All of this *supports* your role in induction. It doesn't replace the need for it. In any case, it may be some time before your new subordinate can attend an induction course — the record wait in a large authority we know of was seven years! Even if it's seven weeks, that's way beyond the point where real induction has to take effect.

So that's the essential skill — communication. It's not a question of whether to communicate or not. You can't *avoid* communicating, by what you do or don't do (silence can be very communicative, as those of you who are married know only too well). The question is whether your communication with your people is conscious, positive and appropriate to the situation and to their needs. Good communication is the cement which holds together all the other aspects of your management and lets you build a permanently productive relationship. If the mixture is wrong, the whole structure of your management is vulnerable to the pressures it will continually have to withstand.

Managing meetings

It was Fred Allen, the American comedian, who described a meeting as: 'a group of people who singly can decide nothing, but who *together* can decide that nothing can be done.' No doubt similar cynical comments are heard in your organisation. The title of the popular John Cleese film seems to sum up most people's attitude — 'Meetings, Bloody Meetings'. Certainly we've all experienced some of the worst examples of the species — meetings which decide little more than the date of the next meeting, meetings devoted solely to discussing the minutes of the last meeting, and so on. Some organisations are so wedded to the idea of spreading responsibility (and blame?) that they function almost entirely through 'committees'. But Jim Hayes, President of the American Management Association, used to say: 'if you *really* have management by committee, why is it that when there's a disaster only one man leaves the company?' (in American companies this would usually be true: almost never in a British organisation, where blame is usually shifted *down* the organisation).

There are plenty of good reasons for improving the quality of meetings. One is simply their enormous cost, which few managers ever really consider. Suppose you have a dozen reasonably well-paid people sitting around a meeting-table for most of a morning. What's the total cost of their time, plus the time of everyone else involved with the paperwork — preparing it, typing it, circulating it, reading it — plust the accommodation, heating, lighting and so forth? It's not likely to give you much change out of £1500. In fact one organisation we know of has made a practice for several years of including in the agenda of internal committee meetings a calculated cost per hour. The idea is not so much to stop people talking as to enable them to reckon whether the value they've achieved by the end of the meeting is really worth the cost. Why shouldn't cost-benefit assessments be applied to meetings as much as to any other kind of organisational activity?

The costs of *successful* meetings can be more than justified by their benefits for you as a manager and for your team. People are far more likely to be committed to decisions they've had a

hand in making (as long as it's a *real* hand, not just a 'rubber-stamping' of something *you've* decided). The more complex your team's activities the more you rely on *co-ordination* to solve (or avoid) problems. Working together in a group may often bring out more of people's talents and experience than solo operations. And, as we said earlier, your chairmanship of a meeting provides *visible* leadership of the team.

Unfortunately, it is true that a lot of meetings achieve little mileage for an enormous amount of gas. As often as not, this is because the members don't seem to be clear about the direction in which they are supposed to be driving as a group, what they are supposed to be trying to do together. And the prime culprit is often the chairman.

What are we here for?

As leader of the group, you must get clear in your own mind what the point of all the talking is. Then you can start playing a useful leadership role instead of just sitting there passive as a figurehead — or worse, actively leading the discussion off the rails. First, you need to be clear about the type of meeting you are running: you can't decide your own role until you've decided this prime question. To start your thinking about the question, here are eight of the more common types of discussion that actually take place in meetings:

1. *Briefing:* One member (not necessarily you) gives the rest of the group a briefing on a situation, a policy, a plan, an approach to future problems. They question him, not to challenge what he is saying but simply to get a clear understanding. If you are not acting as the informant, your role is as a referee to ensure orderly discussion and adequate understanding without time-wasting.

2. *Co-ordination review:* Each member gives a short account of whatever is happening in his own area of responsibility, and is then briefly questioned by the other members to establish the facts and explore their relevance for other members. Any problems of co-ordination that cannot be quickly resolved are noted for later solution outside the meeting. Your role is to see that there are no doubts about what each report implies for the immediate plans of others in the group. You see that problems that can be resolved in private discussions between members are not discussed at length by the whole group. This type of meeting is often a regular weekly or monthly event within a department or project group or across different interlocking functions.

3. *Fact-finding:* This discussion tackles a problem that is common to all members present. Each member contributes his knowledge of facts that are relevant to the problem or issue — facts on which someone (perhaps present, perhaps not) will later have to base a decision. Members' contributions stimulate each others' memories of relevant facts. Your role is to see that the group does not limit its fact-finding by trying to pre-judge the issue or waste time trying to *resolve* the problem before the facts are clear. You must also ensure that the discussion covers all relevant angles, that facts are properly recorded and given appropriate weighting and that they are reported on to the decision-maker.

4. *Brainstorming:* The aim here is to produce the widest possible range of imaginative ideas for solving a problem or for developing some possibility — including ideas that may seem at first sight ridiculous or far-fetched. The group may analyse the problem or question in search of ideas, but it does *not* attempt to evaluate the ideas or to reach a solution. Your role is to prevent negative or destructive comments about any idea put forward, and to see that every idea is recorded. You have to maintain a totally permissive atmosphere.

5. *Evaluation:* The task is to present an assessment of alternatives (or sometimes to recommend a decision) to

someone who has eventually to take a personal decision. The decision-maker may or may not be present, but he wants a variety of opinions and arguments to consider in making his decision. All members present participate in analysing the given alternatives (perhaps produced by an earlier brainstorming discussion) or in considering proposals put forward. Your role is an as impartial chairman — whether or not you are the eventual decision-maker. You see that all members contribute effectively, that they listen to each other in developing points put forward, and that each angle on the question is given proper weight in the group's thinking. You may also have to steer the group *away* from time-wasting attempts to add to the alternatives given.

6. *Joint decision-making:* As in the evaluation discussion, all those present participate in weighing up alternative solutions or in considering proposals put forward. But the aim here is for the group itself to come to an agreed decision (or failing this, a majority decision) about policy, a plan or an action. Your role is again that of an impartial chairman. But here there is no final decision-maker to act as a back-stop for a poor group decision, so you have to ensure that the group arrives at a good decision (not necessarily the decision you yourself would have chosen). You see that the discussion deals with the subject in logical stages, that all contribute effectively and are listened to, that each angle on the subject is given proper weight, and that the group's decision is practicable and one that all members of the group will support in reality. You remind the group of items forgotten, of factors and risks that are in danger of under-rating. You ensure that all are clear about the practical implications of their decision. *This is the most difficult type of discussion to chair effectively — but of enormous value when well-run*.

7. *Action-planning:* This discussion assumes a broad plan or policy already decided on elsewhere, or a state of affairs demanding action. The group discusses the different tasks that will have to be done to achieve the required results, and agrees who will do what. You role is to see that all actions needed are taken into account, that each member is clear about his tasks and about the way they interlock with others' tasks, and that contingency plans are developed for likely snags or failures. You also have to steer discussion *away* from reconsidering the rightness of the given plan or policy itself (evaluation).

8. *Opinion-airing:* The purpose here is to give your people the opportunity to vent their feelings or views about some issue — either as a form of 'blowing off steam', or so that others can assess the force of these feelings and decide what should be done — if anything. Your role is to ensure that members are not inhibited from speaking their minds — and at the same time to see that the group does not confuse facts with feelings. You also have to see that those speaking feel their views are having a fair hearing and will be given proper weight in any decisions that follow.

In addition to these eight common types of discussion, you may occasionally find yourself involved in *negotiations*. Usually the group represents two sides of an argument or 'case'. and tries to arrive at an integrated solution to the problem (i.e. one that satisfies both sides present) — or, failing this, a comprise or *'force majeure'* solution. If you are chairman, your role is as a totally impartial umpire, acceptable equally to both sides as completely unbiased.

Useful meetings nearly alway serve a learning purpose for the members. However, from time to time you may see an opportunity to use a meeting specifically for *training*. Perhaps you give a short briefing or discussion to explore members' understanding and acceptance of the points you've made. The meeting may tackle practical exercises or role-play situations. You act as guide and coach, and aim to stimulate the enthusiasm of the members for applying the knowledge, skills, or ideas they are learning.

Finally, there are two clearly recognised types of meeting which, generally, you would do well to avoid.:

1. *Persuasion:* The discussion begins with a presentation from you, often with strong emotional overtones. It then develops into questioning, argument and verbal jousting. You counter each point of opposition, using both rational argument and your own force of personality to swing the group in favour of the views you are putting forward. You try to isolate any dissidents from the rest of the group so that you can later use the strength of group-feeling to persuade them to come into line. Such meetings can be used to reinforce views already held by the group, as well as to attempt conversions, but are often unsatisfactory in their effect on people's commitment.

2. *Rubber-stamping:* The group groes through the motions of analysing the rights and wrongs of a decision already made, but the real purpose is either to paper over the cracks of dissention or to spread the responsibility for the decision. This is the bogus democracy often in evidence in organisations that haven't the stomach or the will to create the reality of democratic action — but that want the democratic lable nevertheless. Your role is to give an appearance of open-mindedness, but in reality to stifle awkward questions and strong-minded opponents of the decision. You do this by rigidly formalising the discussion ('all comments through the chair', 'points of order') and by adopting an autocratic manner. This type of meeting can cause severe frustration within the organisation if those present realise what is happening.

In any agenda, *different items may call for different types of discussion.* The first item may be a briefing, the second perhaps a fact-finding discussion, the third may be a joint decision-making session — and so forth. Item by item, you have to adjust your role to the type of discussion that each one demands. A lot of time can be wasted when you fail to perceive your proper role and so allow the group to hold the wrong type of discussion. For example, a group may be supposed to plan to implement a policy (action planning) but tries instead to question the policy itself, either constructively (evaluation) or destructively (opinion-airing). As a result, members are frustrated by a pointless discussion, and no implementation plans emerge.

However, you are sometimes wise to change your mind about the type of discussion you are running — if you see you can achieve a better result by doing so. Good chairmanship can't be rigid. It must include a large element of constructive 'thinking on your feet'.

Should we be here at all?

Before setting up a meeting there are a number of important questions you should ask yourself. Is there enough to be gained from a meeting to make its cost worthwhile? What *is* the cost — in the time and effort of preparation involved for all concerned (including secretaries and clerical staff?). In the time of people present at the meeting? In failures to do other things because of attendance at the meeting? In the documentation needed before, during and after the meeting? In the share of general overheads that can be allocated to the meeting? Could regular meetings be run less often? Could some be scrapped altogether with advantage?

But what would be the effect of *not* having a meeting? What would it cost in lack of co-ordination, in poor decision making, in reduced involvement and morale? are *enough* meetings run to achieve all the worthwhile purpose that meetings *can* achieve? Should more briefing groups be held? More training meetings? More co-ordination reviews? More fact-finding and brainstorming sessions? Fewer 'rubber-stamping' meetings?

What shall we discuss?

Does each agenda item have good reason for being included? Have all worthwile items been considered for inclusion? Any items listed for no better reason than that someone is trying to duck responsibility for making a decision? Is this the right point in time for considering each item — will all the information needed be available then? Are there not too many items — can *all* of them be given consideration in the time allowed for the meeting?

Does perceptive thinking about problems, needs, priorities and objectives lie behind each item? Is the item worded clearly? Will all members understand the point of including it? Will they be prepared for the kind of discussion it will involve them in? Should the agenda state, for the more complex items, the key questions to be considered under each?

Do members need any extra information on any item *before* the meeting — a report or a note that will put them in the picture so they can take a full, constructive part in the discussion? Should any documents to be considered at the meeting be sent with the agenda? Is there any item on which a member could be nominated to prepare a short statement — a statement that he can present to gather and focus the group's thinking before it starts discussion of that item? Is the sequence of items well-planned? Are those items needing more discussion and penetrating thought placed near the start, when minds will be fresher? Are items in the right order for sequential decisions, where one decision depends on another? Can you avoid a clutter of 'Any Other Business' at the end?

Does the agenda reach all members in good time before the meeting? Does this give them enough time to read all the supporting information sent?

Who should be here?

Does the membership list include those people directly

involved or with something valuable to contribute, not 'passengers' (however senior)? Can the agenda be arranged so that those involved in only one or two items need not be present for the whole meeting?

Is the membership small enough for genuine group discussion (not more than about 10–12 people)? Are too many levels involved? Any risk of more junior people being inhibited by the more senior people present? How can this problem be reduced or overcome?

Who should take the chair? Must it always be the most senior person present? If that is you, and you need to act as a discussion member on some items, should you step down from the chair for those items and let a more junior member take it? Can you then accept control from the chair? Will the deputed leader have the nerve to control you and the other senior people present? Should the chair be 'rotated' for different meetings — or for different items on the agenda? Could this provide useful training in discussion-leading for more junior people? Will you then use the opportunity to coach the junior people in chairmanship, not to score points off them? Promise?

The arrangements

Does everyone know what time the meeting starts? Where it is to be held? What time it is expected to finish? What kind of outside interruptions will be allowed and what prohibited? Have members made their arrangements to suit?

Is the room booked? Is it suitable — not too small, too dark, too noisy, too hot/cold, too open to interruptions? Does everyone know where to find it? Is the furniture suitable — enough table space? The right sort of seating to encourage the required atmosphere? Any other equipment or materal needed — flip chart, blackboard, overhead projector, paper, pencils, documents? Are any tea/coffee arrangements needed? Should lunch be arranged — if so, for what time? Where can members' secretaries or colleagues send messages? When can they contact them?

Minutes and action

As chairman, do you realize that *you* are responsible for any minutes or action notes that result from the meeting — whoever you may nominate to take notes and write up the minutes? Have you nominated a minute-taker? Or could you better use a dictating machine and dictate brief minutes yourself as the meeting proceeds? Have you selected a minute-taker who knows enough about the issues involved to take sensible decisions about what is important and what trivial? Have you briefed him or her adequately on the form of minute required — layout, amount of detail to be included or omitted, how action is to be indicated, purpose and readership?

Does the minute get sent out promptly to members (say within 48 hours)? Have you as chairman signed it? Are you willing to protect the minute-writer against later criticisms from members of the minutes you've signed ('that's not what I said')?

Does the minute make it explicity clear *who* is going to do exactly *what* by *when*? What arrangements will be made for follow-up to ensure that something *happens* as a result of the meeting? Will a later meeting get a report on action taken and results — or will some member be made responsible for ensuring that action happens?

Maybe you'll dismiss a lot of this as 'only common-sense'. Of course, you're right. But in our experience, this kind of common-sense is an uncommon commodity. More meetings fail from lack of preparatory thinking than from what actually happens during the discussion. Nevertheless, having got all your preparations right, you still face a major challenge to your communication skills.

Leading the discussion

Leaderless discussions, like conductorless orchestras, are rarely as successful as their members suppose. When your people meet for discussion they *need* a chairman or leader. If that's you, your role is different from theirs. Their job is to concentrate their knowledge, experience and thinking ability on the *subject*. Your job is to manage the *process* by which they achieve joint understanding and agreement.

True, the meeting's success depends in part on its members' willingness to listen to each other and to help work out ideas. Sometimes they may not be willing to do this — they may be more concerned to win private battles than to co-operate as a group. You then have an impossible task: 'bad members make bad chairmen'.

But success also depends on your skill as a leader in developing a positive, impartial sense of purpose. Perhaps you forget this role and become involved as a participant. Perhaps you don't listen properly to what the members are saying. Perhaps you fail to recognise what is relevant and what irrelevant. Perhaps you can't point the group towards constructive thinking. Then the group has less chance of success: 'bad chairmen make bad members'.

Leading discussions productively is one of the most difficult communication skills. The higher you rise in the sphere of management, the more valuable you will find this ability. You can develop it only by practice, but you must first learn the principles involved. There are rather a lot of them, but they fall naturally into five major areas. The first three are concerned with *guiding the process*:

Clarity of purpose

— Think out the aim for each item. Everyone must know where the group is going — and be prepared to help it get there. As the leader, your key responsibility is to help them develop this sense of purpose. You have to see that an aim is defined. It must be one the members can all understand and support. It must also be clear enough to keep in mind throughout all the twists and turns of discussion.

Often you can state the aim at the start. Sometimes you might better open with a review of the situation that led to the meeting, and use this to get the group to define their objective. As discussion proceeds, be prepared to modify the aim if it becomes clearly inappropriate or if the group come up with a better idea. Remember — the aim is the *group's* aim, not just yours.

— *Define terms where necessary.* Many a discussion gets bogged down because the members are not clear about the meaning of the words and phrases they are using. They may be using the same words to mean rather different things. They may be using mindless clichés with more emotion than sense. When you spot this problem, stop and *get the terms defined*.

— *Control irrelevance.* With each turn in the discussion, check: 'is this getting us closer to our aim?' Don't jump too soon! Often you will have to listen for a moment or two to see if what a member is saying is really relevant or irrelevant. Don't assume something is irrelevant just because you hadn't thought of it yourself.

Once you realise it *is* off the point, decide what to do. Perhaps you can ask a question about the previous point: perhaps you can summarize progress so far; perhaps you ought deliberately to let the hare run for a short while — groups need some moments of indirection. (Could you warn off persistent ramblers by defining *limits of discussion* at the start?).

— *Probe relevant issues.* Are you after a *good* decision, not any old decision? Then listen for what's *not* being said as well as what is being said. From time to time you'll need to guide members to dig deeper rather than give issues just a surface treatment — asking for facts, implications. And you will need to point up important issues they are overlooking. So, think *through* the subject properly before the meeting and think *around* the issues the group are discussing to see what they are forgetting.

The discussion plan

— *Identify key questions.* An aim isn't enough to guide the discussion of each item. You need a *plan* — a list of key questions that pinpoint the key issues and break the discussion into stages. Get these questions in the right sequence to lead to a conclusion without back-tracking.

— *Run the discussion in stages.* Start by telling the group your list of key questions so they can get a sense of the plan. Then restate the first question to start the ball rolling. Get each one settled before you let the group take up the next key question.

— *'Think on your feet'.* No one is clever enough to see *all* the possible angles minutes before the meeting. Your plan will inevitably have missed some essential point. Its questions may not be focussed sharply enough on key issues. It may even prove to be unworkable — separating things that have to be discussed together or combining issues that used to be treated separately. So don't be rigid with your plan. Be ready to develop it as the talking goes on — and see the group is quite clear about your changes of mind.

— *Avoid topic-hopping.* Don't let the discussion drift on in a series of short speeches that just don't connect with each other. From time to time you may have to say 'Yes, but what do you feel about the point Joe has just made?'. Good points do get submerged. Members don't always listen to each other, and you have to be ready to rescue the contribution that has gone down like a lead ballon. Ask the member to restate his point. Even restate it yourself — and get the group to comment.

A sense of progress

Groups forget what they have already discussed and agreed. The lose sight of the ground they have covered. As a result, they often cover the same ground time and again, getting nowhere. It is up to you to keep them in mind of how far they've come — and how far they still have to go. You do this by your use of *summaries*.

— *Summarise frequently.* At a bare minimum, you must summarise at the end of each stage of discussion (i.e. before moving on to the next key question) and at the end of the meeting — a final review of what the group has achieved and how they've got there. But this may not be enough. *Summarise* long and rambling contributions. *Summarise* points of argument between members. *Summarise* whenever anyone complains of getting lost. *Summarise* the mile-stones of progress every ten minutes or so.

— *Summarise fully and fairly.* Too often, a leader's summaries simply restate the questions the group has talked around. Summaries should contain the gist of what has actually been said. They should point up the main issues raised. They should make clear what the group have agreed — and what they have failed to agree. They should also be fair (not assume agreements you haven't got!) For this, you have to *take notes*. The final summary must be a complete review of the discussion: it must confirm what has been discovered, what agreed, what decided, what action planned. The members may be quite happy to have had an 'interesting' discussion. You must also see that is has achieved something worthwhile.

— *Have respect for time.* A discussion must be kept moving on as fast as is compatible with a fair hearing of relevant points. It must neither rush important issues nor waste time. You have to sense the point at which to clinch an agreement (without using the vote, which leaves the losers resentful and uncommitted). You have to judge when to cut short an argument without agreement.

Throughout, you have to decide how to share the total time between the different aspects of the subject — in terms of their importance, their difficulty and the strength of the feelings they arouse.

The last two principal requirements for leading discussion are concerned not with the process itself but with your *skills with people:*

Group involvement

—*Restrict your talking time.* As a leader, you talk only as much as is needed to get the *group* talking together and to keep them to the point. Rather than getting involved in dialogues (or worse, arguments) with individuals, feed their points back to the group. Make your words of guidance and control crisp and to the point. The ideal is for the members to be so clear about the aim that you can shut up entirely for minutes on end.

—*Make your questions clear:* Questions are your main tool for discussion-leading. Are yours clear and stimulating — not wordy, woolly and muddle-headed? Do you probe members' ideas ('Why?' 'How?') Do you reflect their views ('So you feel . . .?') to open up differet ways of looking at situations?

Some questions will need to go to individual members to draw out relevant experience or to get them involved (*direct questions*). Most should go to the group as a whole to encourage across-the-table talking (*overhead questions*).

—*Stimulate interaction between members.* Do you get members of your meetings to talk to each other, instead of 'through the chair'? Do you watch those who are silent for their reactions to whoever holds the floor (not just watch the ones who are talking)? Do you bring in those who have a point to make? Do you control the over-contributors by insisting that the under-contributors have a hearing? Do you get junior members to speak their own mind — not just echo the senior members? Do you stop the discussion fragmenting into side-conversations? And can you do all this without acting like a whistle-crazy referee?

—*Maintain the quality of listening.* The discussion leader must not only be a good listener himself, he must also be able to get the members to listen to each other. If you can't understand someone's point, stop and clarify it — it's a fair bet that the other members won't have understood it either. Ask him to restate it, or say what you think he means and ask him to confirm. Listen for emotional reactions that are getting in the way of objective thinking. Listen for members getting themselves into win/lose situations, and help them to disentangle themselves without losing face. Allow 'sounding off' if feelings run high — but treat them as feelings, not as arguments. Do stop the group charging on when members seem to be talking at cross-purposes.

Leadership style

— *Show interest in the subject and the members.* To stimulate the group's interest, *you* must show interest. However relaxed your style, you must be *seen* to regard both the subject and the members' ideas as important.

— *Be sensitive to feelings.* Can you sense when people are bored? When they feel frustrated or impatient? When they feel embarrassed or resentful? To lead their discussions successfully, you have to be aware of these feelings — and ensure you don't cause them yourself by putting members on the spot, rudely interrupting their words of wisdom, or failing to keep the discussion moving on.

— *Be impartial.* If every member is to feel he has a fair and unbiased hearing (however unpopular his views), *you* have to stay outside the battle. Can you avoid taking sides? Can you restrain yourself from pressing your own views? Can you conceal your reactions to members' comments — whether you agree or disagree?

— *Control decisively.* You have to be able to command attention for your guidance and control. Your decisions have to be firm — whether on the course of the discussion or on who should have the floor. Your manner has to convey a sense of urgency and purpose.

Let's be practical. You can't hope to develop all these tricks of the trade at one fell swoop. *Don't try to*! First, know where your *strengths* lie — and where you have *weaknesses*. Your strengths because they give you confidence. Your weaknesses so that you can tackle them one by one in the meetings you actually run. This is the whole point of the analysis. Using it, you isolate just one problem at a time in your own technique. You concentrate on developing that one element of skill until it becomes natural to you. Then forget it — and turn to the next element.

Attending meetings

So far we've concentrated on those meetings which you arrange and lead. But what about the many meetings you attend as a *member*?

Meetings can be good for your own management development. They can force you to think more deeply about problems and possibilities. They can balance out your own one-sided views on questions and issues. They can help you avoid making silly judgements. They can be willing to take more risky — but necessary — decisions than you and your colleagues might take by yourselves. But they cannot do these things if you and your colleagues approach them either as battles for personal victories of as mutual back-slapping sessions.

At a problem-solving meeting, your views need both supporters and challengers. The supporters will share your orientation and will help develop and refine your ideas. The challengers will have a different orientation and will point out short-comings and put forward opposing ideas. The meeting also needs a mixture of temperaments — both the high-risk decision makers who will opt for a solution on hunch and rule-of-thumb, and the more cautious souls who want more facts and opinions to back their judgements. The first type supply the motive power, the second provide the brakes and steering. To get full value from these different approaches, there are two key questions for everyone present:

Do you contribute?

A meeting is not an event for wallflowers. No member should have to wait for an invitation to join in. If you are present, presumably you have things to say that can usefully influence the group's thinking. It's your job to say them without prompting.

First, be clear what you are contributing towards. What is the purpose? Are you really clear about it? If not, say so and get it clarified. Does the aim seem right? If not, say so and get it changed. If the direction is vague or pointless, what you say and what others say cannot all be to the same point, except by coincidence. Once everyone is agreed on what you are all trying to do as a group, then you can contribute in several different ways:

— *Contribute your own ideas* on the subject. Perhaps you can offer an initial view to start others' minds working, your own particular angle on the question, a fresh way of thinking about the problem, a different solution to it that you have thought of, a relevant factor you can see in the issue, evidence for an opinion you hold.

— *Contribute your support* for others' ideas — saying you agree, confirming what they say, adding your own arguments for the points they are making, developing their ideas by refining them, adding to them, modifying them, spelling out their implications.

197

— *Contribute your disagreement* with others' ideas — because you doubt their relevance, truth or practicality, or perhaps because you think the group is coming to a decision too soon, before the issue has been properly explored.

— *Contribute your help* to the progress of the group as a whole — asking where a discussion is getting to, helping to clarify what someone is trying to say, recognizing an important contribution, stopping the talk from going round in circles, reminding the group of a comment being forgotten, supporting the chairman's leads, even disagreeing with his guidance when you believe it will not help the group achieve its aim — and suggesting something better.

With each contribution you make, are you helping the *group* towards its aim? Do you make the right contribution at the right time — is what you say relevant to what the group is trying to do at the moment? Do you try to help others to work out *their* thinking, taking a constructive approach to what they say? Do you try to prevent others from being pushed into win/lose situations, perhaps by saying where you agree before saying where you differ? Do you take the trouble to explain your own thinking so that others understand why you think the way you do? Do you try to stop the group jumping to over-hasty and impractical conclusions? Are you prepared to accept ideas that will work and that are acceptable to the group as a whole — even if you have better ideas of your own that you can't persuade the group to accept?

Whether the group listens to you depends on what they've grown to expect from you — what value they expect to find in your contributions. Do you notice if they begin to look away whenever you start up? If they do, perhaps they don't expect you to have a point to make, just an urge to hold the floor. Or perhaps they don't think you make your point crisply enough — you seem to waste their time, strain their patience. Or perhaps they feel you don't know when to shut up and listen to what others have to say.

Do you listen?

A meeting is not an opportunity for compulsive talkers. No member should have to be asked to give others a chance to say something. If you are present, presumably you have things to hear from others that can usefully influence *your* thinking. You come to the meeting with views of your own, ideas and attitudes based on your experience to date. But you don't have

to leave with your thinking unchanged. If you do, it's *your* fault for not listening properly to your colleagues.

None of your colleagues is stupid. Each one has reasons for saying the things he does. Perhaps his reasons are based on less experience than yours, perhaps on more experience — but inevitably on different experience. Some of his judgements may be poorer than yours, some may be better, many may be equally valid — but different. If you don't listen, you can't sort the objective views from the emotional, the clear relevant thinking from the foggy, the perceptive judgements from the hare-brained.

We've dealt pretty thoroughly already with listening as a management tool. But many of those bad listening habits are particularly noticeable at meetings:

- Perhaps you come to the meeting feeling that you already fully understand the problem — and with your mind already made up.
- Perhaps you are so involved in saying your piece that you don't hear what others are saying.
- You may hear only what you expect others to say — not what they actually do say.
- You might listen only to reassure yourself that your thinking on the subject is better than anyone else's.
- Perhaps you view meetings as battle-grounds and direct your main efforts towards defeating your opponents, not towards trying to understand them.
- Perhaps your management position or professional

qualification gives you the foolish notion that the comments of juniors or 'outsiders' can safely be treated with contempt.

— Maybe you subscribe to the common fallacy that strong-minded people (like you, of course) don't change their minds.

— Or could it be that you are simply a lazy listener? Do you close your mind to new ideas that might upset your comfortable habits of thought? Have you got accustomed to parking yourself at the table with your brain idling in neutral and your mouth emitting the occasional cloud of exhausted clichés? If so, you must get very bored.

Listening at a meeting (as in other situations) is hard work. It means trying to understand what others really mean rather than taking their words at face value ('I don't care what you meant. What you *said* was . . .'). It means thinking around their reasons for saying what they say rather than thinking only of your own reactions. It means talent-spotting among their comments for the good ideas they have only half-explained, or maybe only half-understood. It means correlating what one member is saying now with what another said ten minutes ago — perhaps taking your own notes as the discussion develops. It means avoiding making up your mind too soon, refusing to respond to uncertainty by creating a false sense of certainty. It means accepting that you may have to change your previous ideas on the subject. All this demands positive mental effort. But in return you may get ideas you would never have thought of had others' words not triggered them off. You will find the meetings you attend more interesting — *and* you will contribute more usefully to them.

If a meeting is successful, everyone present shares the success. If it fails, don't blame just the chairman. Perhaps he didn't help — but it is you and the group as a whole who have failed. Meetings are only good for you if *you* are good for *them*.

The essential skill

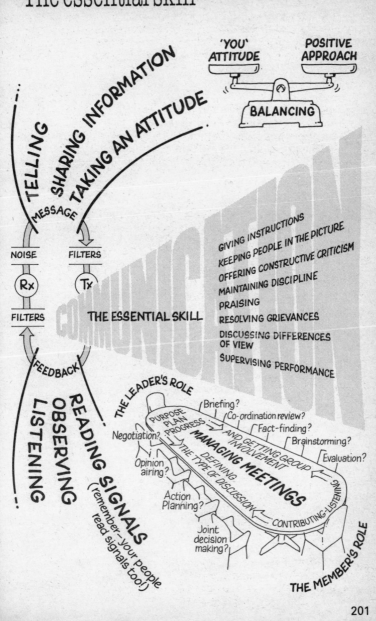

'YOU' ATTITUDE — POSITIVE APPROACH — BALANCING

TELLING — SHARING INFORMATION — TAKING AN ATTITUDE

MESSAGE

NOISE — FILTERS — Rx — FILTERS

Tx

FEEDBACK

READING SIGNALS (remember — your people read signals too!) OBSERVING LISTENING

COMMUNICATION

THE ESSENTIAL SKILL

GIVING INSTRUCTIONS
KEEPING PEOPLE IN THE PICTURE
OFFERING CONSTRUCTIVE CRITICISM
MAINTAINING DISCIPLINE
PRAISING
RESOLVING GRIEVANCES
DISCUSSING DIFFERENCES OF VIEW
SUPERVISING PERFORMANCE

THE LEADER'S ROLE

MANAGING MEETINGS
AND GETTING GROUP INVOLVEMENT
DEFINING THE TYPE OF DISCUSSION
CONTRIBUTING-LISTENING

PURPOSE PLAN PROGRESS

Briefing?
Co-ordination review?
Fact-finding?
Brainstorming?
Evaluation?
Negotiation?
Opinion airing?
Action Planning?
Joint decision making?

THE MEMBER'S ROLE

7. Getting the right people

Managing people is a good deal easier if you can make sure you get the right people in the first place.

When you pick a new member to join your team you are taking the most important management decision of all. Some say that the single *essential* task of a Board of Directors is to hire and fire people in just one role — that of Managing Director. Peter Drucker maintains that the test of whether a job is really a management job or not is the question 'do you select new subordinates or are you told whom you'll have?' If you are to be held accountable for the results they produce, then you ought to have the responsibility for deciding who should join your team.

Who recruits your people?

In practice, as the immediate boss of a vacant position you will rarely be the only person involved in filling it. Personnel people may actually draw up recruitment advertisements. They may also screen applicants and produce a short-list for you to interview. Selection specialists may be able to offer you advice based on personality and aptitude tests. Superiors may want to interview the likely candidates — and can often give you wise guidance. You yourself may have no more than a right of veto on your superiors' choice. But if they take the *final* decision themselves, you are no longer a manager — you're a minder.

As a manager, you have a duty to insist on having a hand in the decision. This is a duty you owe to your other subordinates, to your new recruit and to yourself — you all have to live with its results. But the right to perform it has to be earned. You earn it by developing your ability to pick people who do themselves and you credit as members of your team.

In recent years most organisations in this country have felt the effects of recession. Consequently recruitment has, to say the least, not been a point of emphasis in managers' activities or training. As the situation slowly improves, however, growth is once again becoming a consideration for the survivors. There may even be a temptation for the pendulum to swing too far. Before embarking on expanding your staff, you'd do well to ask yourself a few pertinent questions:

Why recruit?

To refill a job that will soon become vacant? Is that job really needed in your operation? Couldn't your team perform as well without it? Does it have to be done by one person? Couldn't its tasks be shared among the others in your team?

To refill a job that's already vacant? Why didn't you recruit earlier? What will be the costs of the gap until your new recruit is selected, installed and able to do the job competently?

Because some of your people are now overloaded? Are others underloaded? Can't you arrange a better share-out of responsibilities and work-load among your present team? Couldn't you schedule and allocate the work more efficiently?

To reduce back-logs of work? Couldn't you streamline your systems, procedures or paperwork to speed the throughput of work?

To get tasks done that are at present left undone? Couldn't you plan your people's activities to create extra capacity within your present resources?

For a new responsibility within your organisation that will help it work more effectively? Couldn't someone already in your organisation handle that job? Are you sure none of your present people has the abilities it needs — or could develop the abilities, given the chance?

To bring new managerial or specialist strengths into your organisation? Are you sure the answer isn't to develop your present people? Are you prepared to accept the disturbance that a talented newcomer may cause? Will you really get your money's worth from buying in his experience? Perhaps you will — but the question is worth asking.

To increase the scope and power of your operation? Examine your motives. Could you possibly be growing an organisational tumour — your private empire? Or can you honestly say that your recruits will add something to the *total* organisation's output or improve its health and fitness to perform? Will the new abilities or extra capacity they provide outweigh their costs?

Whether or not these decisions are within your area of discretion, they need careful consideration before the expensive process of recruitment begins. Assuming that the decision is taken, there are four key areas of preparation:
- the Ability specification
- the Job advertisement
- the Form of application
- the Selection interview.

What are you looking for?

Aim-setting is basic to management. The first step in recruitment is to set your aim in selecting someone for a job —

thinking through of the qualities that are needed to do it, the experience that's called for, the personal characteristics or circumstances that might prevent someone from doing it effectively.

Many managers skimp this first step. Perhaps they have an excessive confidence in their ability to spot 'a good type' on sight. Perhaps they are ready to accept anyone who can impress them with his qualifications, his acquaintanceship or his personal manner. Perhaps they oversimplify the task — boiling it all down to a search for 'leadership potential' or 'persuasive ability' or 'steady worker' or some such abstraction.

This won't do. The problem needs thinking through, to produce what we call the Ability Specification — preferably on paper. It has to be specific and practical enough to help you do two things: First, to know how to question a candidate to see how he measures up. Secondly, to interpret what he tells you in terms of what you're looking for. If there is any quality you can't specify clearly enough to recognise when it's sitting in front of you, don't include it. It will only cloud your thinking.

The ability specification

You start by looking over the job itself, trying to define the different elements that it demands. Wisely you won't try to specify an impossible ideal — you're more concerned with marking out the area of possibilities.

So you will want to include in your specification any 'no-nos' you can think of — factors that will show that a candidate *doesn't* come within the area. The factors you want to see are best divided into *essentials* and *desirables* among the abilities you are concerned with. Examine them under the headings of the three performance factors we've already identified.

Know-how

What abilities does the job call for?

What kinds of levels of knowledge and skill are needed to create these abilities? Which are essential for the job as a starting condition? Which could be picked up in the course of getting into the job?

What sorts of decisions does the job involve? How can you explore candidates' ability to use judgement in taking such decisions — or to learn how to develop it?

What kinds of experience could provide this know-how? Is any particular experience essential for it? (Don't overspecify here — many a good salesman has come from a non-selling background). What experience is no more than desirable?

What educational attainments are needed as evidence of ability or potential? (Are you sure they're needed? A lot of good people didn't do well at school.)

Where could outside interests reveal useful skills and aptitudes? Where could they clash with interests needed in the job?

Commitment

How does anyone become committed to the job?

What kinds of personal motivation are relevant to this? Pride in skill or craftmanship? Need for responsibility? Desire for achievement? Need for recognition and praise? Ambition for personal advancement? Desire for money? Concern for society? Interest in helping others? Could any of these actually be a disability in the job?

Should you look for any specific attitudes towards others — towards authority, toward colleagues, towards customers, towards unions, towards family? What qualities can you look for in forecasting a candidate's potential response to the job, to his colleagues-to-be, to your leadership? What elements in a candidate's past history might contain clues about these things? To what extent do you have to trust your intuition at the interview?

Calibre

How 'big' a person does the job really need? What sort of nerve does it demand in tackling problems, challenges, decisions? How important is stability and inner strength? WHat kinds of past behaviour might demonstrate these questions?

What balance of personality traits are best suited to the job and to the team? The will to take an independent line or willingness to follow a lead? A liking for working alone or in company? An out-going exuberant personality or an analytical deep-thinking individual? An inclination for quick tempo changes of activity or for steady presistent toil? A nervy energetic disposition or a placid easy-going approach to life? What kinds of past behaviour might demonstrate the traits that are important?

What sort of intelligence does the job really need? To what

extent does the job demand the ability to learn knowledge and skills quickly? To solve complex problems? To use imagination? To visualise how ideas will work out in practice? To what extent does it *not* call for these abilities? (You'll have problems if you pick someone who's too good for the job.) What kinds of past behaviour might demonstrate the abilities needed?

What aptitudes does the job demand? How important is it for the candidate to be a good talker? A good writer? Perceptive about people? Good with figures? Good with visual designs? Good with mechanical things?

How long do you foresee your chosen body staying in the job? Do you want someone who'll stay in it for years, or someone who'll move quickly through it and on to something bigger and better?

One of the problems of writing an Ability Specification — and in interviewing candidates to match it — is in deciding where to place the emphasis. Without doubt, most organisations tend to recruit primarily on the basis of *know-how* — qualifiactions and experience. Which is not surprising, since that's by far the easiest factor to judge or measure.

It is interesting to contrast the comment of the (British) personnel manager of the Japanese Yuasa Battery factory in Ebbw Vale, Brian Butler: 'They (the Japanese) set tremendous store by *attitudes* when they're recruiting; much more than qualifications. They're prepared to teach skills and give people experience, if they've got the right attitude. They're looking for long-term employees.' We believe that many British organisations could improve their management selection enormously by shifting the emphasis from know-how to finding out about people's *commitment*. This should certainly be the major thrust in the face-to-face interview, which is so often devoted to discussing the details of an applicant's technical competence.

However, we're getting ahead of ourselves. Having specified the desired levels of know-how, commitment and calibre, you now need to define the requirements in one further area:

Personal circumstances

Here you are looking mainly for the factors which would make a candidate ineligible or unsuitable. For example:

Is there any *real* limit to how young a person can hold down the job — given that he has the necessary abilities?

Can anyone really be too old for the job? Again given that he has

Selection worksheet

Ability specification (M = must, essential W = want, desirable)	Interview notes
Knowhow Job knowledge and skills? Leadership and social skills? Communication skills? Knowledge of methods and techniques? General knowledge? Work habits? Career record?	
Commitment Personal ambitions? Personal values? Attitude to others? Attitude to work? Career record?	
Calibre Maturity and 'size'? Learning and thinking ability? Relevant aptitudes? Career record?	
Personal circumstances 'Musts' and 'no-noes' Personal history?	

the other abilities? (The main point here may be the question of how long you want your new body to stay. If retirement age is too close, he may not be able to give you the time in the job you want or may block younger talent on the way up).

Does the job demand anything that domestic circumstances could disbar or make difficult? Freedom to move house? Freedom to spend time away from home? Freedom to work 'antisocial hours'?

Are there any important legal or moral qualifications to consider? Possession of a valid driving licence? Lack of a criminal record? Financial stability? Moral stability?

Are there any conditions of background, health, physique or appearance that might create difficulties? How much importance should you attach to them if everything else is right?

By when do you need to have the job filled? Will this give a new recruit enough time for induction and getting to know the ropes before he has to shoulder the full weight of the job?

One word of warning. The law on Equal Opportunities now has to be carefully studied to be sure that no part of your Ability Specification is discriminatory. In the United States, many questions about personal circumstances are completely taboo in recruitment advertising and interviewing. UK legislation may well move in that direction in the future.

You are the one person in the organisation who can know what's needed in this depth — the immediate boss of the job to be filled. So you have the main responsibility for defining the Ability Specification. Get others' ideas and advice by all means, but the final decision on whether to include an item or not should be yours. The next two pages have a suggested worksheet format for producing the Ability Specification.

How will you attract the right people?

Professor Heathcote Parkinson, in his book 'Parkinson's Law', suggested that the ideal recruitment advertisement gets just one person to apply — the person who is ideally suited to the job. That can't happen in the real world. But the principle still holds good: the aim is to attract just those people who come within the range of possibles, and no others. It is not to get all and sundry to apply.

There are other purposes to consider too. The job must be right for the person as well as the other way round; good recruitment doesn't consist of trying to con the job-hunters. And the advertisement has a broad public relations purpose for the organisation itself — to improve or maintain the organisation's status and image in the mind of the public generally.

The job advertisment

Typically the advertisement is headed with the *title* of the job. This isn't the only possibility. But if you start with something else, it is hard to make the real point of the advertisement crisp and clear. The content that follows should be structured to cover:

— *The organisation.* A brief note about who you are. This might explain what the organisation does, what its reputation is, where it's based, what its plans are for the future.

— *The job.* A short outline of what the job involves, its scope, and possibly its potential in the future. It should be written in a style that appeals to the kind of personality that is needed in the job. It should take a balanced view — neither overselling the job nor understanding it.

— *The person.* A thumb-nail sketch of the kind of person needed — abilities, temperament, qualification, experience, etc. — drawn from the Ability Specification. It is, of course, important to be sure your advertisement complies with equal opportunity legislation and your organisation's own policy on this subject.

— *The rewards.* It is becoming more common now to quote

the salary — either as a range or as a minimum. Presumably those organisations that still say 'salary according to experience' don't know what experience they need in the job or what the job itself is worth to them. They often raise the suspicion that a con is being attempted. Besides salary, the advertisement should say something about fringe benefits and promotion prospects, if any). Be truthful in this area — attracting candidates who will subsequently become dissatisfied with the lack of opportunity is bad management as well as immoral.

— *How to apply.* The close of the advertisment gives instructions for applying for the job. There is something to be said for the increasingly common practice of giving applicants a name to contact, not just a position title. This helps to make the organisation less remote and forbidding to the would-be recruit.

The actual drafting of an attractive job advertisement is a fairly specialised business. There may be experienced people in your organisation who will advise or undertake the task for you. However, *you* should retain control. In our experience, personnel departments do not always have people who can produce lively, appealing copy. Since you know the job and the person you want to fill it, it may be better to do the job yourself. Reading other organisations' job ads may give you ideas of how to frame yours (and how not to).

As to *where* to place your advertisement, that is also a subject for specialised knowledge and we don't intend to deal with it here. But, thinking about your potential applicants and what they would be most likely to read — don't just accept the obvious. Remember you're not trying to reach only those who are actively seeking employment. The people you really want may already be employed and not particularly dissatisfied. So the specialist press, for example, in any industry or profession, *may* be a better bet than the well-known mass-circulation media.

Increasing use is being made, especially for middle and senior management posts, of recruitment agencies. They may advertise under their own name or on your behalf under your own organisation's name. There are many pros and cons in this area, but the decision may well be a policy one in your organisation anyway.

Forms of application

There are several ways in which people can be asked to apply for jobs, apart from inviting them simply to turn up for interview:

Application Forms: The most common for all but shop-floor and top management jobs. They usually follow a standard pattern (drawn up by your Personnel Department) asking for information about such things as personal and domestic details, health record, educational history and attainments, employment history, refereces, hobbies and personal interests, reason for leaving last job, and abilities relevant to advertised job.

They do make sure the ground is covered (covered too well sometimes!). The *factual* information is useful for interview. The questions about motivation and ability (the last two items above) are worse than useless. This sort of information is best checked out at the interview. Asking for it here forces the candidate to produce 'respectable' answers that he may feel bound to maintain once he is talking to you face to face.

Personal letters: There are pros and cons here. The pros are that the applicant may reveal something of himself in the way he describes himself and even in the style of his letter. The cons are that he may not stay enough about himself and his history to allow you to sift out the possibles and the doubtfuls among your applicants. There is a danger too that a poor letter may cause a good applicant to be rejected for a job that has nothing to do with writing skills.

Telephone calls: You may ask your applicants to 'phone you or your organisation. There and then, his or her call is used for an initial brief 'interview', to check whether it is worth going on a face-to-face interview. The main use for this method lies — obviously enough — in selecting for jobs that involve a lot of telephone work: telephone operators, telephone sales staff and the like. It can in fact be used far more widely, to prevent the long queues of candidates who have been asked simply to 'turn up for interview', or to encourage people to apply who just don't like writing.

Using the application

In whatever form the application is made, it has two main uses. The first is for initial screening of applicants, to decide who should be asked to attend for interview. The second is to help you plan for the interview. You use the hard facts of each candidate's past history and present circumstances to decide what aspects to explore in depth for the 'soft' information needed (know-how, motivation and calibre, or sensitive details of personal circumstances).

The initial screening is quite often done by the Personnel Department (sometimes with the help of selection specialists). The aim is to separate out those applicants who seem likely to come within the area of possibles, as far as the *factual* information will allow. It is a mistake to allow candidates to be crossed off the list because of the reason they give for leaving their last job is because one of their references suggests a clash of personalities, or other such subjective judgements.

Personnel departments sometimes conduct initial interviews too. The Ability Specification should enable them to judge from these interviews which applicants match most nearly the needs of the job and the immediate boss.

But you, the immediate boss, should interview *all* the applicants short-listed, not just the one or two that a superior has picked. From Personnel you should get their comments, plus suggestions, hints and pointers on each of the applicants to be followed up in your interviews. Add these to your own ideas based on the application form or letter.

Selection interviewing

An interview is a conversation in rather special circumstances. The circumstances do demand some specific skills, but the first point to remember is that it *is* a conversation. It is not a grilling. Not a quiz. Not a kind of oral examination. Not an exhibition of the interviewer's superiority or the interviewee's submissiveness. The interviewer has to be as natural, as courteous, as considerate as in a conversation with a friend.

There are three particular differences between an interview and an everyday conversation:

— First, *the atmosphere at the start* is more tense — certainly for the interviewee and often for the interviewer. You have to relax this tension to the extent needed for the interviewee to begin talking easily and openly about himself, revealing details that are too personal for most conversations. You need skill in getting the interviewee to trust you, and in stimulating an easy, natural flow of conversation.

— Secondly, each person has a *consistent purpose* throughout. The interviewee to be acceptable and accepted. The interviewer to get enough information on specific questions that are relevant to the Ability Specification. You need skill in framing the questions and guiding the conversation to get the information you need, without wasting time or upsetting the interviewee.

— Thirdly, *the interviewer talks far less* than he would in normal conversation, the interviewee far more. In this sense, the conversation is very one-sided: the interviewee should be talking for at least 75% of the time. You need skill in listening perceptively — in reading between the lines, in watching for expressions, in understanding how the information you are getting tallies with the Ability Specification.

Preparing for the interview

Check the Application. Note any information or pointers you can get from those who have already interviewed the applicant. Read any references available.

Compare what you know against the Ability Specification. Which points are already answered fully enough? Which points should you explore further? What aspects of the applicant's past career might contain the best evidence on the things you want to check?

Think out the *key questions* you want to ask and make a note of them. Decide how you will explore past experience: will you work from schooldays forward (the only possibility for younger people with little job experience)? Or will you start with the last job and work backwards (better perhaps for older people whose early job experience may no longer be very relevant)?

Prepare where and when you'll conduct the interview. Perhaps your office isn't the ideal place. A conversation of fits and starts punctuated by telephone bells and heads-round-the-door is not on. Nor is it reasonable to expect an interviewee to wait for an hour or two in a daughty and prison-like corridor with a herd of other unfortunates. Arrange your interviewees' reception to show them a suitable human respect.

Here's an example of how a plan can be drawn up for conducting a selection interview.

The job to be filled was that of a Deputy News Editor in a regional daily newspaper. It involved regularly taking over and running the daily activity of a busy News Desk with a team of

INTERVIEW PLAN

1   What does his operation do?
    what sort of sports are covered?
    what types of reporting? any investigations?
    or critical articles?

2   How is his operation organized?
    how many people in his team? what are their
    roles?
    what sorts of people in the team? how does he
    choose who does what task?
    what relationship between sports reporters and
    sub-editors?

3   What is his role?
    what are his responsibilities? how much free-
    dom of action does he have?
    how does he allocate his time between team
    leadership/admin/writing?
    what relationship with colleagues? with his
    Editor?

4   What are his journalistic abilities?
    what does he see as important in a good story?
    how does he get information from unwilling
    sources?
    what experience of legal issues?

5   What is his leadership style?
    how does he delegate? how much does he
    maintain control?
    how does he plan and lead a large-scale
    reporting project?
    how does he develop the interest and skills of his
    people?

6   How does he view his paper's social purpose?
    how does he see its role in the local community?
    how does he attack local issues and problems?
    how maintain his relationship with his contacts?

7   What is his motivation?
    what does he find satisfying about his present
    job? what dissatisfying?
    why is he applying for this job?

some twenty reporters. From time to time it included local investigations — forming and heading up small teams of reporters to probe local issues and suspect going-ons in the community, and to produce in-depth stories and leaders. Such work was also used to sharpen the professional skills of the newspaper's more experienced reporters, so there was a training element in the role. The interviewee was a sports journalist of many years' experience.

Preparing the interviewee

He's not your employee yet! He is still a member of that 'Public' that your organisation is supposed to have 'Good Relations' with.

Do make the tone of your letter inviting him to the interview pleasant and warm. His feelings are probably more intense in this rathe intimidating situation. What feelings will the letter help to stimulate? Mute resentment of a cold summons? Or interested anticipation?

Conducting the interview

'One at a time please' is a good rule for interviewers. Don't fall for any suggestions about sitting in on someone else's interviews of the candidates whether he's a Personnel man or your own boss. Let him run his interviews and you run yours. That way there is less strain on the interviewees, and you force yourself to plan your questioning properly.

Of course it may be very good sense for an applicant to be interviewed by more than one person — you and your boss, say. But at *separate* interviews. Maybe your organisation is one of those that insist on 'panel' interviews. If you've been interviewed *yourself* by a panel you know the drawback. They *can* work — but usually only if the panel members operate together regularly, know each other's thinking and plan their lines of questioning.

Allow time for each interview. Half-an-hour is a minimum. Many good interviewers insist on forty minutes at least, even for fairly junior posts.

Establishing 'rapport'

You might start the interview in any of several ways: perhaps ask him about his journey, perhaps show some interest in his present locality or tell him something about your Company's; perhaps mention some interest or experience you've found you have in common; even talk about some mutual acquaintance you happen to know about. Establishing rapport need not take more than a few minutes, but don't go and spoil it by jumping abruptly into the interview proper. You might lead in by explaining the form of the interview: you want to ask him about various points in his application that interest you, and then you'll explain more about the job and give him a chance to ask any questions he has.

Questioning the interviewee

During this main part of the interview, remember: he talks — you listen. Your job is to keep the conversation flowing that way easily and naturally. You do this by your *manner*, your use of *questions*, and your ability to *listen* and *respond*.

1. *Your manner*
   Try to act naturally. Sit in a relaxed, easy posture. Let your tone of voice suggest your interest in the questions you ask and in the interviewee's replies. Look pleasant! A smile helps the tense and nervous interviewee to relax.
   Don't turn the interview into a test — demanding for instance that a candidate for a sales job 'sells' you something, or adopting a deliberately aggressive and unconciliatory manner to test the interviewee's nerve or stability. 'Stress interviews' usually rely on the false assumption that the candidate's behaviour at an interview

represents his normal behaviour in a job. They can sour the relationship between interviewer and interviewee — perhaps permanently. And if the candidate knows something about interviewing technique he may be able to turn the tables on the interviewer. If the interviewer then loses his temper, whose stability is most in question?

2. *Your questions*
Use broad questions to open up each area you want to explore: 'could you tell me about . . . ?' 'What sort of thing did . . . involve you in?' 'How did you tackle . . . ?' 'What did you feel about . . . ?' 'Why did you . . . ?' (*open questions*). These get the interviewee taking fluently. They prevent the uncomfortable jerky exchanges that some interviewers get trouble with.

Use specific questions to probe particular points for the details you need: 'How many subordinates did you have there?' 'How often did you do that?' 'Over what period did this go on?' (*closed questions*). And *do* probe. Don't let vague or generalised statements go unquestioned. Interviewees criticise interviewers more often for failure to probe properly than for probing too deeply.

Balance your use of closed and open questions. In this way you can keep the conversation flowing easily *and* maintain the guidance and control of it that you need.

Question only the candidate's experiences to date. Don't ask questions that ask him to guess his future behaviour in a situation that is for him unknown: 'How would you deal with . . . ?' 'How would you feel if . . . ?' 'How do you think you could cope with . . . ?' The suppositious answers you get will be totally unreliable. All the valid information that's available lies somewhere in the candidate's past, present or his existing plans for the future.

3. *Your ability to listen and respond*
Almost any interviewee responds to a good listener, to an interviewer who seems pleasantly interested in what he's got to say, whose face and eyes look responsive, who helps the conversation along with small comments: 'Uh-uh' . . . 'I see' . . . 'That's interesting' . . . 'And then?' . . .

Listen for more than the face value of the interviewee's words — listen for what his statements mean for him. Listen for intonations in his voice. Watch for expressions on his face. They give you clues to the ways his attitudes and feelings colour the situations and incidents he describes.

Check that you have understood the implications

behind the interviewee's statements: 'So you found this was ...?' 'If I understand you properly, you felt ...?' ('reflecting' his meaning). You demonstrate your interest in him, and his responses give you added insights into what makes him tick.

Listen without revealing your personal preferences or your reactions to the candidate's views. Don't ask questions in a way that suggests the sort of answers you expect or feel are correct. Don't let your comments imply criticism of the candidate. There is an important reason for this: if you show your bias, your interviewee will begin to tailor what he says towards what he thinks you want to hear. This is no criticism of his honesty or sincerity. The slanting is usually quite unconscious — and you may not even realise you are getting limited and unreliable information.

Listen without making snap judgements about the candidate's suitability. Otherwise *you* start to tailor your questions towards confirming your over-hasty conclusions. Keep an open mind until you are positive you have all the evidence you need.

Genuine, attentive listening is tiring and a strain on the memory. If you have several candidates to see, make notes as you go. Otherwise, at the end of the last interview, you'll find you can't recall what you've discovered from which candidate.

Discussing the job

Once you have found out enough to check how far the interviewee suits the job, he needs a chance to interview you — to find out how far the job suits him. Don't talk about the job *before* this, or you run the risk of getting information about his experience that is tailored to suit.

You might begin by explaining what the job entails. But be ready to let him interrupt with questions (and listen to his questions — they may tell you yet more about his interests and motivations). Make your description a fair one, showing the scope for challenge and achievement, but not ignoring the hard facts of life in the job.

Finally explain what happens next, how long it will be before he hears from you again, and show your appreciation of the time and trouble *he's* given to the interview.

The decision

Perhaps the decision seems an obvious one — one candidate

stands out head and shoulders above the others. Don't rush your fences. Are you sure he isn't *too* good for the job? Are you reasonably satisfied that he won't back out when the job is offered to him — and leave you in the lurch?

Perhaps two or three are fairly closely matched. Then you may have to work out some sort of scale of importance for their strong points and their weaker points. In the final analysis, your own gut-feelings about the candidates count. Selection is as much art as craft.

Offers and rejections

Whatever formal stuff your letter to the successful candidate has to contain — terms and conditions, salary scales etc — give it a note of sincere welcome. Particularly in its opening and closing paragraphs, introduce some human warmth and pleasant anticipation.

Warmth is equally — perhaps more — important in the letters of rejection, though tinged with a note of regret. Your company probably has to reject far more candidates than it accepts, and you don't want to turn any that you have dealt with into sources of ill-will for the company. Suggest the job's unsuitability for the candidate rather than the other way around, and give him some encouragement for wherever his future career may lie.

See yourself as the candidate sees you

None of the advice we've given on recruitment is new or revolutionary (although we've encountered very few organisations where *all* of it is followed with any great consistency).

Maybe there's just a slight danger that we've given the impression that recruitment is simple if you follow the rules. When all's said and done, the selection of people is a difficult, imprecise art and — interviewing, the heart of the process, a very complex communication skill.

One of the specific difficulties seems to be honest self-assessment by interviewers. So often *our* idea of what we're doing is apparently quite different from the way the candidates see it. A few years ago a leading employment agency conducted a survey of 750 job applicants and 450 employers of clerical and secetarial staff throughout the country. It revealed almost unbelievable disparities between the perceptions of interviewer and interviewee. For example:

- Over 90% of employers said they tried to create a relaxed atmosphere in interviews; less than half the applicants found this to be true.
- Nearly 90% of interviewers said their interviews started punctually; fewer than half the applicants said interviews 'usually' started on time.
- Hardly 10% of employers admitted purposely asking 'difficult' questions; more than 60% of applicants said such questions were put to them.
- Four out of five interviewers said they allowed no interruptions during an interview; three-quarters of all applicants said interruptions did take place. And so on.

It's pointless to surmise whose perceptions were 'right'. The point is that, regardless of accuracy, they are so different. No one had any reason to falsify their evidence, so we have to accept that these are genuine views of the *same* situations. How do your applicants see you as an interviewer? For that matter, how effective is the interview as a selection tool?

What else can we do?

The fact is that, despite the fact that at least 90% of jobs are filled on the basis of performance at interview, the interview itself has been shown to have very low reliability and validity as a selection device. (This has been tested by comparing the level of agreement among different interviewers of the same candidates, whom they are asked to rank in order of merit. Generally there is statistically little agreement on the ranking.)

The relative inefficiency of the interview has led to quite a wide use of various psychometric tests. Many hundreds of such tests are now available and your organization may use some of them. If you decide to supplement your own recruitment resources in this way, there are three important steps to take:

- First, find out *exactly* what any test you use is designed to measure, for example, intelligence, introversion/extroversion, specific personality traits etc. It is in the nature of a test to be very narrowly specific, yet we often see people drawing all kinds of quite unjustifed conclusions from the tests their organisations use.
- Secondly (obviously?) be sure that the trait or characteristic is actually relevant to the job for which you're recruiting.
- And thirdly, find out how the actual performance of candidates chosen by this test compares with that of people chosen by other methods. Only when a test can be shown to pick more successful people than otherwise can it be said to be validated.

Just one other approach which we must mention because you yourself may quite possibly become involved in it. It is the so-called 'assessment centre' method. This has gained enormous acceptance in the United States and is now being used by more and more British companies. Because of the time it demands from the candidates (probably not less than a whole day) it is more often used for internal selection than external recruitment.

The assessment centre

The term originated from the development of the method by the Bell Telephone Company in the late 1950s. For their widespread use of the technique (eventually applied to over 100,000 employees) they set aside a separate building in Michigan known, of course, as the 'Assessment Centre'. The widespread publicity it received resulted in the term being attached to the *method*, as opposed to the place.

More accurately, an assessment centre is a *multiple* assessment process. Its key features are that a *group* of participants (managers or others undergoing assessment) take part in a *variety* of activities, observed by a *team* of trained assessors who jointly evaluate a *number* of pre-determined job-related abilities.

The activities or exercises are designed to parallel or *simulate* those demanded by the job or the management level for which assessment is being made. They are *not* psychometric tests, but management tasks — reaching decisions, solving problems, dealing with mail, etc. — carefully structured to required behaviour which can be objectively observed and reliably evaluated.

The assessors are not 'experts' or consultant psychologists. They are line managers, at least one level above that for which they're assessing, who have undergone intensive, professionally-designed training in the techniques of objective observation and evaluation.

An important safeguard for the reliability of results is that assessors' evaluations are made *separately* from their observations — usually at a special 'evaluation meeting' immediately after the conclusion of the simulation exercises. The assessors make individual evaluations, which are compared to ensure consistency and guard against unintentional bias. They then pool their information (but *not* on a jury system basis) to reach a final judgement.

The outcome is an objective measurement of the amount of ability actually displayed by each participant in such areas as leadership, communication, judgement, creativity, flexibility, etc. These measurements have been consistently found to be accurate and reliable in a great many different organisations and industries.

In addition to these measurements of specific abilities, an evaluation may be made of each participant's *overall* management ability and, for example, the level in the organisation at which he or she is capable of succeeding, immediately and after a specified period of time. This information is usually given to each participant in the form of a feedback interview.

If your people are asked by your organisation to participate in an assessment centre you should give this your support. Because of the demonstrable objectivity of the process, the feedback he receives is a powerful influence on each individual. It can give him a clear understanding of the abilities he needs for future progress and success, and of the importance placed upon these abilities by the organisation; he will also become more aware of personal strengths on which to build, and of areas on which to focus his own improvement and development efforts. All of which, apart from any question of his promotion, can only make that person a more effective member of your team and contribute to your success as a manager. Assessment centres not only act as a possible recruitment aid they also help you in the final area of your people-management — your people's development.

Getting the right people

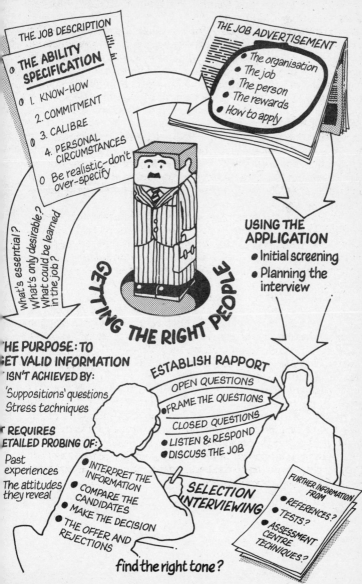

THE JOB DESCRIPTION

THE ABILITY SPECIFICATION

1. KNOW-HOW
2. COMMITMENT
3. CALIBRE
4. PERSONAL CIRCUMSTANCES

Be realistic–don't over-specify

THE JOB ADVERTISEMENT

- The organisation
- The job
- The person
- The rewards
- How to apply

What's essential? What's only desirable? What could be learned in the job?

GETTING THE RIGHT PEOPLE

USING THE APPLICATION
- Initial screening
- Planning the interview

THE PURPOSE: TO GET VALID INFORMATION ISN'T ACHIEVED BY:
- 'Suppositions' questions
- Stress techniques

IT REQUIRES DETAILED PROBING OF:
- Past experiences
- The attitudes they reveal

ESTABLISH RAPPORT

OPEN QUESTIONS
FRAME THE QUESTIONS
CLOSED QUESTIONS
- LISTEN & RESPOND
- DISCUSS THE JOB

- INTERPRET THE INFORMATION
- COMPARE THE CANDIDATES
- MAKE THE DECISION
- THE OFFER AND REJECTIONS

SELECTION INTERVIEWING

FURTHER INFORMATION FROM
- REFERENCES?
- TESTS?
- ASSESSMENT CENTRE TECHNIQUES?

find the right tone?

225

The attributes which decide a person's calibre and commitment are mostly deeply entrenched in his personality and character. Know-how on the other hand, is the sum of what he has learned — his qualifications, experience, knowledge, skills and habits. Some of this he has learned because it has been taught. Most of it he has acquired from his experience of life and work — he has learned it without being taught. Norman Evans, Senior Fellow at the Policy Studies Institute, actually suggests, in his book 'The Knowledge Revolution' that untaught learning could be enough to fit people for degree-level study: 'Office workers could well have learned enough about internal and external communication systems, the behaviour of individuals and groups of political and government procedures, to provide a good basis for studying Business Studies, social psychology, Politics and Government or perhaps Computer Studies'.

For a manager, the important thing about this 'untaught learning' is that it continues throughout peoples working lives. The old saying that 'you can't teach an old dog new tricks' is quite true — but only about dogs. The human animal has a lifetime learning span (the principal characteristic which distinguishes us from other species). Which is not to say that some people's *desire* to learn has not been extinguished by negative experiences. We'll return to that point a little later.

In the work context, people are learning all the time — often without themselves realising it. The trouble is that much of this learning is not only untaught but also unguided. With no help or encouragement to learn what might be useful and constructive in their jobs, they often learn the wrong things — how to avoid work, how to cut corners, how to 'defeat the system' and so on.

Development — or, as we are more likely to call it in a working environment, training — is something that many managers do not see as part of their responsibility. Just as they leave advertising to the advertising department or accounting to the accountants, so they leave training to the organization's training 'specialists'. But, just as 'war is too important to be left to the generals', so training is too important to be left to the trainers — and we speak as a couple of life-long professionals in the field. As such, we spend a good deal of our time trying to convince our clients' managers of the overiding need to become concerned and involved in their people's development.

Managing people's abilities

If management really is 'getting things done through other people' then your success as a manager must depend to a large extent on how good your people are at doing the things. The greater their abilities, the better a manager you are. So developing people's abilities could be said to be a fundamental part of the *purpose* of management — and the more senior the management, the more fundamental it is.

How do you go about managing your subordinates' abilities? We find managers attitudes in general tend to fall into three groups. Compare *your* approach with the views of these three managers:

1. *I don't think I do have a problem* with my people's abilities. Most of them seem to cope with their work without my worrying about them. I don't get any complaints about the way they do it. They'd resent it if I started running around looking for reasons to criticise them.'

   'Anyway, people ought to be competent to do their jobs, otherwise they shouldn't be there. It isn't my job to teach them — that's what we've got a Training Department for. In any case I haven't got the time. I've got a department to run.'

   'When we promote anyone into management, I work on the principle that the best worker makes the best manager. If he's good at the work of his section he shouldn't have any problem supervising it. If he does make a mess of things, it just proves he wasn't as good as we thought. That *is* a bit of a problem because you can't get rid of useless people so easily these days.'

2. *'You've got to push people* if you want to get really high standards of work out of them. They'll learn to do it all right if you keep the pressure on them. If I didn't do this in my own department, they'd soon start slacking and letting me and the department down.'

   'Ability only comes with experience, of course. Most of the people who've joined us here seem to pick it up after they've been in the job for a while. I tell them it's up to them to learn it for themselves — and they can always come and see me if they've got any problems. I don't suppose they do get any, because they hardly ever accept the offer. Once they've got the experience, there isn't much more for them to learn.'

   'The same goes for anyone who gets a promotion into

management here. I had to find out for myself how to cope when I became a manager, so I don't see why anyone else can't. If any of my new supervisors does run into trouble, it's usually because he's done something stupid that he should have had the sense to avoid. You've just got to point out his mistakes until he gets it right.'

3. '*Helping my people to develop their abilities* is one of the most important parts of my job as their manager. I try not to let them get complacent — anyone can learn to do his job better, however good he is. But there's no point in pushing them if you aren't willing to give them some positive leadership.'

'For me, the trick is to get them to see their work as something to continually learn from. I talk with each of my people regularly about the standards we want to try and achieve in the department, and ask him how he thinks he could contribute. That seems to create a challenge. Then we can go on to work out the kinds of knowledge and skill he'll need to work on, and draw up a plan of action for him to follow. Usually, most of it is based on things he'll be doing in his job where I can play a part in coaching him.'

'Well before we promote anyone into management, I talk with him about his future responsibilities. I also begin to involve him in things that enable him to learn the abilities he'll need as a supervisor. I was dumped into my first management job and that's no way to learn. It's hard to become a good manager, but my people seem to get themselves into fewer serious difficulties in their early days if they've had some help to prepare themselves beforehand.'

There's little point in our asking you to decide which of these managers you agree with most. The question is far too heavily loaded. But what you *do* speaks louder than what you say. And you'll be an exceptional manager indeed if you don't have to admit that there have been times when the way you *behaved* towards your people was based on the first or second of these attitudes. The third you may in fact regard as impossibly idealistic. Yet we *have* known managers who actually operated on this basis — with quite outstanding effect. Helping people to develop their abilities can, in fact, affect all three performance factors. As their *know-how* increases, so people are able to make better use of their intelligence, creativity and capacity for application — their *calibre*. At the same time, their growing know-how in their jobs leads to achievements which reinforce and strengthen their *commitment*.

Teaching versus learning

It's really not surprising that managers don't always see themselves as trainers. It has a lot to do with the way industry regards training. Training is concerned with change — and change is a personal process. As Nancy Foy has written: 'There are pessimists and optimists regarding change. The pessimists say you can't change human nature. The optimists say you don't have to change human nature; you just need to change some of its habits'. As a manager, you *have* to be an optimist — otherwise you can't really manage in the full sense. So what we have to examine is how best to change habits or behaviour. Training is concerned with changing what a person can *do*, not what he *is*. It is therefore quite distinct from (although it may be a part of) the wider concept of 'education'.

The confusion of education and training has persisted for many years. As a result, too much emphasis has been placed upon 'teaching' and a good deal of maytique built up around this supposedly highly specialised activity. Even today, it is often still regarded as a process of 'pumping-in' to the 'student' a great many facts and techniques. For you to be able to see yourself and function effectively in the role of trainer, the emphasis must be shifted away from 'teaching', towards *'helping people to learn'*. This is the starting point for acquiring the skills and abilities needed to be an effective trainer as well as a manager. And this in turn means knowing something about *how* people learn.

How we learn

Learning has been defined as 'a process which leads to a relatively permanent change in behaviour'. There are four major ways in which this process can be seen to take place:

1. *Discovery*
A child's first approach to learning, the result of taking an interest in his surroundings, exploring and 'trying-out'. In adult learning this method is often characterised as 'trial and error' and thought to be inefficient or wasteful. In fact it's unavoidable. And, it may be used very effectively in training if the learner's discovery is *guided* along carefully planned lines.

2. *Imitation*

Children learn by copying the behaviour of others. Much adult training too is in effect little more than the planned imitation of the behaviour of more experienced colleagues (the training method often rather contemptuously called 'sitting by Nellie').

3. *Rote learning*

A great deal of knowledge is acquired in schooldays by memorizing — arithmetical tables, historical dates, etc. Most adult training contains some basic element which has to be acquired by this method, and new behaviour patterns *can* be acquired by constant repetition, until they become habitual.

4. *Reasoning*

Another characteristic which distinguishes man from the other animals is his ability to reason — to make deductions from given facts. Closely allied to and often an extension of discovery learning, this is often the most effective means of achieving 'relatively permanent' behaviour change. This is primarily because of the mental involvement required and because the process of reasoning things out for ourselves motivates us to adopt new behaviour.

For all practical purposes, learning is a voluntary process — you can't force people to learn. The first step in behaviour change is not to learn — it is to *want* to larn. Wanting to learn is natural to human beings — curiosity is a strong element in our make-up. Regretably, this curiosity has often been suppressed by the time maturity is reached. A child doesn't have to be taught to be curious. The tragedy is that he is so often taught *not* to be.

Motivation to learn

Adults often suffer from a set of attitudes towards learning which have to be changed before training can succeed. Many of these are derived from experiences in school; others are created or reinforced by the work environment. They may include the ideas that:

- learning is unpleasant (the result of poor experiences in the past)
- learning is 'non-work' — time devoted to it specifically is regarded as unproductive, or even as shirking
- learning is impractical — the activities involved seem too far removed from the real-life demands of the job

- learning is a waste of time — better to spend the time tackling practical problems there's *no* time for learning (maybe it *should* be done, but too many other things always come first)
- learning costs too much ('I can't afford to have my people sitting around.')
- learning can be done by 'magic' — an unending search for the short-cut method or the miracle one-day course.

If these attitudes are deeply ingrained in any of your people, changing them is going to be a difficult and lengthy task. But, you have working for you the basic human need to know, to understand, to grow and develop one's full potential — Maslow's 'self-actualisation'. True, it may temporarily have been partly or even wholly extinguished, but it remains a fundamental fact of human personality and offers hope in the hardest case!

To stimulate your people's motivation to learn, you have to try to:
- set a good example, by both your attitude and your actions
- establish a clearly discernible link between what is learned and what happens on the job
- ensure that learning is in no way associated with negative influences, such as fear, anxiety or humiliation never allow people in a learning situation to be embarrassed or ridiculed

- ensure that learning doesn't cause exhaustion
- ensure that learning *does* result in positive influences — reassurance, social acceptability, esteem, a sense of achievement and growth
- show that there is a 'pay-off' from learning — that it provides some concrete, specific, useable knowledge or skill which is clearly related to job achievement
- make it as *interesting* and *enjoyable* as possible.

Individually, people *will* learn if they are interested and have an incentive to learn. Incentives may be infinitely varied, according to individuals' character and circumstances. They could include ambition, curiosity, personal pride, the desire to achieve, to win recognition or praise, competition and rivalry, the wish to increase earnings, to avoid criticism or censure, or simply to survive.

Motivation will be affected not only by incentives but also by such factors as the organisational climate and management attitudes. When the *organisation* accepts training as a real force in the company's growth or survival plans (rather than as a socially-acceptable but time-consuming irrelevance) your training role as a manager will be much easier.

Two kinds of learning

Behavioural scientists have undertaken a great deal of research into methods by which people can be encouraged or induced to learn. The theories they have produced broadly fall into two groups, which identify two approaches to learning:

1. *Mechanistic learning* rests primarily on the belief that behaviour can be conditioned and shaped, by reward on the one hand and by punishment on the other. 'Punishment', in this sense, may be no more than indicating to the learner that his answer to a question is wrong; 'reward' may mean the opposite, that is, confirmation of its correctness.

This form of learning is accomplished by a number of steps or stages:

First, there must be a *readiness* to learn on the part of the learner — in other word he must feel motivated to learn. He is then ready to receive a *stimulus* — an input of information, a mental challenge, or a variety of other possible forms. He makes a *response* to that stimulus in the form of a reaction of some kind, and his response is *reinforced* if correct or *negatively reinforced* (ignored or punished) if incorrect.

Correct responses are encouraged, repeated, developed and practised until they become part of the learner's behaviour pattern. When he is able always to give the right responses to particular stimuli, he can be said to have learned. This approach might employ any or all of the four methods we describe, but probably places emphasis on imitation and rote learning. It is the basis for all kinds of 'programmed learning', texts, teaching machines, etc.

2. *'Organic learning'* is described as 'primarily experiential, significant or meaningful'. It has a quality of personal involvement and makes a difference not only to the behaviour of the learner but perhaps also to his attitudes, temperament and character — for example he may gain new insight into his own potentialities or be able to see himself in a different role. Again all four methods might have a part to play but the essential emphasis is on discovery and, especially, reasoning. It is almost certainly a lengthier process than mechanistic learning.

What these theories really say is that there are two ways to modify behaviour: to reward certain types of behaviour and punish other types, so that through practice, correction and repetition the former types become habitual; and to help the individual change his perception of his environment, of himself, of his values and attitudes, which in turn will give rise to new patterns of behaviour.

As a manager you most often employ a mixture of these two types of learning, the emphasis being decided by what has to be learned. This will also decide the point from which you start.

The learning process

Many managers and 'professional' trainers start from the formulation of *rules* — 'this is how you should carry out this task'. Their subordinates then put the rules into *practice* and in so doing they gain *experience*. At this point they may decide that the 'rules' don't work and revert to the former way of accomplishing (or avoiding) the task. Or, if they really *want* to learn, they may *reflect* on their experience and *modify* the rules to suit their own situation. They then again apply the rule in its modified form, gain more experience, reflect further and maybe even modify again, until the new and successful method becomes the norm. The process takes the form of another 'cycle'.

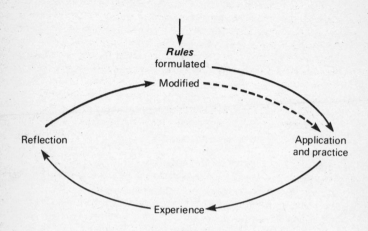

For certain kinds of learning your starting point probably has to be the 'rules'. Precise technical procedures, accounting practices, administrative systems, may be satisfactorily learned mainly by imitation or rote, with a certain amount of reasoning. In these cases your planning of your people's development will emphasize *teaching* — arranging courses, using lectures, films, video or audio tapes, written instructions — methods which the educationalists call 'didactic' (reading this book is a didactic way to learn something about management).

On the other hand, ask yourself where and how you learned *most* of what you actually use in your job. The answers will almost certainly be from experience. So with your people. *Most* of what they need to do their jobs they learn in the act of doing them. This might therefore lead you to plan their development from a different starting point in the cycle. By *reflection* on their *experience* they may be able (with help) to *formulate* the *rules* before *applying* and *practising* them. From there on the process of *modifying* can be the same; although probably easier.

This will lead you to plan your people's development quite differently, looking for ways of helping them *learn by experience* — coaching, delegating, experimenting, giving them new responsibilities — methods which the educationalist calls 'experiential' (only when you try out the ideas in this book to see how they work in practice will they *really* be of value in developing your management ability).

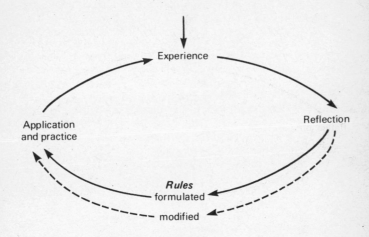

Learning by experience

So people often develop practical abilities best by 'doing'. Yet managers can, and commonly do, leave this learning process for their subordinates to chance. People's development is not their business. They give all their attention to getting operational things done, financial results achieved, leaving their subordinates to learn their jobs as best they can for themselves.

True, people *do* develop abilities without any particular guidance or pressure. Self-taught by experience, by private study and practice, by trying things out for themselves, they acquire skills and knowhow, sometimes to high levels of competence. All they need is the motivation, the luck to get the right opportunities, the aptitude and persistence to learn from them — and time. Often considerable time! But this doesn't necessarily apply to all your people in their jobs. Once someone has learned the basics, he may see little need to widen the range of his abilities or improve his competence further. There may be few pressures on him to do these things — and few opportunities in the routines of his job. He may well resnet the idea that he has anything more to learn, and be unwilling to devote the effort required. And there may be ready excuses in the other prssures on his time. He learns slowly and ineffectively.

People's learning by experience must be managed. It is influenced in any case by the things you give them to do, the way you act with them, the kinds of pressure you apply in the normal course of their work. But this is not managing the *learning* process. They gain more from their experience when you consciously encourage and guide their development.

You can probably recognise in your team both the 'learners' and 'non-learners'. Here is an analysis of what the *learner* does as he learns by experience — the five steps through which he gains or improves an ability — and the various problems that lead the *non-learner* to avoid learning, or that limit the extent to which he learns. Then there are suggestions for *managing the process:* ways in which you, the manager, can encourage the learners among your subordinates and stimulate the non-learners' development:

1. *The learner **realises** there is something to learn.* He becomes aware that something could be done better than he can do it now. There are two conditions for this to happen: first, he has *opportunities* to do it himself, to make mistakes, to get into difficulties. If the opportunities don't happen in the normal course of the job, they have to be created. Secondly, he has something to *compare* his performance against. He sets himself a standard that is above his present ability, but one that he feels is within his potential capability.

   The non-learner is complacent about his present level of performance. He *knows* he is fully competent already (in fact he hardly ever questions his own competence and ability). The situations he is involved in and his own behaviour in them are too familiar for him to consider the possibility of any change in his approach. He avoids situations where he risks failure. He blames any failures on the situations themselves or on other people involved. He is never at fault. He sets himself easily-achievable standards. He has a limited perception of his own potential: 'I'd never be able to do that' or 'I'm too old to learn' etc. He regards a low ability in himself as inevitable and permanent.

   To manage the process, keep talking about your people's development (including your own) as a normal part of your management of them. Make changes in working arrangements, systems, procedures, etc., that you can claim improve efficiency, but that also upset comfortable routines and established working habits. At the same time, begin to give guidance and coaching on the approach and skills that need to be developed. Delegate clearly-defined responsibilities to the non-learner. Give him tasks and assignments that test his ability and that expose him to the risk of personal failure. Don't take over yourself if he gets into trouble — allow him opportunities to make mistakes. Insist he accepts a personal responsibility for the outcome. Demand high standards — but not too high for him to eventually achieve. Discuss them with him to develop his ideas of what he could become capable of. Give him opportnunities to observe the way a more competent person performs.

2. *The learner* **reflects** on his past peformance, on mistakes he has made, on difficulties he has run into. He thinks through the way things happened and his own thoughts and behaviour at the time. He identifies the problem in his approach.

The *non-learner* doesn't reflect on his experiences, merely remembers them. He finds it too uncomfortable to think over past mistakes and inadequacies, and so avoids doing it. He cannot identify any problem in his approach.

To manage the process, discuss with him the past situations, the gap between the standard and his achievement, his reasons for his approach and actions. Do this *objectively:* avoid personal criticism or arguments about who was to blame for failures and deficiencies. Help *him* to define the problem for himself — don't tell him what you know (or think) it was.

3. *The learner* develops **insight** into the problem to see other ways of tackling the situation. he sees factors that he didn't recognise at the time; he acquires new knowledge that is relevant; he thinks out a possibly better approach for the future.

The non-learner is too negative to search for solutions — he can only produce justifications for his failure to solve the problem. His attitudes are too rigid for him to look at the problem from different angles. He is too set in his ways to consider trying other lines of action.

To manage the process press him into develop solutions, not further difficulties. Talk over ideas with him: encourage him to produce his own. To help him to do this, offer him your ideas based on your experience. Provide ways for him to get further information and knowledge that he discovers is relevant. Help him to work out his own best approach — don't impose your own.

4. *The learner* **practices** what he has learned. He has opportunities to tackle the situation again and again, and to develop the skills he now sees are relevant. Perhaps he gets into other kinds of difficulty — followed by further reflection, further insights.

   The non-learner's habits are too strong for him to change his approach as he had intended — he is stuck in a rut of fixed reactions to familiar situations. His earlier experience has demoralised him — he lacks the confidence to try again. Even if he does try, his tentative approach makes failure more likely.

   To manage the process change the situation in which he is trying to carry his learning into practice. Involve his colleagues in the process. Don't interfere as he repeats the task — but do run postmortems afterwards: how well does he feel his new approach works out in practice? Show *your* confidence in his ability to tackle the situation successfully.

5. *The learner* gets **reinforcement** of his improvements in ability. He has success through applying what he has learned, and gets a feeling of achievement. This gives him an incentive to continue practising, and to develop the ability further.

   The non-learner finds it difficult to be objective about his ability: he is over-critical of himself. He sets himself impossible ideals and demoralises himself when he cannot reach them. He doesn't recognise the success he does achieve. After a short-term improvement, he reverts to his old approach.

   To manage the process, praise his improvements in ability and performance — try to get others (his colleagues? superiors?) to do the same. Discuss with him the difference between his earlier performance and what he is now actually achieving. Supervise his work regularly for a period to ensure that he maintains his improved approach.

Appraising people's performance

In managing your people's learning by experience you will obviously have regular contacts with each of them to discuss

A guide to the appraisal of subordinates

PERFORMANCE	Outstanding	Highly capable	Average	Sub-standard	Totally incapable
Dexterity	Vaults over canyons with the greatest of ease	Leaps rivers after a running start	Can jump ditches with a following wind	Falls into ditches	Ditches colleagues for his own ends.
Mental capabilities	Thinks quicker than lightning	Thinks	Avoids thinking	Needs to avoid thinking	Requires a brain transplant
Efficiency	Catches rockets in flight with bare hands	Moves as fast as a rocket	Would you believe a slow rocket?	Needs frequent rockets	Accidental suicide
Resourcefulness	Walks on water	Only occasionally gets wet feet	Manages to stay in the swim	Cannot keep his head above water	Passes water in emergencies
Negotiation ability	Argues with the angels	Argues with Sir Robin	Argues with himself	Loses arguments with himself	Cannot understand himself
Personal attributes	As strong as a bull	Amateur matador	Talks bull	Thinks like a bull	Smells like a bull
Managerial ability	God-like	Believes in God	Plays God	Believes he *is* God	God!
RECOMMENDED ACTION	Hide this assessment from the Chief Executive	Watch out for	Sweat	Recommend for inter-departmental transfer	Ready for recruitment by a competitor

performance, their future in the organisation and ways in which they can grow in ability and competence. Every time you do this you are in fact carrying out an *appraisal*.

Many organisations, of course, have formalized this process and established an Appraisal System, which requires that an appraisal form be completed after an annual appraisal interview. That this particular road is paved with good intentions doesn't necessarily mean it has to lead to Hell, but unfortunately it frequently doesn't lead where it should. If your organisation has such a system, of course you have to abide by it and operate it to the best of your ability. Perhaps you may even be able to get some improvements made if they're needed.

Quite often the biggest problem is the design of the appraisal form, asking for a lot of very subjective ratings of personal attributes. You may have seen this 'Guide to the Appraisal of Subordinates' which has been around so long we've forgotten where we first saw it:

Although this still gets a lot of laughs, it also makes a serious point. The kind of arbitary judgements it contains really are not all that unlike those called for by a great many appraisal forms. Conversely, forms often contain little space for what should be the most important aspect of the annual appraisal — the plans for performance improvement.

Rules for appraisal

If you want to check over your company's Appraisal System, here briefly are ten key issues:

1. *The first purpose of appraisal is to improve a person's performance in his present job.* It is accomplished by working ideas out together, not by filling in an appraisal form and then telling him what it contains.

2. *A second purpose is to see what potential he might have for other jobs in the organization.* No rash promises should be made about promotion. Good performance in the present job doesn't prove anyone's potential to do a higher-level job. But his personal goals and the abilities he'll need to develop are an important area for discussion.

3. *The manager doing the appraisal should be the immediate boss of the person appraised.* No one else is likely to know the person and his work in enough depth. The topics to be discussed should have been talked over with the appraiser's boss first.

4. *Discussion of peformance should be based on objective standards.* There should be no surprises at the appraisal stage. And no need for argument about whether standards have been met or not. That should be evident. What needs to be discussed is where help is needed.

5. *Both the person and the appraiser need to prepare for the interview.* Not the case for the defence and the prosecution, but thinking through what needs to be discussed to make the interview of value.

6. *Criticism doesn't actually improve anyone's abilities.* This doesn't excuse the manager from constructively pointing out failings in performance or behaviour, but this isn't enough by itself. It makes anyone feel defensive — whether he shows it or not. The most effective form of criticism is a person's self-criticism. The discussion should encourage him to be self-analytical.

7. *The appraiser needs to listen.* He should be prepared to consider ideas and views that differ from his own — and even to learn where he can improve his own management of his people.

8. *The aim is to work out a plan.* Performance improves most when the person participates in planning *goals* for self-improvement and specific *actions* that will develop his abilities.

9. *Helping anyone to do a job better is a day-to-day responsibility for his manager.* It is not a once-a-year task. The annual appraisal should summarise discussions of performance throughout the year and plan long-term action.

10. *Pay is not a subject for discussion during appraisals.* It diverts attention from the main purpose — to improve performance. Increases should be awarded at a different time of year.

Setting performance standards

One of the 'rules' for appraisal needs particular emphasis. More appraisals fail because of the absence of pre-agreed standards than for any other reason. Actually, standards exist for every job. *Your* job for instance: you have your own idea of what constitutes good performance in it — and so does your boss. So do your colleagues, your subordinates and everyone else who is affected by the way you do it. The trouble is that the ideas of the different people may not agree. Setting standards is a process of drawing the ideas together.

The purpose of standards is to *motivate people to perform well*, not to provide opportunities for you to criticise. Much depends on your way of setting them and of dealing with any problems they reveal. Low performance may be due to problems in the job rather than in the person; even if it does stem from personal failures, the person may need training rather than discipinary action.

Standards are *unique to the individual*. For each person, the standards he works out with you are a separate, individual agreement — even though he does similar work to his colleagues. The yardstick may be the same. But the standards should be set in terms of *his* abilities, *his* working conditions, the problems and opportunities *he* is likely to meet in *his* job. Attempts to make everyone match up to the same standards ignore individual strengths and limitations; they also ignore differences between the specifics of different people's jobs.

Both you and your subordinate should be involved. Ideally the subordinate proposes his standards to you. He is more likely to commit himself to his own proposals than to yours, however tentatively you put them forward. At the end of the day he must be convinced that the standards are achievable by *him*, not by your department's star performer.

Setting standards *tests people's ideas* about what good performance is. The subordinate who sets himself low standards may need counselling or training to raise his sights. But a subordinate will often set himself higher standards than you would. Perhaps they are unrealistic and you are wise to counsel caution. Perhaps they *are* realistic, and you may yourself learn something from the discussion.

The aim throughout is to *lift people's ideas about the norms of performance* generally considered acceptable in the organisation. Standards are a *minimum* condition of acceptable performance, calling for management action when they are not achieved. But they should not be easy to achieve without care, effort and attention. For each subordinate, his standards should provide a challenge, a stimulus for the growth of his abilities.

The yardsticks for standards

The standards of performance of a job are the ways used to gauge how well a person is doing in its various aspects. To set the standards, the first thing is to decide what yardsticks to use.

Yardsticks are rather like the indicators a doctor uses to gauge the state of his patients' health — temperature, pulse rate, blood pressure, etc. Like the doctor's checks, they should be valid indicators of the state of the person's performance in the job: fair to the person, reliable for you, and simple and easy for both to check.

Deciding the yardsticks is a critical management decision. To help in thinking out the possibilities for any job you are looking at, here are a number of alternative ways of choosing them. Yardsticks may be:

either *measurements:*
things that can be objectively *counted*: numbers, amounts, incident counts, percentages, ratios etc. As many yardsticks as possible should be of this type. They give more accurate contol and are seen to be fair.

or *assessments:*
things that involve subjective *judgements* based on experience or skill (or often, unfortunately, the halo-or-horns effect). Not to be ignored — they exist anyway, and important areas of the job may not lend themselves to arithmetic.

either *comparative:*
based on *variances* from a previous period's performance or from others' per-

or *engineered:*
based on calculations of what is *inherently possible* given the facts of the situa-

formance. Popular and easy, but the variance set is often a 'wet finger' guesstimate that may be unjustified.

tion. They can be difficult to specify but often give a more reliable guide to the quality of performance.

either *positive:*
based on the *existence or abundance* of some desireable feature of performance: output levels, good quality work, revenues gained, required things done etc.

or *negative:*
based on the *absence or rarity* of some undesirable feature of performance: wastage, losses, poor quality work, complaints, incidents, needs for correction etc.

either *periodic:*
regular features of performance: sales calls per week, monthly materials usage, annual staff turnover etc. The period must be defined — whether by the week, month, quarter, half-year or year.

or *unique:*
isolated features of performance: completion by a specified date of a special project or report, a sales campaign, a new installation etc. Total avoidance of something.

either *results:*
features that can be reckoned only at the *end* of a period or task.

or *activities:*
things to be *done*. The requirement is simply that they are performed.

These alternatives are of course combined in any particular yardstick. One standard may be an engineered, positive measurement of activities, another may be a comparative, negative assessment of results. There are many other appropriate combinations.

For *fair and reliable* standards, two criteria should apply to the choice of each yardstick: it should be one that you and your subordinate understand in exactly the same way. If you differ about its meaning during a review of performance, there is little point in arguing about the person's performance on that point. The yardstick has to be clarified first. And it should be one for which you both have the same control information. Each should know independently whether the standard has been satisfied. If either of you have relevant but private information sources not available to the other the yardstick is either unreliable for you or unreasonable for him.

Standards of performance are, of course, related to the

tasks or responsibilities of the job. As such they could form part of that Job Profile you completed towards the beginning of the book. Go back and look at it again, especially if you completed the 'Priority-centred' profile. For each Key Task you listed, now decide what would be an acceptable standard of performance. Ask yourself questions like: 'How much? 'How often?' 'By when?' This will help you guide your own people when they start developing standards for discussion with you. Standards are a way of increasing people's motivation to perform consistently well. They are an indispensible pre-requisite for any review of performance, such as an appraisal interview.

Comparing performance with standards

The managing director of a medium-sized company we know recently decreeed that there should be no more annual appraisals. He had come to the conclusion that the inability of his managers to conduct an appraisal interview without arousing rancour and dissention meant that the process was doing more harm than good.

As we tried tactfully to point out, he had arrived at a 'solution' to the problem without really analysing its causes. We suggested two possible reasons for the situation. One is that the managers had got the wrong idea about the purpose of appraisals: they found themselves simply repeating their criticisms of incidents they'd already dealt with during the year. The other is that they weren't sure *how* to run an appraisal interview and found in an uncomfortable thing to do.

If these are problems for you, the following simple four-stage plan may help:

1. *Prepare:* Both you and your subordinate need to think ahead about the points you each want to discuss. When you brief him to do his preparation, talk about the appraisal as a constructive exercise so that he approaches it in a positive frame of mind.

   In your preparation, think back over the whole of the last year with two questions in mind: what have been the main strengths and limitations of his performance throughout the year? Where have his difficulties and successes had more to do with the situations in which he has been working than with him? Then think what problems and opportunities his job might hold in store in the coming year.

   Your aim in doing this is to draw up a short-list of key

247

point about the job and about his abilities and behaviour that you want to discuss with him. Keep the list short: at most, a couple of strengths that could be exploited more fully, two or three key weaknesses he can learn to overcome, and whatever points you've got on the job itself.

2. *Review:* Have a meeting with *your* boss to talk about your subordinates and the future possibilities for them. This may sometimes be difficult to arrange — but if you can, it's worth doing. You need to be fully in the picture on anything that could affect your people's futures before you start interviewing them.

3. *Interview:* Keep the aim in mind — to come up with a plan of action for future improvements:
   - *Review the job.* It is often easier to begin with the job itself — its responsibilities, tasks, difficulties and opportunities in the past year. See if there are any aspect that could be changed for the better.
   - *Review his performance.* Approach this by asking him how *he* assesses himself. What is he good at? What abilities has he improved over the year? Where does he have problems? What does he think causes them? Introduce your own points in discussing his self-assessment.

     Don't criticise his personality or character traits. Stick firmly to questions of *ability* and *behaviour*. Involve him in defining the further knowledge and skills that would enable him to perform better. And be ready to pick up hints on where your own management of him could be improved.
   - *Build the learning plan.* In discussion, work out goals for the comming year and specify actions to achieve them. Prepare a *written* plan, along lines we'll suggest a little later.
   - *Look into the future.* Finally you might consider some longer-term questions: What are his ideas and ambitions for his future? What are the likely possibilities for him — being realistic about his calibre and the way the organization is heading? Are there any practical steps that could be taken to broaden his experience or test his potential? How can they be built into the plan?

All of this may well take two or three hours with each of your subordinates. Don't begrudge the time. Such personal discussion can't be rushed. And surely it's *worth* spending that time once a year on your key resource — your people?

4. *Follow through:* If you fail to implement an operational or financial plan you've prepared, you've wasted your own time. Failure to implement a plan you've developed with someone for his future is worse. It damages his respect for you and his interest in doing the job well. You are telling him he doesn't matter.

Having made the plan, you're both now committed to carrying it through. You may have to change it if circumstances change. But whatever you do, don't let it become merely a set of Good Intentions. As his manager, you've got to see that during the coming year he gets the development you've mapped out.

Planning for learning

The principal outcome of a successful appraisal (although you don't have to wait a year for it to occur) is the learning plan for each of your people. Even if your organization has no formal system of appraisal, you should still be jointly planning with them how they can improve their ability and competence. This plan needs to be agreed between you and your subordinate and put into writing, so that you both understand it and can monitor progress. To produce the plan, follow three simple steps:

1. *Define the development needs*
The first thing is to establish the aim: what abilities should he try to develop? You and your subordinate might consider:
   —*Performance improvements* he could achieve in his present work, given further knowledge, understanding or skill. Don't include aspects of his performance that have more to do with his temperament, calibre or motivation — concentrate on *know-how*. Decide which improvements are the most important: which will have the biggest effect on his success in the job?
   —*Further abilities* he could gain, with an enlargement of his responsibilities or promotion in view.

2. *Specify the missing knowhow*
Analyse the knowledge and skills that he is now lacking — the

specific things he needs to learn that will enable him to improve his performance or gain the further abilities you have defined. Be as precise as you can. It is essential that you are both absolutely clear about exactly what he is to learn, otherwise you can neither plan the learning methods nor check whether he has eventually learned it.

3. *Build the learning plan*
   — *The learning tasks:* Think out ideas on *how* he can acquire each element of the knowledge and skill you have specified: will attending a formal course be the answer, or are there other more effective ways?
   — *Timing:* Decide when he should undertake each of these learning tasks. How can they be fitted in with his operational work? How should they be sequenced? How much should he aim to learn by when? See that the timings are reasonable and realistic for the amount he has to learn (the 'learning load'), his capacity for learning (intelligence and aptitudes) and his normal work pressures.
   — *Monitoring:* Plan how you will check, stage by stage, what he has learned. Can you use your normal supervision of his work to check any behaviour skills involved? Should you arrange meetings with him to question him about the knowledge he is supposed to have gained? Could you ask him to prepare a report on information he has acquired?

Learning tasks

Training courses are not the only ways of learning to improve performance — nor even the most important. Your learning plan should use off-the-job methods only as a support for the subordinate's on-the-job development. Among the more common types of learning tasks that are available are:

1. *Learning on-the-job.* This means building a learning element into some part of the *normal* job. It is so basic and important a learning method, it deserves an example to illustrate how it works.

A sales manager had tried for some time to train his salemen to improve the way they handled what are often called 'buying objections' — the reasons put forward by customers for refusing to place an order. A good salesman will probe to find out whether an objection is valid or whether it's caused by a misunderstanding — or indeed by a customer who's simply being difficult. But in this case the salesmen were taking any objection at face value: the first hint they received that a customer had any doubts would cause them either to start an argument or to pick up their hat and leave. Classroom training sessions run by the sales manager had had no effect whatsoever. They were all older men, long experienced in their particular methods of selling (poor though they were), and resistant to any changes.

The sales manager started an on-the-job learning exercise for his team. For the first fortnight, every salesman was to make a list of all the objections made by customers he visited. During each weekly sales meeting, the lists were reviewed and compared. The aim was twofold: first to get the salesmen to realize what objections they were actually getting (they had never done this before *on the job*); secondly to see how common each type of objection was. This enabled the sales manager to identify the three most common types of complaint (only three — he wanted to avoid a learning overload).

At the next training meeting the manager got the salesmen to act out role-plays of how to respond to those particular objections. Then for the following fortnight they were asked to try out these approaches whenever they recognized one of the three objection-types. Again they were to notice the way customers reacted, whether positively or negatively, list the reactions and produce their lists at each weekly sales meeting. This idea — of *monitoring* what is happening in an on-the-job learning exercise — is absolutely crucial. Without it, the learning is quite likely not to happen.

In the next training session, the salesmen analysed what they were doing that made each approach successful or unsuccessful. Having done so, yet another exercise was planned for the next fortnight to try out in practice what they had learned about making the approaches successful. By this time the message had started to get through: what they were learning was good practical stuff if the salesmen *applied* it in the right way. But there was only one place they could learn how — in actual on-the-job practice.

2. *Specific learning tasks* related to the job's operational work: reading files, reports, minutes, books; collecting and analysing information (keeping a diary of one's own use of time for example).

3. *Observing others' working methods:* 'sitting by Nellie' but with a difference. The subordinate has *specific* things to observe, and the learning is *monitored* by you.

4. *Study projects:* The subordinate investigates the working of a system, a method, a machine perhaps, and reports back on what he has been able to find out.

5. *Job rotation:* properly planned as a learning exercise, not just to fill vacancies or absences.

6. *Inter-departmental transfers and secondments:* again, properly planned; just getting the subordinate to kick his heels or do dog-work in another department may provide a change of scenery, but little enlightenment.

7. *Getting the subordinate involved* in aspects of your own tasks: for example, discussing with the subordinate a problem you have to tackle or a decision you have to make — explaining your reasoning or your method of approach.

8. *Attending departmental meetings* (or better still, inter-departmental) can provide a broadening experience: as always, you must afford time to check what the subordinate is learning about the organisation and its workings.

9. *Visits to other departments* (those visited must be prepared to co-operate in the training, and must know what specifically the subordinate is to learn from his visits) or *to other organisations* (probably best run as a type of Study project). The aim of such visits may be directly job-related, or it may be to broaden the subordinate's thinking.

10. *New responsibilities* in the job, properly delegated, not dumped: the responsibilities should stretch the subordinate, not simply add to his work-load; this may mean carefully defining the limits of authority within which he must take his new decisions.

Delegating to develop

We discussed delegation at some length as an element of your organisation's pressure system and as one of your essential management skills. Like so many aspects of this complex business of management, delegation fulfils more than one purpose. It can make a major contribution to your people's development.

Used in this way, delegation requirs a careful step-by-step approach, in which decision-making by the subordinate is built through five levels:

Level O: Observe
The subordinate watches you (or someone else) doing the job. You check what the subordinate is learning.
Level D.1: 'Discuss with me — we decide — you act'
The subordinate helps you decide and has himself to put the decision into effect.
Level D.2: 'You decide — tell me — then you act'
The subordinate thinks out his own decision, but cheks it with you before acting.
Level D.3: 'You decide — then act — then tell me'
The subordinate decides and acts without referring to you. But he checks with you after each time he does so.
Level D: 'Delegation'
The subordinate takes the full responsibility and assumes authority himself. You now have only your normal controls as feedback on how things are going (*not* an incident-by-incident check). This staged approach to full delegation allows for the development of the subordinate's self-confidence and of *your* confidence in *him*.

Coaching your team

Perhaps one of the most valuable ways for you to manage your people's develoment is the one we've left till last. If you're in agreement with what we've already written about managing people, and if you're making a conscientious effort to shape your personal management approach along these lines, it's almost unnecessary to discuss it at length: you'll automatically be *coaching* your people.

Every sportsman knows the value of the coach. But people in work have an advantage over the boxer, the athlete and the tennis player: they can actually have their coach alongside them in the ring, on the track or the court, helping them tackle each challenge and opportunity as it occurs.

Coaching really consists simply of using work as an opportunity to help people learn. being a good coach is part of the everyday activity of the effective manager, not a separate task to be undertaken. It relies mostly on skills we've dealt with already: understanding people and their motivations, using leadership and communication skills, listening and responding, constructively criticising and giving feedback, building on people's ideas, suggesting alternative approaches.

Perhaps one of the few additional things it's worth pointing out is the need to identify *opportunities* for coaching. The late Hawdon Hague was a consultant totally committed to the idea of 'training for real' — building training into his clients' normal working situations. In a 'Management Today' article he cited a managing director who 'said he was too busy for training, because one of his major products was fast becoming obsolete; a small firm he had just taken over was producing a conflict of management styles: and he had a pressing liquidity problem. In about six months time, however, he hoped to have some time for training. In other words, three ideal teaching projects were staring him in the face, together with demonstrable management shortcomings'. Coaching opportunities are often missed because they look more like operational difficulties requiring the superior expertise of the manager (who probably caused the mess in the first place). In fact they're frequently problem-solving projects from which people at lower levels could usefully learn something, while at the same time solving the problem.

Development projects

Such projects can be a valuable source of development, not only for individuals, but for the organisation. A lot of 'internal consultancy' can be done by people working, either individually or in teams, on organisational problems, needs and opportunities. The ideas they produce are often more practical than those of professional consultants. And the people involved get some useful broadening of their experiences and their thinking in the course of the project.

But to get full value for both the organisation and those involved, a project needs to be tackled systematically. This is a simple method for the person or project-group who'll be involved. Suppose that's you:

1. *Define the aim*
Write down a statement of what the project is trying to achieve. Don't make the statement too specific yet. You may later need to refine or even re-define your aim as you get a clearer understanding of what you are tackling.

2. *Analyse the problem*
What is the *real problem*? This is often a very difficult thing to define. You will probably find that in your first attempts

you are stating *symptoms* of the problem (or of several inter-related problems) rather than the problem itself. So you may need to do a lot of hard thinking and detailed investigation before you can identify the core of the problem and the different factors you have to take into account. List *all* the factors you can think of.

Also review the information and knowledge you have available that are relevant to the problem. If yours is a team project, pool the knowledge you already have available within the team. Decide what further information you will have to get fromewt sources: files, interviews, visits, meetings, direct observation, reading, etc.

Now review the aim. Does it need re-thinking in the light of what you now know?

3. *List what has to be done*
List *everything* that will have to be done to achieve the aim, taking into account all the factors in the problem. Put the tasks down as you think of them — don't worry yet about their sequence or who should do what. Make sure the list is complete. You may have to include getting specialist advice or help among the tasks. And don't forget information-collecting tasks and the need to lobby people or involve them at some stage. One task may be to keep a written record of the project stages.

4. *Plan*
Now plan the sequence of tasks — who will do what by when. If the project is for a team, then you must decide how you will all organise yourselves and who will take responsibility for what. Use the resources of the team to best effect, but don't forget the learning element: someone other than the team's best report-writer may gain most from keeping the written record of the project, for instance.

5. *Action*
Be ready to revise the plan if things do not turn out as you expected. As you work on the project, try to get your people to recognise *consciously* what you are learning from it and from the problems of implementing the plan.

6. *Review*
Have regular reviews of progress with your people. Remember — these should not be reviews of just the project itself but also of what they are *learning* from it. This is your coaching in action.

If it is a team project, you should include in your reviews an appraisal of how they are working *as a team*. Don't let their interest in the project itself cause them to ignore what they are learning about the way they co-operate (or fail to): to what extent does the group support its members? Does it really operate as a team, or more as a loose collection of soloists? Whose ideas are taken up? Whose aren't really listened to? What does the group seem to react to — the quality of the idea, the way it is presented, or the status of the person putting it forward?

What roles do the different members take at different stages of the project? Do the roles seem to change? Who takes the lead — when and how? Does the lead change, and what seems to decide it? Human issues like these are major factors in how organisations actually work. Becoming observant about them is a valuable step for your people towards themselves undertaking a leadership role in the future.

Don't let us give the impression that coaching is concerned *only* with this kind of project. Your people can learn from you continually — by seeing how you do things, by working with you on everyday tasks, by asking for your help in solving their problems (and by offering you their help in solving yours if they know what they are) and from the regular feedback you give them as a result of your observation of their performance. But this will happen only if you make if happen, by seeking opportunities and making sure they are taken.

Although on-the-job coaching is an indispensible development tool, formal courses, run either within or outside your organisation, will also offer opportunities for your people to learn. Whoever actually runs them, *you* still have a vital role to play. Firstly, you should be the one to decide which courses your people attend. Find out as much as you can about the content, methods and track record of any course before allowing your people to go. Make sure it really does match their learning needs (in some cases it will be worth attending the course yourself before sending members of your team).

Secondly, talk to your people before they go. Help them define what they can get out of it, what specially to look for and how to prepare for it. Thirdly, very importantly, talk to them again *very soon* after they come back. Find out what they've gained and help them plan how to apply it (the application may be another opportunity for you to act in coaching role).

And finally, on the principle that the best way of learning something is to teach it, consider occasionally getting some of your people to plan and run training sessions for the rest of the team. In doing this they'll also be developing their communication and leadership skills.

In all this managing of people's development, bear in mind that the *authority* which is, hopefully, implicit in your normal working relationship may inhibit some people from revealing their uncertainties and need for help. In this area of your management you have to be accepted as a 'mentor' — an experienced and trusted adviser: a very exacting but very rewarding role.

Developing people's know-how

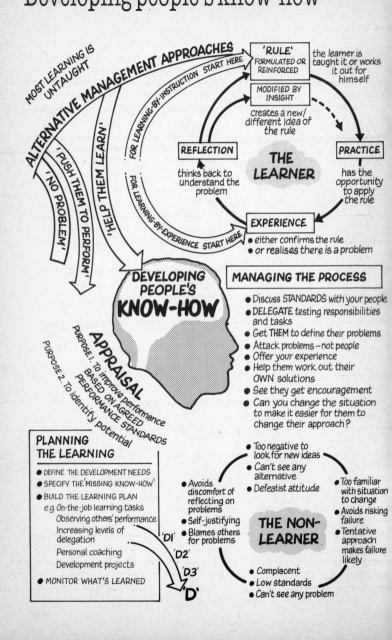

MOST LEARNING IS UNTAUGHT

ALTERNATIVE MANAGEMENT APPROACHES

FOR LEARNING-BY-INSTRUCTION START HERE

'NO PROBLEM'

'PUSH THEM TO PERFORM'

'HELP THEM LEARN'

FOR LEARNING-BY-EXPERIENCE START HERE

'RULE' FORMULATED OR REINFORCED — the learner is taught it or works it out for himself

MODIFIED BY INSIGHT — creates a new/different idea of the rule

REFLECTION — thinks back to understand the problem

THE LEARNER

PRACTICE — has the opportunity to apply the rule

EXPERIENCE
- either confirms the rule
- or realises there is a problem

DEVELOPING PEOPLE'S **KNOW-HOW**

APPRAISAL
PURPOSE 1: To improve performance BASED ON AGREED PERFORMANCE STANDARDS
PURPOSE 2: To identify potential

MANAGING THE PROCESS
- Discuss STANDARDS with your people
- DELEGATE testing responsibilities and tasks
- Get THEM to define their problems
- Attack problems – not people
- Offer your experience
- Help them work out their OWN solutions
- See they get encouragement
- Can you change the situation to make it easier for them to change their approach?

PLANNING THE LEARNING
- DEFINE THE DEVELOPMENT NEEDS
- SPECIFY THE 'MISSING KNOW-HOW'
- BUILD THE LEARNING PLAN
  e.g. On-the-job learning tasks
  Observing others' performance
  Increasing levels of delegation
  Personal coaching
  Development projects
- MONITOR WHAT'S LEARNED

'D1' 'D2' 'D3' **'D'**

- Avoids discomfort of reflecting on problems
- Self-justifying
- Blames others for problems

- Too negative to look for new ideas
- Can't see any alternative
- Defeatist attitude

- Too familiar with situation to change
- Avoids risking failure
- Tentative approach makes failure likely

THE NON-LEARNER

- Complacent
- Low standards
- Can't see any problem

NOTES

WHAT IS A MANAGER?

The first of the Effective Management Skills books, *What is a Manager?* answers that question.

Even at a fairly junior level in an organisation you may be responsible for staff and projects and thus, a manager.

It also tells you who is not a manager. Once defined, the book helps the manager to develop essential management skills: organisation, delegation, innovative thinking.

All this written in a bright and accessible style, wittily illustrated by Paula Youens' cartoons.

MANAGING WORK

Managing Work in the Effective Management Skills series deals with the four letter word! The psychology of work: earning a living, self-respect, purpose. What the organisation wants from you.

The book encourages the manager to define the results he is after — why work needs to be managed — and how to achieve that management.

There is detailed information on company systems, policy statements, writing a job description and forecasting.

In a lively and practical style, wittily illustrated by Paula Youens.